SWATI PAL

Look

SWATI PAL

Look Back At Anger: Agit Prop Theatre in Britain

Red Ladder Theatre Company From the 60s to the 90s

VDM Verlag Dr. Müller

Impressum/Imprint (nur für Deutschland/ only for Germany)
Bibliografische Information der Deutschen Nationalbibliothek: Die Deutsche Nationalbibliothek
verzeichnet diese Publikation in der Deutschen Nationalbibliografie; detaillierte bibliografische
Daten sind im Internet über http://dnb.d-nb.de abrufbar.
Alle in diesem Buch genannten Marken und Produktnamen unterliegen warenzeichen-, marken-
oder patentrechtlichem Schutz bzw. sind Warenzeichen oder eingetragene Warenzeichen der
jeweiligen Inhaber. Die Wiedergabe von Marken, Produktnamen, Gebrauchsnamen,
Handelsnamen, Warenbezeichnungen u.s.w. in diesem Werk berechtigt auch ohne besondere
Kennzeichnung nicht zu der Annahme, dass solche Namen im Sinne der Warenzeichen- und
Markenschutzgesetzgebung als frei zu betrachten wären und daher von jedermann benutzt
werden dürften.

Coverbild: www.purestockx.com

Verlag: VDM Verlag Dr. Müller Aktiengesellschaft & Co. KG
Dudweiler Landstr. 125 a, 66123 Saarbrücken, Deutschland
Telefon +49 681 9100-698, Telefax +49 681 9100-988, Email: info@vdm-verlag.de
Zugl.: New Delhi, Jawaharlal Nehru University, India, Diss., 2005

Herstellung in Deutschland:
Schaltungsdienst Lange o.H.G., Zehrensdorfer Str. 11, D-12277 Berlin
Books on Demand GmbH, Gutenbergring 53, D-22848 Norderstedt
Reha GmbH, Dudweiler Landstr. 99, D- 66123 Saarbrücken
ISBN: 978-3-639-07839-8

Imprint (only for USA, GB)
Bibliographic information published by the Deutsche Nationalbibliothek: The Deutsche
Nationalbibliothek lists this publication in the Deutsche Nationalbibliografie; detailed
bibliographic data are available in the Internet at http://dnb.d-nb.de.
Any brand names and product names mentioned in this book are subject to trademark, brand or
patent protection and are trademarks or registered trademarks of their respective holders. The use
of brand names, product names, common names, trade names, product descriptions etc. even
without
a particular marking in this works is in no way to be construed to mean that such names may be
regarded as unrestricted in respect of trademark and brand protection legislation and could thus
be used by anyone.

Cover image: www.purestockx.com

Publisher:
VDM Verlag Dr. Müller Aktiengesellschaft & Co. KG
Dudweiler Landstr. 125 a, 66123 Saarbrücken, Germany
Phone +49 681 9100-698, Fax +49 681 9100-988, Email: info@vdm-verlag.de

Copyright © 2008 VDM Verlag Dr. Müller Aktiengesellschaft & Co. KG and licensors
All rights reserved. Saarbrücken 2008

Produced in USA and UK by:
Lightning Source Inc., 1246 Heil Quaker Blvd., La Vergne, TN 37086, USA
Lightning Source UK Ltd., Chapter House, Pitfield, Kiln Farm, Milton Keynes, MK11 3LW, GB
BookSurge, 7290 B. Investment Drive, North Charleston, SC 29418, USA
ISBN: 978-3-639-07839-8

CONTENTS

Acknowledgements

Much has happened in the years that have gone into the writing of this book and the joy of seeing it take shape has been no less than seeing my son, Divakar, grow along side. Needless to say, the nurturing of both has often led to traumatic moments in the lives of each!

Standing by me always has been GJV, my guide, mentor and friend of many years. If it could be acknowledged in words what I owe to him not just in guiding me along this rocky road of research, but also for his persistent positive outlook, he would surely be swamped!

This research would not have progressed at all without the timely support of the Charles Wallace Trust Scholarship and the unstinted co-operation of Rajni Badlani, then in the British Council that enabled me to collect archival material from Red Ladder at Leeds. Of course, for being there, literally, I am completely in Red Ladder's debt. Thank you for staying alive!

There are a number of RL people whose generosity I must acknowledge: Kully Thiarai, Stefanie Gascoigne, Noel Greig and Ann Cross. What has been remarkable has been the sharing of more than intellectual space with all these wonderful people.

There are others in England who need to be thanked: Amit and Jayati for being caring hosts; Jonathan Meth (NPT), Professor Trevor Griffiths (University of North London) and Michael Anderson (IFTR) for volunteering as much information as possible; Roland Rees (Foco Novo), the late John McGrath (7:84), Roland Muldoon (CAST), Ann Louise Wirgman and the people at the Theatre Museum Library for their time and engagement with my work. Theatre Companies like Cheek by Jowl, Half Moon, Grass Market and so many others who willingly shared information – Thank you.

My three elder sisters and their families, particularly my niece Pooja and nephews Gagan and Saurav whose impatience and obviously biased admiration goaded me on – I hope this book makes you proud. Thanks are due also to my husband's family, especially my late father-in-law, for their support.

For all the teachers who taught me: MM, Gill, Dr Sareen, KK, HN, and Rimli; for everything that the years at JNU have woven into the tapestry of my existence: I hope that this book bears adequate witness to all that I have gathered epistemologically and ontologically.

For a relationship that keeps me going, thank you Abhi.

Perhaps this book would have remained a distant dream if Uttam had not pitched in: for being, truly, my 'significant other', I cannot even begin to thank him.

VDM has been a real blessing and has prevented my manuscript from collecting dust: a heartfelt thank you.

This book is dedicated to my parents. In memory of Baba who always believed I could do 'anything' and for Ma who feels I can do 'more than anything' – this is 'something' for you both.

Introduction

WHY BRITISH AGIT PROP THEATRE?

Studying an area as vast as agit prop theatre is a marathon task and one that raises many questions from the viability of the research area to its focus and its conclusions. One of the first questions that such research is bound to encounter is: "Why BRITISH and then, why British AGIT PROP theatre?" Especially since one is residing in a country where agit prop theatre abounds. The answer is not insignificant.

In the first place, though rich in agit prop drama, one rarely comes across plays of this genre in the English language in India. For the purpose of this study then, it would involve a translation of the plays into English; and translation is inevitably problematic creating its own web of socio-historio-culturo signifiers. But of larger consequence is ones own location as a post-colonial subject in choosing not just British but agit prop theatre over and above other theatres in Britain. Subjected as one had been to an English Literature curriculum where the study of the (now much intellectually bashed) English canon was sacrosanct, where Shakespeare was iconicised to the extent that his plays were seen as cutting across historical space and time, one failed to realise that this was misleading. That one had unwittingly become an accomplice in abetting the vision of a sanitised British culture, an ordered entity. One failed to observe the agenda behind the English Literature curriculum imposed in schools and colleges which was to suppress peripheral voices including as this study focuses on, that of the alternative theatre groups/movements in Britain which dared to challenge the Establishment and to prove by their very existence that they were a viable option against the mainstream.[1] Such groups though dealing with a space/system quite different from those in our country had politically subversive aims that were similar to theatre groups of the same ilk here (and in fact elsewhere in the world).

It was only with the burgeoning of post modern and post colonial studies in the late 1980s and 90s and with such hall markers as The Empire Writes Back: Theory and Practice in Post Colonial Literature (1989) by Bill Ashcroft, Gareth Griffiths and Helen Tiffin (followed in 1995 by their Post Colonial (Studies Reader); Colonial Discourse and Post Colonial Theory (1993) ed by Patrick Williams and Laura Chrisman; and Nation and

Narration (1990) ed by Homi Bhabha – that English Literature students of my generation in India gradually awakened to challenge and negotiate with the literary manipulation that they had been subjected to.

Apart from the valorisation of Shakespeare one discovered that most English Literature curriculums for undergraduates within the country concluded with either TS Eliot's Murder in the Cathedral or at the most John Osborne's Look Back in Anger as part of the drama course. Such a rounding off inevitably led the unsuspecting graduate, especially one not inclined towards further studies, to believe that post John Osborne (and by extension, post the well-made play) theatrical activity in Britain became sterile. It is true to some extent of course that there was a relatively dull theatrical period in Britain in the 50s. But it is also true that this inertia was broken in the 60s by such a spate of theatrical performances/movements that critics are still trying to categorise them into such types as "expressive realism", "utopian realism", "socialist realism", "drama of conversion", "agit prop" and so on. Such attempts at categorisation only serve to highlight the vastness, heterogeneity and alterity of Post World War II British theatre. It also serves to point out that the objective of a lot of theatrical activity in the late sixties was non-commercial and therefore distinguishable from West End Theatre or the circus and music hall which aimed at financial gain (Davies, 1987, Preface). Thus for me, the process of selecting 'an' area for study was steered in the direction of that theatre which has been effective in more ways than one and which has changed the whole nature of the theatrical enterprise. Such a theatre is the agit prop.

While it is true that agit prop theatre has not accompanied or generated major revolutions in Britain as it has done in other countries, it has stood in the vanguard of political and social change and has justifiably been the model of alternate theatre used by the WTM (Workers Theatre Movement). Perhaps the most interesting facet of the British agit prop theatre movement is that it has a diverse nature. Christopher Innes puts it clearly when he says that many stylistic features were shared by various groups since a Marxist ideological line had come to be identified with the agit prop. Aims however ranged from conveying information for example on the social and economic implications of new laws to shaping political consciousness (by promoting support for industrial action or exposing Establishment corruption) to aggressive protest (through the use of violent images to

4

bring home the corrupting effects of pornography or to assert the public complicity in the bloodshed of Northern Ireland). (Innes, 1992)

Or again, to quote John McGrath who identifies three main areas of activity. Loosely speaking, they are:

> first, the struggle within the institutions of theatre against the hegemony of the 'bourgeois' ideology within those institutions; secondly, the making of a theatre which is interventionist on a political level, usually outside those institutions; and thirdly and most importantly, the creation of a counter-culture based on the working class, which will grow in richness and confidence until it eventually displaces the dominant bourgeois culture of late capitalism. (Bigsby, 1981: 33)

This study recognizes that contrary to popular, uninformed belief that post the Fall of the Soviet Bloc and subsequent events, agit prop theatre too declined, in actuality such theatre continues to thrive whether practiced wholly or partially, by Theatre Companies interested in investigating political/social/cultural concerns. The study also perceives that there is no single formula responsible for the survival of such theatre, indeed of 'any' theatre—mortality rates of theatre being as high as they are.

If agit prop theatre, in whatever form, has succeeded in surviving, it is significant to analyse the reasons for its survival. The most obvious reason of course is the nature of such theatre i.e. its immediate emotional appeal during a historically charged situation and time. But the question is, how is this emotional response elicited? If Performance Studies can be seen (and it has been, primarily by cultural anthropologists such as Victor Turner and Richard Schechner) as synchronous with Ritual Studies, the answer to the question becomes more manifest.[2] Even when only reading the text of agit prop plays, one discerns certain patterns emerging in various aspects of the plays—be it the language, the form or the themes. It is these elastic patterns that this work will address as 'Rituals'.

Because Ritual Studies are a focus of study in disciplines as diverse as Religion, Sociology and Cultural Anthropology[3], it is necessary to chart out the parameters within which the term Ritual will be used from Chapter Three onwards. Even though critical approaches to Ritual Studies are wide, there are certain points of convergence. To begin with, Ritual is considered as a symbolic action which, while on the one hand is temporarily discontinuous with routine activities by enforcing itself spontaneously, on the other hand reveals a tremendous capacity for routinisation. At once the connection between this definition of Ritual and Theatre becomes clear. As Eugenio Barba says:

> It is the performance not the theatre which lasts only a short time. The theatre is made up of traditions, of conventions, of institutions, of habits which endure throughout time. The weight of this endurance is so heavy that it often prevents life from emerging and replaces it with routine. Routine is another of theatre's natural boundaries. (Barba, 1990: 96)

Hence 'drama' or a 'play' which is defined as a mode of fiction represented on stage and constructed according to certain dramatic conventions may be replaced by another. But 'theatre' which is a complex of phenomena associated with the performer-audience transaction, i.e. with the production and communication of meaning in the performance itself and with the systems underlying it, endures conceptually. (Kier Elam, 1980: 2)

Such a definition of Ritual ushers in notions of the 'sacred' and the 'profane': while 'profane' embraces the routine aspect of a man's activities, the 'sacred' is that aspect of a community's beliefs, myths and material objects that is set apart and sacrosanct. The function of ritual in the community is that of providing the proper rules for action in the realm of the sacred as well as of supplying a bridge for passing on into the realm of the profane. It would be useful at this juncture to refer to Van Gennep who in his Les Rites de Passage speaks of the 'pivoting of the sacred', i.e., he says that nothing is inherently sacred or profane.[4] These are not substantive categories but rather, situational or relational categories, mobile boundaries which shift according to the map being employed. There is nothing that is in itself sacred, only things sacred in relation to. It is perhaps easy to recognize this feature of Ritual as an intrinsic characteristic of all Theatre but especially of agit prop theatre.

Ritual can also be studied as non-verbal communication disclosing its own structure and semantics.[5] The space, spatial orientation and location of the ritual setting are essential features of the semantics of ritual action. Examples of ritual time and ritual space orientation can be found in the rituals for building the sacrifice in Brahmanic Indian ritual texts; for the building of a Hindu temple or a Christian Cathedral; and for consecrating those structures that symbolize a definite space-time orientation in which rituals are enacted. Man's use of space in his architectural, domestic, urban, workplace and aesthetic activities is neither casual nor merely functional but represents a semiotically loaded choice, subject to powerful rules which generate a range of connotative cultural units. The three principals 'syntactic' systems distinguished by the American anthropologist Edward T Hall, and which are an important basis for the study of drama and theatre, are the 'fixed feature', the 'semi fixed feature' and the 'informal' (Kier Elam, 1980: 62-63). In Halls' own terms the fixed feature space involves 'static architectural configurations' which relate to the playhouse itself, be it the opera house, the proscenium-arch theatre, the open square or the street—the shapes and dimensions of stage and auditorium. The semi fixed feature space involves such movable but rather static subjects such as furniture or the set and other auxiliary factors like the lighting. And the informal space is concerned with the ever shifting relations of proximity and distance between individuals in the theatre viz. actor-actor, actor-spectator, and spectator-spectator. Such proxemic analysis can reveal how drama and in this case, agit prop affects and transforms dramaturgic space.

While there are many conflicting views about whether ritual is prior to explanatory belief, a view propagated primarily by Robertson Smith, or whether there is a priority of belief over ritual as Taylor believed; there can be no doubt that ritual can be seen as an expression of the urge for integration with the whole that transcends it and transfigures it. This 'integration' (read variously as allegiance/binding/affiliation and affinity) however, seeks not just to reinforce notions of the collectivity but also serves to impart a sense of belief in individual identity to all the members within the collectivity because within it, the members have their own status and role. Ritual is thus oriented to the need dispositions of a collectivity and requires the participation of a community. Bearing this aspect of Ritual in mind and recalling the discussion of the nature of agit prop as will be detailed in subsequent chapters; the parallels between the two become only too visible, for after all, the aim of agit prop theatre is to integrate a community by propagating a certain ideology. As Kertzer says:

> Ritual is a means by which we express our social dependence; what is important in ritual is our common participation and emotional involvement, not the specific rationalization by which we account for the rites. (Kertzer, 1988: 67)

7

It follows then that Ritual has both a hierarchical as well as an egalitarian structure. It is hierarchical when the sacred is outside the person of the communicants who reach out to it as individuals approaching factual objects. And it is egalitarian when the sacred is inside the person of the individual communicants who listen within and join together in a group. Theatre may wield its power over spectators; agit prop theatre attempts to literally hand over power to the spectators.

Ritual has a many layered or tiered structure, each level having many sectors so that it becomes an instrument for carrying out and communicating many messages at once, even of subverting at one level what it appears to be saying in another. The full meaning of the ritual emerges from the union of the text of the ritual with the performers at a given moment in a group's ongoing social process. The performative genre does not merely 'reflect' or express the social system or the cultural configurations or their key relationships but has a reciprocal relationship i.e., it is either a critique (direct or veiled) of the social life that it grows out of or an evaluation of the way society handles history. This critiquing and evaluating has been and is a need disposition of most collectivities. Agit prop theatre carries this a bit further and uses the register of active protest in its performative process. This protest occurs in two broad formations: one in which the propagandists speak *for* the ruling opinion (or dominant power structure of the times) and treats the audience as a passive existent; the other speaks *against* the ruling opinion, *for* the people as individuals or grouped into associations and in which the audience is (apparently) regarded as a subject or co-creator. In the former, the propagandist seeks to exhort or correct the listeners so that they move perfectly according to the ruling opinion. In the latter, the propagandist seeks to realise in the listener, a consciousness, latent until then, of necessary change which is done by exciting the imagination of the listeners to conceive of difference; once difference (disharmony, division) is recognized and the idea of belonging to two 'opposite' factions becomes clear, a successful reducing of accord between the listener and the ruling party will have been achieved.[6]

Repetition, emotionality, drama and symbolism are the other principle features that most rituals share; along with is the whole process of order-disorder-reorder which is embedded within rituals.

While it is relatively simple to deduce the connections between Ritual and Agit prop Theatre as described in this section, it is certainly not conclusive enough. Any research on drama invariably involves confronting the whole issue of 'performance', i.e. questions about the validity of conclusions in the light of not having watched the actual performance of the plays. Undeniably, as all theatre researchers will agree, there are disadvantages in being thus situated. With agit prop theatre, this difficulty is compounded by such problems as an unavailability of scripts (few have been published; many have fluid texts with missing sections/pages). Besides, the kind of historicity which this thesis intends to explore cannot be located only within the scripts of agit prop theatre companies—other factors such as the policies of the theatre companies, finance, the government, etc—cannot be ruled out. However, in spite of such problems it is possible to discover the protests, the ritualistic features of the protest and an evolution of the rituals of protests over a period of time through a semiotic study of the texts that the thesis will use as case studies. Proxemics one has already mentioned earlier on. A few more primary aspects of the kind of semiotic study that will be involved need to be mentioned here.

The two most important aspects are in Roman Ingarden's terms, the 'Haupttext' (main text) which comprises of the words spoken on stage by the actors and the 'Nebentext' (subsidiary text) consisting of stage directions, etc. (Esslin, 1987: 80). That the Haupttext is crucial is obvious but the significance of the Nebentext can hardly be overstated for it decides the infrastructure of spaces which 'determines the paterns of the actors' movement' and 'express a multitude of moods and meanings.'[7]

The language of both, the Haupttext and the Nebentext will be studied according to what, semiotically speaking, can be called the 'denotation-cannotation dialect'. The mechanism of connotation in language and other sign systems has been much discussed, but the most satisfactory formulation remains that provided by the Danish linguist Hjelmslev, who defines a 'connotative semiotic' as one 'whose expression plane is a semiotic. Connotation is a parasitic semantic function, therefore, whereby the sign vehicle for one sign-relationship provides the basis for a second-order sign relationship (the sign vehicle of the stage sign 'crown' acquires the secondary meanings 'majority', 'usurpation', etc).' (Kier Elam, 1980:10-11)

9

Apart from analysing changing ritual patterns within the scripts, it is imperative to study the developments in the Artistic Policies of the Theatre Company under consideration. The Theatre Company that this book will be studying is one that has withstood the test of time and financial tide, i.e. the Red Ladder Theatre Company. This theatre company emerged in 1968 (originally called Agit Prop Street Players) sharing theatrical space in Britain with equally effective agit prop theatre companies like Cartoon Archetypal Slogan Theatre (CAST), InterAction and The Other Company. As time went by, however, Red Ladder persisted in its efforts and is a major fringe company in Britain even today.

Obviously no theatre form is conceived overnight. It grows out of past and existing trends and is influenced by theatre theorists, philosophers and practitioners. Chapter One, **Theory and Praxis: Historicising Agit Prop Theatre** is divided into two sections. The first section traces the history of agit prop theatre till the immediate post-World War II period. This necessarily involves a study of those historical movements or unique situations especially the Russian Revolution that have facilitated the progressive growth of agit prop theatre. Such a background serves to provide the parameters for defining the way that agit prop theatre will be perceived in this study.

The second section of this chapter seeks to elucidate the ideas of those who have most influenced agit prop theatre practitioners. While it is true that many philosophies have helped agit prop theatre proponents, for the process of selection, it would be more meaningful to take on in particular those to whom agit prop theatre activists have themselves acknowledge a debt. So, while not neglecting the work of such cultural anthropologists as Victor Turner and Richard Schechner who are vital to this study in terms of examining the roots of theatre in the 'lived experience' and as part of a 'ritualised lifestyle' of many cultures (therefore as not only an isolate art form); or in the theories of Jerry Grotowski and Augusto Boal with their Poor Theatre and Theatre of the Oppressed (Boal is especially interesting in his projecting the spectator as spect-actor and in his propagation of Image Theatre, Invisible Theatre and Forum Theatre with special attention to the last); the chapter also concentrates on Romain Rolland (1866-1944), Vsevolod Meyerhold (1874-1890), Erwin Piscator (1893-1966), Vladimir Mayakovsky (1893-1930) and Bertold Brecht (1898-1956). Finally, the growth of such theatrical movements as Dadaism and Futurism and Artaud's Theatre of Cruelty has also been dwelt upon.

Proceeding from the view established in Chapter One that agitprop theatre originates from unique moments in history; Chapter Two, **An Overview of Agit Prop Theatre** then traces the birth, profession and decline/success of agit prop theatre/s in Britain from 1968 onwards. This chapter makes a close and detailed study of historical developments in post-World War II Britain and how these in turn affected political theatre, in particular the agit prop theatre enterprise. That different Companies employed different technical methods for a consummation of their ideological aims and different tactical measures for their survival, is central to the analysis of these Companies in this chapter. Apart from outlining the career graph of different agit prop theatre companies (including the one that this study takes up as a case study: Red Ladder), the chapter also briefly looks at individual playwrights who have written meaningful agit prop plays or plays that have been used effectively by agit prop theatre companies.

Chapters Three, **Red Ladder: The First Rung** and Chapter Four, **Climbing to the Eighties** then examines the first two decades of Red Ladders existence. In order to formulate a certain system to analyse the plays in the face of a complete lack of criticism on them, both chapters use such bases as historical realism/parallelism; Schechner's theories of performance; the politics of discourse and Feminist theories to delve into the plays at length. The chapters also carefully carefully follow the changing dimensions of the Company under different circumstances over the years. Factors such as the differing attitudes of changing governments towards Theatre (and therefore a poverty of/insecurity about funds); failed productions; administrative bungling etc that led not just to an improvement in both, form and content of the plays so that they became artistically more complex and fulfilling, but also resulted in the conversion of Red Ladder from a collective to a hierarchy; from an aggressively political Theatre Company to one concerned primarily with community development and social welfare, have been chalked out in these two chapters. That in the final analysis, youth in the multicultural situation of Britain with their problems of race, class, sex, gender, tradition, modernity, etc has become the main area of concern which Red Ladder consistently addresses, is firmly established as well.

Chapter Five, **Between Two Centuries: Red Ladder in the Nineties** continues to engage with the same aspects as the preceding two chapters but with a shift in emphasis from the plays proper to the other pre and post production devices deployed by Red Ladder, i.e., such stratagems as leaflets, fanzines (magazines for fans), ragazines (literally 'rags' or scraps of information relating to the theme/s and the actors of a production, interestingly collaged in magazine form), interactive sessions with members of the target audience/organisers or hosts of a particular production, both before and after the performance. The chapter   highlights the increasing professionalism of all these measures complemented by the growing complexity/artistry of the scripts, especially in terms of language.

In the Conclusion, **Red Ladder at 40,** there is a quick recapitulation of the changing trends and emergent patterns in the functioning of Red Ladder and an evaluation of how far it has succeeded in sustaining itself as an agit prop theatre company. Through such a reassessment, the altered parameters of the agit prop in theatre are   redefined.

Most critics devote only a few sections upon agit prop theatre in their books on political/social theatre such as for example the collection of essays edited by Sandy Craig, Dreams and Deconstructions Alternative Theatre in Britain (Craig, 1980). Even more thorough works as Catherine Itzin's Stages in the Revolution Political Theatre in Britain Since 1968 (Itzin, 1980) or Andrew Davies' Other Theatres The Development of Alternative and Experimental Theatre in Britain (Davies, 1987), provide only a comprehensive historical mapping. They do not unravel the inner complexities within such theatre; the battles for survival waged by such theatre companies and certainly there is no   analysis of the plays performed, available. Consequently, the sheer immensity of the work done by such theatre companies is barely perceptible and is perhaps the most significant reason for the flawed understanding the layman has of agit prop theatre as one that arises out of historical contingencies, and dies once these are resolved. When combined with other factors such as the unavailability of scripts (un/published) and the incomplete information that theatre companies are furnished with, the former due to financial constraints and the latter possibly due to a negligence in handling archival records, it is small wonder that in epistemological terms, there are so many misconceptions about agit prop theatre.[8]

In the face of such lacunae then, this study aims primarily at initiating a critical tradition regarding agit prop theatre and acknowledges that there is a definite need for contesting views about how the plays performed by agit prop Theatre Companies are perceived.

Notes

[1] The introductory pages of <u>Post Colonial Drama theory, practice, politics</u> by Helen Gilbert and Joanne Tompkins, Routledge, London and New York, 1996 were helpful in formulating my position.

[2] Victor Turner's methodology has been followed closely in Chapter Three. He is best known for formulating such concepts as 'liminality' in his book <u>The Anthropology of Performance</u> PAJ Publications, New York, 1986, while Richard Schechner's Environmental Theatre is briefly outlined in Chapter One. Eli Rozik's <u>The Roots of Theatre: Rethinking Riual and other Theories of origin</u> University of Iowa Press, Iowa City, USA, 2002 is a useful book to refer to if one wants to study those who believe the exact reverse.

[3] Among the cultural anthropologists Victor Turner and Richard Schechner are important while Durkheim, Radcliffe Browne and Malinowski are significant sociological thinkers on the subject of ritual.

[4] Jonathan Z Smith, 'Bare Facts of Ritual', <u>History of Religions</u>, Vol 20, 1980-81

[5] The New Encyclopedia Britannica: Macropedia, Vol 15, p 866

[6] See Roger Howard's 'Propaganda in the early Soviet and Contemporary Chinese Theatre in <u>Theatre Quarterly</u>. Vol VII, No. 27, Autumn 1977, p.59

[7] <u>Theatre as Sign-System: A Semiotics of Text and Performance</u> by Elaine Aston and George Savona, Routledge, London and New York, 1991, firmly asserts the importance of the Nebentext.

[8] These misconceptions have been outlined in Chapter One.

THEORY AND PRAXIS: HISTORICISING AGIT PROP THEATRE

If in the beginning was the word, theatre showed how the word could be used meaningfully. It showed how a community can be formed through the force of emotions generated by an acting unit in close communion with a receiving unit through a mode of fiction represented within a certain space and time.

Much research has gone into the word 'play' both as noun and verb form. Of the many synonyms of this word, what is of significance to this study is 'recreation', i.e. if interpreted in one sense: we create ourselves anew through 'playing'. 'Theatre is by its very nature play, for the audience as well as its creators; in fact the audience are creators, players in the game' (Goodman and Gay, 2000, Chapter 20). For art to be fully appreciated and realized or for effective 'recreation' to take place, it is obvious that the spectator cannot remain merely a passive observer. The spectator must necessarily be involved in the play at least at an emotional level. The linguistic equation between 'acting' and 'playing' holds good with both, actors and audience: both 'act' while 'playing' their role. It is the interactive relationship between actor and audience, the engagement in a communal activity that demarcates theatre from all other art forms. As with any form, artistic or otherwise, that helps create a social group, it is this interactive and communal nature of the theatrical experience that makes it a forceful political agency.[1] In this study, 'The theatres explored...are those that self consciously attempt to transform consciousness and initiate active struggle' (Goodman and Gay, 2000) to which we give the name 'agit prop theatre.'

If theatrical space is the 'qualitative ensemble' whose different dimensions signify various ideological ways of perceiving possible societal relations (Suvin,1984:5), 'agit prop theatre' declares its own intent. This is the creation of a radical and progressive politics of theatre in/as action. Following Phillip B. Zarilli's lead, what I mean by such theatre is not only in the narrow sense of those dramas whose subject matter deals with the staging of a social crisis or a revolution; but the entire spectrum of publicly enacted events such as rallies, meetings, marches, protests and the like that often take place during, and/or inspired by periods of social and political crisis and/or revolution. Such 'theatres' not only reflect or mirror contemporary social and political turbulence but are

14

'instantiated in the potential to effect a process of change in the individual and/or social consciousness' (Zarilli; Goodman and Gay, 2000).[2]

In this context it would be pertinent to remember that theatre in itself doesn't cause revolutions. But it allows like-minded people to gather together and through a recognition of the theatrical event as well as of each other's and their own presence, reinforce their beliefs. It may also provoke the consciousness of 'others' to think along hitherto not-so-acceptable lines.[3] Even a casual glance at world events is enough to confirm the dramatic role played by agit prop theatre in almost every continent/country. To mention a few—the tremendous power of street theatre in the overthrow of the Marcos dictatorship in the Philippines; the resistance theatre in South Korea (especially against the Japanese invasion) called Madang which is the South Korean version of agitational street theatre based on traditional folk drama and western agit prop:

> ... The word agitational should be taken quite literally in this context:
> many Madang performances succeed in getting the audience in such
> a state of ecstatic frenzy that they are spontaneously transformed from
> spectators into slogan chanting political demonstrators. Many mass
> demonstrations were initiated or animated by Madang performances
> (VanErven, 1988:158)

Hwang Sok Yong's <u>Sweet Potato</u> or Kim Chitta's <u>The Funeral Ceremony of National Democracy</u> performed in 1965 at Seoul University would serve as good examples of Madang Theatre. Again, the activists of the Velvet Revolution in Czechoslovakia found agit prop theatre a useful tool in mobilising the people into action.[4] In Australia, street performances in the mid-seventies with a strongly political content that usually voiced the despair of tribal cultures found an emotionally charged audience.[5] Agit prop has remained a consistent part of the Chinese government's education programme in rural areas.[6] The techniques of agit prop groups were emulated by the Teatro Campesino, the first of the Chicano Theatres in the United States, which was founded in California as part of the farmworker's union campaign for recognition in the mid-1960s.[7] Black Theatre in Africa and America (as for example Matsemala Manaka's group, Soyi Kwa's performance of <u>Pula</u>) relies largely on agit prop means in theatre to arouse the sympathy of the spectators.[8] Agit prop troupes have been used by the North

Vietnamese during the Vietnam War.[9] All over India street theatre using agit prop techniques is hugely popular and such theatre exponents as Badal Sircar and Safdar Hashmi are almost household names in the north. In England, in fact, agit prop theatre can be traced back to as early as the tenth century when the church in the form of simple narrative plays designed to bring to life the basic legends of Christianity; they were in fact political propaganda on behalf of an organization in hot pursuit of temporal as well as spiritual power (Lambert, 1977).

In spite of this evidence of the obvious impact of agit prop theatre however, it does not always conjure up a positive response. When one talks about such theatre as it has been practiced in recent times, what immediately comes to mind are masses of people indulging in an exercise of violent lung power, generally in a public arena, armed with many pamphlets sticks and stones and vicious slogans, and inciting spectators to behave in like manner. This vision of agit prop theatre is not untrue.[10] Nor are the accusations that often follow such performances: that they are usually cliché ridden with rehashed plots, weak story lines and unskilled acting. Of course, one could argue that this nature of the agit prop plays is intentional; recalling Erwin Piscator's dictum would be relevant here:

> … theatre must be run on these lines:
> simplicity of expression and construction, with a clear and unambiguous impact on the emotions of the … audience; any artistic intention must be subordinated to the revolutionary purpose of the whole …(Quoted by Lambert,1977)

But a major reason for discrediting such theatre arises from the term 'propaganda' itself.

The origins of this word as it has been in use in recent centuries, is traced to the title and work of a group of Roman Catholic Cardinals called *Congregatio de Propaganda Fide* (Congregation for the Propagation of Faith) instituted in 1622 to carry on missionary work. For many Roman Catholics then this word may have at least in ecclesiastical terms, a highly respectable connotation. To a vast majority however, the term is usually a pejorative one tending to connote such (mis)deeds as the atrocity stories and deceptively stated war aims of World Wars I and II, the operations of the Nazi's Ministry of Public Enlightenment and Propaganda and the broken campaign promises of

16

a thousand politicians. Also, it is reminiscent of countless instances of false and misleading advertising (especially in countries using Latin languages in which 'propaganda commerciale' or some equivalent is a common term for commercial advertising).

If we trace the history of the theory of propaganda we find that it has ancient but firm roots. In the East, towards 400 BC in India, Kaultilya, a Brahmin believed to have been the chief advisor to the Emperor Chandragupta Maurya reputedly wrote the Arthasastra (Principles of Politics), a book of advice for rulers that has often been compared with Machiavelli's The Prince. Kautilya discussed in some detail, psychological warfare, both overt and clandestine to disrupt an enemy's army and capture his capital. Overtly, he said, the propagandists of a king should proclaim that he can do magic, that God and the wisest men are on his side, that all who support his war aims will reap benefits. Covertly, his agents should infiltrate his enemies' and potential enemies' kingdoms, spreading defeatism and misleading news among their people, especially in capital cities, among leaders, and among the armed forces.

In the west the theory of propaganda began in Athens, in about 500 BC as the study of rhetoric (in Gk. 'the technique of orators'). Teachers such as Isocrates, Plato and Aristotle compiled rules of rhetoric to (i) make their own arguments and those of their students more persuasive (ii) design counterpropaganda against opponents and also (iii) teach their students how to detect the logical fallacies and emotional appeals of demagogues. These measures proved so successful that they were further developed in Rome by such figures as Cicero and Quintilian.

In the early twentieth century, the word propaganda had a new term conjugated to it to give it further substance—this was the word 'agitation'. The two terms were first employed by the Marxist theorist Georgy Plekhanov and later elaborated upon in doctrine form by Vladimir I. Lenin in a pamphlet entitled What is to be done? (1902). This doctrine aimed at achieving political victory by blending the strategies of: 'agitation', defined by him as the use of political slogans, parables and half truths to exploit the grievances of the largely uneducated masses and thereby mobilize public support;

'propaganda' or the indoctrination of the educated and enlightened sections of the populace through a reasoned use of historical and scientific arguments.

Immediately after the Bolshevik Revolution of 1917, this agit prop methodology was put into practice and various arts were enlisted to further the propagandist aims of the Bolsheviks. Be it posters or poets reading from their own work, a number of communicative devices were used to deck ships and trains crisscrossing the country. Since few in the country could actually read the newspapers, authors cited out news stories in a Living Newspaper. In 1921, a group of actors from Moscow formed the Blue Blouses Company drawing its name from the blue workers overalls that its members wore as their basic costume. This company inspired the birth of other professional and amateur factory groups throughout the Soviet Union. The work and techniques of these groups, in turn, set the stage for political theatre groups in other countries between 1921 and 1939.

The montages of the Blue Blouses were brief—not more than an hour and a half long—and comprised of dramatic monologues, sketches, dialogues, mass declamations and movement derived from dance and gymnastics. Since the aim of the company and others of its kind was to be able to perform anywhere, staging demands were extremely simple. The performances invariably began with a parade in which the actors presented themselves to the audience. Music, be it instrumental or folk/popular songs especially those with satiric lyrics featured prominently in the presentations. Animated posters (similar to photographer's dummy boards with cut out faces) were frequently made use of for rapid cartoon characterisation. Though the use of film was a rarity, the Blue Blouses specialised in the art of using flickering light on slowly moving actors to create the illusion of a silent film. Of the many devices used by the company the seemingly conventional and politically neutral dance and gymnastic routines were in reality their most positive strengths; the actors could, in the process of moving scenic pieces, acrobatically combine to compose pictures, diagrams and structures.

Though the method of juxtaposing overtly political pieces with the more entertaining ones was not new as it had been used for many years by music hall and variety theatres; what was new was the ideological purpose behind the combining of these skills which sought more than the applause of the audience. Part of the ideological aim of the Blue Blouses was to attack the inequities that followed the Revolution and the survival of pre-revolutionary thought and class distinctions through satire which the company saw as a legitimate part of their repertoire. In 1928, however, such a programme was considered counterproductive by the Stalin government that suppressed the movement and replaced it with Socialist Realism, a derivative of Naturalism, where state intervention converted the typical figures in a typical landscape into idealised figures in an idealised landscape.

However, just before disbanding, the Blue Blouses made a tour of Germany in 1927 to celebrate ten years of the Revolution. Coincidentally a communist backed congress of representations from many other countries was present in Germany at that time. The performances of the Blue Blouses consequently inspired an international movement of workers' theatre groups performing with varying degrees of skill, agit prop in the Blue Blouse mode.

In spite of the decline of the Blue Blouse movement, until recent events in Russia, every unit of a communist party used to have an agit prop section. Though reorganized several times, this section continued its functions of deciding the content of all official information; supervising political education in party schools and in the regular school system; overseeing all forms of mass communication and mobilizing public support for party programmes. Therefore, a standard Soviet manual for teachers of social sciences was entitled 'Propagandist Politekonomi' (For the Propagandist of Political Economy) and a pocket sized booklet which used to be issued weekly to suggest timely slogans and brief arguments to be used in speeches and conversations among the masses was called 'Bloknot Agitatora' (The Agitators' Notebook).[11]

This overview of the history of agit prop allows one to venture on a preliminary definition of agit prop as the more or less systematic effort to deliberately manipulate people's beliefs, attitudes and especially actions by means of symbols—words, gestures, banners, movements, music, insignia, hairstyles and so on. Theatre is one of the vehicles of the agit prop. Three aspects clearly emerge at the outset, that agit prop theatre is in essence (a) an interventionist theatre (b) a historical phenomenon (i.e., it emerges in conjunction with certain historical situations and events) and (c) it is generally Communist-backed since its origins and continuing ideology and techniques seek primarily to grant power to workers or other underprivileged sections of society.

To proceed a step further, while actual political or other events directly spark off agit prop theatre, a more significant contribution towards the active growth of such theatre is provided by a suitable intellectual or cultural climate. This is prepared by theatre theoreticians who are invariably also theatre practitioners and who at every juncture in theatrical experimentation attempt to formulate certain ground rules according to which the new theatre may run. In the case of agit prop theatre, no such canon of theatre theoreticians has ever been formalized. However, among those who played a more visible role in the development of such theatre are Bertolt Brecht, Jerzy Grotowski, Erwin Piscator, Vsevolod Yemilyevich Meyerhold, Vladimir Vladimirovich Mayakovsky, Richard Schechner, Romain Rolland and Augusto Boal. While it is tempting to include in the ensuing discussion such theatre practitioners as Badal Sircar, it must be remembered that this thesis aims at reviewing 'British' agit prop theatre which is largely informed by the ideas of 'Western' theatre practitioners. Nonetheless, it must be acknowledged at this point that Eastern/Oriental theatre (especially Indian and Japanese) forms and practices are a subject of tremendous theatre research not just in Britain but in the entire western world. To include these theatre activists, though justifiable, would then stretch the boundaries of this study considerably; hence it is only possible to mention their importance perfunctorily.

In an interview with Duncan Wu, Howard Brenton on being asked how influential Brecht had been to his work, answered that he too, like Brecht believed "in people in action, that human nature is very difficult to find out. He doesn't have the Ibsen like view that the human soul is an onion which you can peel; he thinks that in some ways we have to make our own lives, so he's a story teller" (Wu, 2000:40). Statements such as this only testify to the fact that Brecht's theories of stage presentation exerted more influence on the course of mid-century theatre in the West than did those of any other individual. This was primarily because he proposed the major alternative to the Stanislavsky oriented realism that dominated acting and the "well-made play" construction that dominated playwriting.[12]

That Brecht absorbed (and in turn perpetuated) many influences in the modern theatre can be seen through his essay "On Experimental Theatre" (1940) in which he reviewed the work of Vakhtangov, Meyerhold, Antoine Reinhardt Okhlopkov, Stanislavsky, Jessner and other Expressionists. Brecht traced through the modern theatre the two lines running from Naturalism and Expressionism. Naturalism he saw as the "assimilation of art of science" which he felt gave great social influence to Naturalistic theatre, but at the expense of its ability to arouse aesthetic pleasure. Expressionism (and by implication the other anti-illusionist theatres) he confessed had "vastly enriched the theatre's means of expression and brought aesthetic gains that still remain to be exploited."[13] Though heavily influenced by German Expressionism, it was however Brecht's preoccupation with Marxism and the idea that man and society could be intellectually analysed that led him to develop his theory of "epic theatre".

Brecht believed that theatre should appeal not to the spectator's feelings but to his reason. While still providing entertainment, it should be strongly didactic and capable of provoking social change. In the Realistic Theatre of illusion, he argued, the spectator tended to identify with the characters on stage and become emotionally involved with them rather than being stirred to think about his own life. Brecht proposed an alternative direction for the theatre where it could project a picture of the world by artistic means as well as offer models of life that could help the spectators to understand their social environment and master it both rationally and emotionally. The main concept of Brecht's program was that of Verfremdungseffekt ("alienation effect") i.e., the use of anti-illusive techniques to remind spectators that they were in a theatre watching an enactment of reality instead of reality itself; thus dispensing with the empathetic involvement with the stage that the illusionary theatre sought to induce. Such techniques included flooding the stage with harsh white lights, regardless of where the action was taking place, leaving the stage lamps in full view of the audience; making use of minimal props and 'indicative scenery'; intentionally interrupting the action at key junctures with songs in order to drive home an important point or message; and projecting explanatory captions onto a screen or employing placards. When it came to actors and acting, Brecht acknowledged in his work the need for the actor to undergo a process of identification with the part and he paid tribute to Stanislavsky as the first person to produce a systematic account of the actor's technique. But Brecht demanded of his own actors a going beyond Stanislavsky; he wanted them to incorporate a social attitude or judgement into their portrayal—to become in a sense, objective or detached observers.

Generally, the Verfremdungseffekt has been understood as a deadening coldness in the productions but such an interpretation proceeds from a general ignorance of Brecht's own writings on the subject. Rather, he insisted, as Appia, Craig and the symbolists did before him, that the audience must be reminded that it is watching a play. Brecht's idea can be approached through the image presented by the theatre he chose to work in on his return to East Germany in 1947. The auditorium of the Theatre am Schiffbacnerdamn was lavish to the point of fantasy, decorated with ornate plastic figures. The stage by complete contrast was a vast mechanized scenic space in which everything was clearly exposed to view as theatrical and man made. In the contrast between the comfort of the auditorium and the science of the stage, lay the condition of Brecht's theatre. The audience was there to be entertained but also to think scientifically.

Many of the techniques of Brecht's staging were developments of earlier work. The use of 3-dimensional set pieces in a large volume of space clearly derived from Jessner. His delight in the use of machinery and in particular the revolving stage came from Piscator. The insistence on the actors' demonstrating through the physical disposition of the body, their gestus ("attitude") toward what is happening derived from Meyerhold, though with Brecht the gestus was always socially based. The clearest of his alienation devices, the projection of captions preceding the scene so that the audience knows in advance what will happen and, therefore, can concentrate on how it happens derived from Piscator's jotter scenes and film captions.

Though the Brechtian principle of critical observation instead of emotional identification has not been successfully achieved by modern dramatists, nonetheless the Marxian ideology behind the Verfremdungseffekt which Brecht outlined in Kleines Organon furdas Theater (1949; "A Little Organum for the Theatre") is one of the major aims of agit prop theatre groups. The essence of Brechtian drama is the idea that a truly Marxist drama must avoid the Aristotelian premise that the audience should be made to believe that what they are witnessing is happening here and now. For he saw that if the audience really felt that the emotions of heroes of the Oedipus, or Lear or Hamlet could equally have been their own reactions, then the Marxist idea that human nature is not constant but a result of changing historical conditions would automatically be invalidated. Though agit prop plays generally do away with the aspect of no empathetic involvement on the part of the spectators, they do remain true to Brecht's Marxian beliefs and his theory that the spectators must be reminded that they are being presented with a demonstration of human behaviour in scientific spirit. As has been mentioned earlier, Brecht adopted and advanced many of the ideas and methods of his precursors and towering above them was the work of Piscator.[14]

Piscator began his dramatic career as a volunteer at the Hoft Theatre after studying at the Konig School of Dramatic Art and the University; he became in turn an actor and director, working in Berlin during the Weimar Republic. Piscator clearly used the theatre to convey radical political instruction; though not a communist, he sympathized with the German working class parties. His first efforts at establishing a theatre brought him into association with the Dadaists.

Dada began as an oppositional movement in Zurich and the Dadaists took on from where Alfred Jarry had left: whereas Jarry had assaulted the audience through an unusual play, the Dadaists began the disintegration of form entirely. Dada's contribution lay in destroying all accepted notions of what the stage should be and should express and in attacking the cultural values of the audience in particular and society in general. This set a precedent for many anti-establishment groups and artists after 1968 whose objectives have been described as "offending the audience" or "disrupting the spectacle". One of the art forms that the Dada engendered was that of photomontage in which graphics and edited photographic images were combined to convey propagandist images. The principle of montage became important in Piscator's work. Piscator felt that though a step ahead, Dada was not enough; a more overtly political and direct form of theatre was required, one that was allied to the political struggle of the proletariat. The proletarian theatre, consisting of both, amateurs and professionals, played in workers' halls and established the principle of free admission for the unemployed, which freed the theatre from its bourgeois status as an economic commodity.

Piscator further eroded traditional relationships with numerous innovations in staging as for example in the Rob Rummel Revue ("Red Riot Review", 1924) produced for the German Communist Party, Piscator began the action with a fight in the auditorium. The protagonists came out of the audience to argue their points of view and commented on the action of the various scenes. In Tai Yang Erwacht ("Tai Yang Awakes", 1931) the setting designed by John Heartfield extended from the stage along the walls of the auditoriums. A conspicuous feature of Piscator's propagandist production was the climatic singing of "L' Internationale", the socialist and communist anthem by both actors and audience.

To establish the political relevance of his work, Piscator devised a number of ways. In a revolutionary production of Schiller's Die Rauber (The Robbers) performed at Jessner's Staats theatre in Berlin, Piscator costumed and made up the minor character Spielberg, a noble character driven by society to crime, to resemble Trotsky. Then, in his production of Sturm ubber Gottland ("Storm over Gothland", 1927) set in the fourteenth century, a filmed prologue showed that as the major characters moved towards the camera, they metamorphosed from historically costumed characters to representations of modern historical figures; the protagonist, for example, turned into Lenin. Theatre the world over, especially German theatre has since tended to interpret classic plays in a contemporary light. Another play Paragraph 218 (1929), dealing with abortion reforms, was toured such that the performances were used to initiate discussions. Such associated discussions have since that time become a strong part of women's theatre and other political forms.

In several productions, Piscator dramatized or inserted verbatim political documents, news reports or direct quotations from public figures. Direct comment of this kind was used frequently by Joan Littlewood and the Theatre Workshop Company in Britain in the 1950s and 60s to comment on political actions and to establish common cause with the audience. Piscator also used the projected film to lend an added authenticity to the documentary material presented in front of it and to establish a principle, which has been built on by other political and documentary playwrights and directors that one function of the political stage should be to make manifest what is concealed in politics.

Piscator established three distinct uses of film in his productions. The 'didactic' film as he called it provided the spectator with objective information about the subject through both, historical as well as up to the minute facts. The dramatic film saved time in the play by illuminating a situation with a few quick shots, thus it contributed to the development of the action. Addressing the audience in much the same way as a chorus, film commentary that accompanied the action drew attention to important developments, leveled criticism, made accusations and provided important facts. Piscator should also be credited with the innovation of the jotter scene, a small auxiliary screen onto which facts, figures, titles, dates and other bits of information can be projected.

There are two other innovations that Piscator added to the repertoire of staging devices. He conceived that the postwar world was too complex in its political and economic operations for any one playwright to comprehend it totally. He took the concept of the dramaturgic collective from Reinhardt and extended it to make it the basis of his production method. Writers, dramaturges, economists, politicos and statisticians worked together to produce a script. Existing playscripts were subjected to analysis and restructuring by the collective. The second invention was the "stage of destiny". A great deal of Piscator's life was spent trying to realise a project for staging Tolstoy's novel *War and Peace*. When he finally accomplished this ambition, the judgements of history were incorporated into the narrative.

The style of theatre that Piscator propounded using montage and juxtaposition of short independent scenes to create dialectical and often contradictory effects and to which he gave the name 'epic theatre', opened new theatre vistas not just for his best known follower, Brecht, but political playwrights and theatre companies the world over.

Like Piscator, Meyerhold too experimented with the use of film, projected images and graphic in his productions and there has been a lot of irrelevant controversy as to who copied whom.[15] Meyerhold is, however, best known for developing an anti-realstic system of dramatic production in the USSR in the 1920s called biomechanics. The actor, whose role was subordinate until he was a mere instrument of the director's will, was supposed to eliminate all emotion from his highly stylised portrayal. Coached as gymnasts and acrobats and emphasizing pantomime rather than words, the actors threw themselves about in puppet like attitudes at the director's discretion. For these productions the stage was exposed to the back wall and was then furnished with sets consisting of scaffoldings, ladders and ramps that the actor used with every strut and bolt displayed to view. The aggressive functionalism of this type of setting was regarded as having considerable propaganda value when the Soviets were being taught to reverse the machine as part of their training to become a great industrial nation.

Meyerhold's system drew on a variety of influences including commedia dell'arte, Kabuki theatre, the ideas of Craig and Ivan Petrovich Pavlov, the psychologist. He constructed a set of sixteen etudes as the basis of biomechanics; these were sequences of precise muscular movements intended to evoke particular emotions in the performer. This process attempted to systematize the kinesthetic relationship between outer movement and inner feeling, to enable actors to experience this relationship, and to train them to control it. Even after so short a time, it is not easy to reconstruct Meyerhold's biomechanics from remaining evidences because of his fall from favour under Stalin. But, if the exact form of biomechanics has not survived, many of the underlying principles of Meyerhold's studies have, and the example of his training programme is embodied in the work of many of the present day advanced theatre groups. Less well known is the work of Vakhtangov, which is important because of the ways in which he combined the inner techniques of Stanislavsky with the external expressive techniques of Meyerhold. An investigation of the work of Jerzy Grotowski shows the continuation of this process and many of the specific techniques.

Against the prevailing approach of Stanilavsky, epitomized in the "building" of a character, Meyerhold instituted a holistic approach whereby the actors did not "mark" the actions but gave prototypical performances in rehearsal. Each rehearsal then produced a more complex prototype, and the process continued into the public performances. According to Meyerhold such a process underlined the "unindividuality" of man whereby he felt that the principles of propagandist theatre conformed with those of Marxism. It is Meyerhold's refusal to submit to the constraints of artistic uniformity and his defence of the artist's right to experiment that led to his arrest, imprisonment and rejection by the Stalin regime but it also made him one of the spiritual gurus of modern political theatre. However, more than Meyerhold's impact has been that of Mayakovsky, the leading Russian poet of the Russian Revolution and of the early Soviet period.[16] Influenced by Marinettis' Futurism and as part of the first group of artists to identity wholeheartedly with the Bolshevik Revolution of 1917, Mayakovsky sought with others of his ilk to create the new proletarian art. The key lay in "depoetising" poetry by adopting the crude language of the man in the street, using the most daring technical innovations and being declamatory for mass audience to which he gave readings on streets, at cafes and at meetings.

Tracing Mayakovsky's artistic career can itself reveal both, his ideological as well as methodological principles that assumed larger proportions in subsequent agit prop movements, especially theatre. At the age of fifteen, he joined the Russian Social Democratic Workers' Party and was repeatedly jailed for subversive activity. He started to write poetry during solitary confinement in 1909. On his release he attended the Moscow Art School and joined, with David Burlyuk and a few others, the Russian Futurist group and soon became its leading spokesman. In 1912 the group published a manifesto, Poschochina Obshchestvenomukusu ("A Slap in the Face of Public Taste") and Mayakovsky's poetry became conspicuously self assertive and defiant in form and content: the manifesto advocated the abandonment of Pushkin, Dostoyevsky and Tolstoy and of course, bringing the language poetry down to that of the streets. Mayakovsky's first poetic monodrama <u>Vladimir Mayakovsky</u> was performed in St Petersburg in 1913.

Between 1914 and 1916, Mayakovsky completed two major poems "Oblakovshtanakh" (1915; "A Cloud in Trousers") and "Fleytapozvonochnik" (written 1915; published 1916; "The Backbone Flute"). Both record a tragedy of unrequited love and express the author's discontent with the world in which he lived. When the Russian Revolution broke out, Mayakovsky was wholeheartedly for the Bolsheviks. Such poems as "Oda Revolutse" (1918; "Ode to Revolution") and "Levy Marsh" (1919; "Left

March") became very popular as did his Misteriya Buff (first performed 1921; "Mystery-Bouffe"), a drama representing a universal flood and the subsequent joyful triumph of the "Unclean" (the proletarians) over the "Clean" (the bourgeoise).

As a vigorous spokesperson for the Communist Party, Mayakovsky expressed himself in many ways. From 1919 to 1921, he worked in the Russian Telegraph Agency as a painter of posters and cartoons, which he provided with apt rhymes and slogans. He poured out topical poems of propaganda (agit poetry) and wrote didactic booklets for children, while lecturing and reciting all over Russia. In 1942 he composed a 3,000-line elegy on the death of Lenin. After 1925 he traveled in Europe, in the US, Mexico and Cuba, recording his impressions in poems and in a booklet of caustic sketches Moye Otkrytiye Ameriki (1926; "My Discovery of America"). He also found time to write scripts for motion pictures, in some of which he acted. In his last three years he completed two satirical plays Klop (performed 1929; The Bedbug, 1960) lampooning the kind of philistine that emerged with the New Economic policy in the Soviet Union, and Banya (performed in Leningrad on January 30, 1930; "The Bathhouse"), a bantering tale of bureaucratic stupidity and opportunism under Stalin.

Though it is true that much of Mayakovsky's utilitarian and topical poetry is now out of date, he was in his lifetime one of the most dynamic figures of the Soviet literary scene. It is evident from this largely biographical note how Mayakovsky has become almost an icon for the true agit prop activist.

In terms of furthering the actor's techniques, the Polish director Jerzy Grotowski stands as one of the key figures of the twentieth century.[17] He made the most thorough effort to rediscover the elements of the actors' art. Though he acknowledged Stanislavsky's contribution in this sphere, he was not satisfied either with the way Stanislavsky allowed natural impulses to dominate or with Brecht's over concern with the construction of the role. To Grotowski, the actor is a man who works through the medium of his body, offering it publicly. Hence the actor must undergo physical, plastic and vocal training to guide him toward the right kind of construction, to commit himself totally and to achieve a state of "trance". The actors concentrate on the search for "signs" which express through sound and movement those impulses that waver on the borderline between drama and reality. By means of such signs, the actor's own psychoanalytic language of sounds and gestures is constructed. Though the actors of Grotowski's troupe are excellently trained physically and vocally and commit themselves to their task with tremendous energy, they have been accused of conveying too little human emotion. More than his Laboratory Theatre group, what Grotowski is significantly known for is his theoretical pronouncements in *Towards a Poor Theatre* (1968).

The 'Poor Theatre' recalls Corpeau's idea of the "greatest possible effect from the least possible means" and its name is derived from the simple circumstances in which it takes place. Rejecting the paraphernalia of the "rich theatre", Grotowski stripped away all nonessential scenery, costumes and props to shift the focus only on the unadorned actor. Sharing with Artaud the concept of the performer as a 'holy actor' and the theatre as a 'secular religion', Grotowski felt that theatre must go beyond mere entertainment or illustration: it must be an intense confrontation with the audience.[18] Though Grotowski preferred a limited audience of not more than sixty people (from 1976 in fact he excluded the audience altogether) whereas political theatre addresses huge audiences, it is easy to see why agit prop theatre companies turned to poor theatre especially in the late 1960s and early 1970s.

The spirit of poor theatre has been most theatrically conveyed by Peter Brooks, famous for such vivid productions as Ubu Roi (1977), a scaled down version of Georges Bizel's opera Carmen (1982) and Le Mahabharata (1985), a nine-hour revision of the epic Mahabharata. Again, a pupil of Grotowski, Erugenio Barba of Odin Theatre in Holstebro, Denmark, has formulated the ideological position of their theatres under the term 'third theatre'. In his book The Floating Islands (1979), he examines a theatre existing independently that creates from whatever material resources are at hand. Barba has sought to return to theatre as a way of life seeing this pattern in the origins of the commedia dell'arte, the wandering players and in Moliere's Company. The third theatre groups give performances, but they insist that the relationships engendered by their work, inside and outside the company, are the criteria by which they judge it. The members of the Odin Theatre have established a form of bartering in which they exchange their work for some cultural offering from the people of the regions they visit. Because the third theatre is a way of life, the actors' work is a fulltime activity. Actors have their own daily training regimen and their work is enriched by the acquisition of other skills especially the techniques of Oriental theatre.

Grotowski's use of psychological conditioning exercises for actors, the collaging of texts and the shaping of theatrical space were inherited by Richard Schechner in his theatrical experiments.[19] Schechner is best known for his development of environmental theatre, a branch of the new theatre movement of the 1960s whose aim is to heighten audience awareness of theatre by eliminating the distinction between the audiences and the actors' space.

Believing in the principle that "Text, action and environment must develop together", Schechner and the Performance Group (founded 1968) shaped the theatre to conform to each play, constructing different audience frameworks for each production (Schechner,1983:77). The sets were usually based on multilevel platforms, balconies, ramps and scaffolds surrounding a stage that encroached on the audiences' territory, providing a wider range of space for the actors and a greater flexibility of interaction between the audience and performers. Schechner felt "...Spaces ought to open to each other so that spectators can see each other and move from one place to another. The overall feel of a theatre ought to be of a place where choices can be made. The feel I get from a successful environment is that of a global space, a microcosm, with flow, contact and interaction."(Schechner, 1983:79).

The audience of the environment theatre was invited, even expected, to participate. The minimum involvement for the production of Commune, for example, was the audience' removal of its shoes upon entering the garage. Schechner wrote that theatre was an "unliterary art" and saw its finest expressions as "immediate gestural, involved, inclusive, participatory."[20] To enhance the immediacy of experience, the multiple-focus theatre replaced the traditional single focus allowing more than one scene to be staged at the same time. This was because Schechner was sure that though "chased from Plato's republic as non-rational and subversive, but existing always, sometimes marginally, theatre is now showing itself everywhere: in social dramas, personal experience, public displays, political and economic interaction, art."(Schechner, 1983: 121)

It must be obvious by now that no chronological order has been followed in this ongoing discussion on theatre theoreticians and practitioners; the prioritising has been done only according to the strength of the impact (direct or indirect) that the aforesaid have had upon agit prop theatre. Romain Rolland's efforts at democratizing theatre in France occurred as early as the 1890s but his influence on agit prop theatre *per se* is not really palpable.[21] Thus this section will be brief.

With both ideological aims and theatrical tastes in mind, members of the German middle class theatre audience formed an organisation called the Freie Volksbuhne in 1890 for the purpose of buying blocks of tickets and commissioning performances and even productions for its membership which included a large working class element. Early in its history the organisation split between the Freie Volksbuhne, who were attempting to make theatre available to a wider audience and the Heue Freie Volksbuhne, who had specific socialist attachments and policies. Eventually the two arms recombined and were able not only to subsidise socialist performance but also to build their own theatre and mount their own productions. During the 1890s in France, a similar programme of democratisation was attempted. One of the prime movers in this was Rolland whose book The Peoples Theatre (Le Theatre du Peuple, 1903) inspired similar movements in other countries.

In this book Rolland speaks of the three requisites of the Peoples Theatre: the first being that it must be a recreation, i.e., he felt that the task of the playwright was to provide pleasure and joy to the audience rather than to burden them with sadness and tragedy. The second requisite according to Rolland was that theatre ought to be an energising agency; he wished that the audience treated dramatist as a congenial fellow traveler. "It is the duty of this companion to take the people straight to their destination— without of course neglecting to teach them to observe along the road."[22] The third requisite that Rolland stated as fundamental was that theatre should provide an "incentive to thought." He felt that since the working man did not as a rule think while his body worked, it was necessary for theatre to provoke him to exercise his brain. This would not only afford him pleasure but would also help him to see and judge 'things' as well as his own 'self'. Rolland also cautioned against the two excesses of moral pedagogy and mere impersonal dilettantism. He believed that the existence of a permanent theatre where emotions were shared would create a bond of brotherhood and that people were more ignorant than bad; thus theatre ought to dispel ignorance. In his beliefs, Rolland was not alone and he acknowledged the debt he owed to the ideas of Rosseau, Diderot and Mercier.

While Rolland had his precursors, he had followers too. His assumption that theatre was an effective arena of action and that people could be manipulated by theatre is a formative principle of all politically viable theatre.

Nearer our times, the Brazilian director and political activist turned politician, Augusto Boal raised the stage/spectator contradiction to an ideological level, of one between authority and people.[23] Believing that since all activities of man are political and that, therefore, theatre too is political, he showed how theatre in the West had been used by the dominant class to project their own norms and values, their ideology. To counter this enterprise, Boal developed the Theatre of the Oppressed, a system which not only surmounted the stage/spectator contradictions but through the conquest of the means of theatrical production was intended to serve the triple function of entertainment, education and consciousness raising.

In his book Games for Actors and non Actors (1992), Boal devised a series of theatrical strategies in the form of games and exercises to effect change in the lives of individuals in all fronts, personal, social and political. As Boal puts it, his aim was that the "spectator is freed from his chains, finally acts, and becomes a protagonist."[24] Thus he was interested in forms of 'rehearsal theatre' the kind of theatre practiced by the proletariat and oppressed classes versus the bourgeois which presents a closed spectacle theatre. A brief look at some of the theatrical games would suffice in showing how theatre can intervene in almost every walk of life; newspaper theatre, for example, involves transformation of daily news items and any other non-dramatic material into theatrical performance. Again, in 'Invisible Theatre' a scene is presented in a non theatre environment by actors who do not reveal their profession throughout the performance to spectators, in such a manner that the spectators are clueless about the fact that they are spectators. During rehearsal every possible intervention from the spectators is included so that these possibilities form a kind of optional text. Thus the 'theatre' element is 'invisible', the spectators act freely as though in a real situation, and the effects last long after the skit is ended. Yet again, in the use of Rituals and Masks, Boal shows that if the ritual is retained but the social masks of those involved in the ritual keep changing, then countless variants throwing up endless options are made visible to spectators.

As Member of Parliament of Rio de Janiero's Workers' Party (PT), Boal developed his most recent theatre form—the legislative theatre. The purpose of this form was to allow communities to propose laws which they wished the Council (Chambre de Vereadores) to formalize by using theatrical strategies. It is evident then that Boal's work aims at providing an 'alternative means of training and of restoring theatre to a meaningful role in society outside theatres; a democratic forum for potential change in peoples lives'.[25]

Perhaps such an overview of theoretical standpoints of theatre practitioners might mislead one into actually seeking exact imprints in British agit prop theatre. But such has not been my aim. This section intends to isolate possible ways to read, view and interpret British agit prop theatres (their texts and their practices) from around certain techniques articulated by those I have mentioned. There are surely many other theoretical nuances that have been overlooked here and may crop up in the course of this thesis, but at this juncture we have at least a broad framework with which we can approach British agit prop theatre and appreciate its changing shapes.

From Brecht to Boal, from conscious Verfremdung to the conscious entry of theatre into every arena of life, is a vast discourse to have chalked out showing that political theatre has indeed come a long way. It may seem that Brechtian techniques are now passé but there can be no denying that much of political drama since Brecht's death has been written with his formidable theoretical example in view; even those dramatists who have refused Brecht's political aesthetic have done so in the wake of its radical reconfigurations of theatre art. Those dramatists who draw upon Brechtian theory have participated in the broader reinterpretation of this theory in terms of evolving political, cultural and theatrical milieux. "We should begin with Brecht", Edward Bond has remarked, but we shouldn't end there." In Heiner Miller's words, "To use Brecht without criticizing him is to betray him"(in Garner, Jr, 1990:146).

Thus while retaining the fundamental Marxian ideology believed in by Brecht as also his views that theatre must engender a spirit of social criticism, agit prop theatres have sought methods other than the Alienation Effect. Discussions with the audience during or after the 'act', singing rousing songs or an instigating poetry, staging mobile plays in unconventional theatre sites ranging from the street, shopping malls to workers' halls, lampooning public figures, using actual facts or quotations of contemporary power holders, creating a script through team effort, using the 'unpoetic' language of the common man or proletariat, breaking through the constraints of artistic uniformity, using lec-dem formats, making spectators participate and, therefore, realize that action in the theatre is only a beginning and not a conclusion, resisting political censorship—all these post-Brechtian features and more which have not just been theorized upon but also practiced by the theoreticians dealt with in this chapter, are characteristic of British as well as global agit prop theatre. Because it embraces aspects of Dadaism, Futurism, Poor Theatre, Laboratory Theatre, Biomechanics, Environmental Theatre, Feminist Theatre and is successful, effective and here to stay, agit prop theatre is possibly the most open ended theatre in our times and makes for a challenging study.

Notes

[1] Anuradha Kapur puts it rather well in her article 'Notions of the Authentic' in the Journal of Arts and Ideas, Nos 20-21, March 1991; "All theatres create their spectators into communities one way or another; the point is to consider what sort of community we should create today. Neither voyeuristic as is done in some forms of naturalism; nor one in the likeness of what we imagine traditional theatres make in their own contexts; but one that queries ourselves, displaying to us the ways in which our past and our future may be conjoined. But not without placing that wedge of contemporary perception that over and again relocates the parts that would be too easy to congeal into a false organicity."

[2] It would be useful to quote Diana Taylor here, who in her article 'Theatre and Terrorism: Griselda Gambaro's Information for Foreigners', in Theatre Journal, Vol. 42. No.2, May 1990, says: "Watching, potentially empowering when it forms a part of a broader network can be extremely disempowering when reduced to the spectator's passive "just watching". She continues: "in order to be empowered by seeing, to be able to look back at the monstrous gargoyles without turning into lifeless stones, we must see beyond the theatrical frame and decode the fictions about violence, about torturers, about ourselves aas audience, about the role of theater in this "pathetic drama", p. 178

[3] As Michael Huxley and Noel Witts quote Augusto Boal in their edition of The Twentieth Century Performance Reader, Routledge, London and New York, 1996, "Perhaps the theatre is not revolutionary in itself; but have no doubts, it is a rehearsal of revolution", p.97

[4] See Drama Review, Nos 125-128, 1990, section entitled 'On Stage with the Velvet Revolution'.

[5] See Theatre Quarterly, Vol. 17, 1977, section on Theatre in Australia, pp.47-70

[6] See The New Encyclopedia Britannica: Macropedia, Vol.28, pp.591-92

[7] Ibid.

[8] See The Drama Review, Vol.30, Nos. 2-4, 1986, section on Black Protest Theatre'.

[9] The New Encyclopedia Britannica: Macropedia, Vol.28, pp.591-92

[10] To quote an example: Nathaniel Buchwald, the director of the Yiddish Artef group, reviewed the winning entry, John Bonn's Red Revue in Worker's Theatre. His criticism is applicable to most of the work of the period. "In general the work of Prolet Buehne, though outstanding in the field of Agit Prop theatre, leans too heavily on direction and delivery of lines and too little on the dramaturgical shaping of its plays. The Prolet Buehne players speak their lines with a ringing galvanic forcefulness, and the director marshals them up on the stage in perfect rhythm and in a variety of group patterns, with changing tempo building up to a spectacular climax. But the plays themselves are frequently devoid of effective theatrical form and the vocabulary leans to the conventional propagandist jargon." From Stuart Cosgrove's 'Prolet Buehne: agit prop in America' in David bridby, Louis James and Bernard Sharratt, eds, 1980: 209-210.

[11] The New Encyclopedia Britannia, Macropedia, Vol.1, p.149 and Vol.28, p.591 were useful sources of information.

[12] Eugen Berthold Friedrich Brecht (b. February 10, 1898, Augsburg, Germany; d. August 14, 1956, East Berlin), German poet, playwright and theatrical reformer whose epic theatre departed from the conventions of theatrical illusion and who developed the drama as a social and ideological form for leftist causes. His notable plays include Baal (produced 1923), Driegroschenoper (1928; The Three Penny Opera), Mutter Courage and ihre Kinder (1941; Mother Courage and her Children), Leben des Galilei (1943; The Life of Galileo); Der Gute Mensch Von Sezuan (1943; The Good Woman of Stezuan), Der Aufhaltsame Aufsteig des Arturo ui (1947; The Resistible Rise of Arturo Ui), Herr Puntila and sein Knecht Matti (1948; Herr Puntila and His Man Matti); The Caucasian Chalk Circle (first produced in English, 1948; Der Kaukasische Kriede Kre is, 1949). His most important work is Kleines Organon Furdas Theatre (1949; A Little Organum for the Theatre).

[13] From 'On Experimental Theater' by Brecht, reprinted in The Theory of the Modern Stage: An Introduction to Modern Theatre and Drama,ed., Eric Bentley, Penguin, reprinted 1992:100

[14] Erwin Piscator (b. December 17, 1893, Alm, Germany; d. March 30, 1966, Starnberg, West Germany), theatrical producer and director famed for his ingenious Expressionistic staging techniques; the originator of the epic theatre style, later developed by Brecht.

[15] Vsevoldo Yemilyevich Meyerhold (b. February 9 [January 28, old style], 1874, Penza, Russia; d. February 2, 1940, Moscow), Russian theatrical producer, director and actor whose provocative experiments in nonrealistic theatre made him one of the seminal forces in modern theatre.

[16] Vladimir Vladimirovich Mayakovsky (b. July 19 [July 7 old style], 1893, Bagdadi, Georgia, Russian Empire; d. April 14, 1930, Moscow), the leading Russian poet of the Russian revolution and of the early Soviet period.

[17] Jerzy Grotowski (b. August 11, 1933, Rseszow, Poland), international leader of the Experimental theatre, who became famous in the 1960s as the director of productions staged by the Polish Laboratory Theatre of Wroclaw.

[18] Antonin Artaud (b. 1896; d. 1948), outstanding writer and actor of the French theatrical avant-garde. He was vehemently hostile towards Realism and naturalism. He believed that theatre could through the power wielded by its immediacy create such a total upheaval in all senses in the population that it would broaden perceptions to a revolutionary level. According to him theatre does away with a rationale that is constricting. Based on his understanding that everything that acted was cruelty and that theatre ought to rebuild itself on a concept of this drastic action pushed to the limit, he developed his idea of the theatre of cruelty. Such theatre, he felt, contained the scope to test 'our entire vitality, confronting us with all our potential.'

[19] Richard Schechner (b. 1934) is director, writer, theorist and the founder of the Performance Group (1967-1980). His environmental productions including Dionysius in 69, Makbeth and Commune were performed in his performing garage on off-Broadway in New York City.

[20] Quoted in The New Encyclopedia Britannica: Macropedia, Vol.4; 512

[21] Romain Rolland (b. January 29, 1866, Clamency, France; d. December 30, 1944, Vezelay), novelist, dramatist, essayist and one of the greatest mystics of the twentieth century French literature. He was, in his life and writings, deeply involved in the major social, political and spiritual events of his age; the "Dreyfus Affair" which exposed anti-Semitism in the French army; pacifism; communism; the fight against Fascism, and the search for world peace.

[22] From The Peoples Theatre by Romain Rolland, excerpt entitled 'Three requisites' reprinted in The Theory of the Modern Stage, ed., Eric Bentley, Penguin, reprinted 1992: 456

[23] Augusto Boal (b. 1934), Brazilian director, political activist and Member of parliament of Rio de Janeiro's Workers' Party; evolved a system known as Theatre of the Oppressed which makes use of games and exercises; image theatre; invisible theatre and is currently developing legislative theatre. His theoretical standpoint is clear from is Games for Actors and non-Actors (1992) and The Rainbow of Desire (1995).

[24] From 'Poetics of the Oppressed: Fourth Stage; The Theatre as Discourse' in Theatre of the Oppressed, Augusto Boal, reprinted in The Twentieth Century Performance Reader, ed., Michael Huxley and Noel Witts, Routledge, London and New York, 1966: 85-86.

[25] Ibid., p.98

AN OVERVIEW OF BRITISH AGIT PROP THEATRE

That the aims of various agit prop theatre groups in Britain differ testifies to the fact that agit prop theatre is conjunctural and it intervenes in a historical context, as elucidated in Chapter One. Since 'historical context' or in other words, 'politics', is by nature dynamic, agit prop theatre too, then, cannot be enslaved to a particular political stance/view/message. This chapter intends to pursue the changing political situation in Britain from the sixties to the nineties and dwell upon the various alternate especially agit prop theatre companies that sprung up at different times.

While the term post World War II would imply a time period beginning from after 1945, critics are unanimously agreed upon considering the sixties as the most 'happening' years.[1] This was not just in terms of evolving political events but also in terms of the development of a counter culture movement around the world including Britain. The counter culture movement did not cause the emancipatory and libertarian movements of the seventies and eighties (such as the women's lib and feminist movements, the black consciousness movements, gay rights and community activist movements or movements that fought for the rights of the disabled, the old or other socially disadvantaged groups). Yet, this

> ...initial counter culture did provide a 'model' for oppositional action
> against hegemony on a grand scale...the British alternative theatre
> movement was only one, relatively small part of the counter cultural
> and emancipatory movements of the 1960s, 1970s and 1980s...its
> chief tactic was allied to the emergence of the aesthetics
> of anti nuclear, anti war and civil rights demonstrations in Britain
> and the USA...a new mode of celebratory protest ...challenged
> dominant ideologies through the production of alternative pleasures...[2]

In terms of political activity, 1968 has been traditionally accepted as the most eventful of years: in her Introduction to <u>Stages in the Revolution</u>, Catherine Itzin has detailed the events such, that an attempt to describe that year would appear to be almost a rewriting of her work. At best one could summarise her informative chapter through the words of Bigsby who appropriately commented that the events in Vietnam, Ireland, France, Germany and even Czechoslovakia were responsible for infusing a political component into public life and rhetoric which had never been present before. (Bigsby, 1981: 32)

The events that stand out in the political front of the year 1968 include the opening of peace talks between USA and North Vietnam at Paris; student unrest in France; liberalisation movement in Czechoslovakia; the occupation of entire Czechoslovakia on 21st August by the Warsaw Pact nations excluding Rumania; the establishment of a puppet regime at Prague; Britain's announcement of her intention to withdraw from all her bases East of Suez by 1971 (with the exception of Hong Kong); the assassination of Martin Luther King on March 5; the beginning of war in Northern Ireland following the banning of a Civil Rights March in Derry.

> Across the world, large scale revolutionary demands by students, workers and peasants were answered by massive and brutal repression ordered by governments of every political leaning—capitalist, communist or social-democratic...In 1968, as now, the world overflowed with milk and honey, yet the majority of its inhabitants were starving. Economically, the world's unrivalled prosperity led to demands for the equal distribution of the world's wealth. Ideologically, the possibility of material freedom was complemented by demands for cultural and creative freedom: one of the most significant calls from the barricades of Paris was for 'power to the imagination. (Craig, 1980:15).

Among those who responded to this ideological calling, it was the politically awakened radicalised student community that became socially the most identifiable of groups. This youthful student community, poised as it was between a world just beyond its grasp that promised all the affluence and advantages that society could offer and facing a real world that could give only struggle, pollution and Cold War imperialism responded not just with resentment but with anger. And this anger did not fizzle out but was channelised such that it

> became a movement of the political left, appealing (however confusedly) to Marx as a symbol of the revolutionary transformation of society. All of this came to be reflected in the theatre. (Itzin, 1980:3)

While the moment of 1968 is clearly perceptible in its contribution to the growing theatre revolution, it would be both unjust and misleading to ignore the earlier harbingers of this radical change. Of these precedents the two most notable were the Unity Theatre which grew out of the Workers Theatre Movement of the thirties and Joan Littlewood's Theatre Workshop at the Royal Stratford in East London. There was also the Centre 42 (named after the 1962 TUC resolution proposing support for the Arts) project of Arnold Wesker. All these theatre movements had ambitions that were similar to those of the alternative theatre companies of the late sixties and early seventies. In fact, as Itzin and Craig among others point out, the work of CAST, The General Will, the early Red Ladder, Broadside Mobile Workers Theatre and North West Spanner was an offshoot of the Unity in terms of form, content and political leaning. Centre 42's dream of bridging the gap between performer and audience and providing a theatre that was accessible to the working class was converted into a reality by Companies like 7:84, Belt and Braces, Foco Novo and Monstrous Regiment. Ed Berman's Inter Action and his contribution in the creation of the Ambiance Lunch Hour Theatre Club and the Almost Free Theatre— which aimed at proving that theatre was not only an evening leisure activity indulged by a small theatre going public or that a community was not one bound by topographical space but by shared interests—drew their inspiration from Joan Littlewoods Theatre Workshop.

The political/theatrical landmarks that impacted the dramatic developments in the theatrical front of 1968, do not end here. For there are other contexts that are equally significant in shaping the nature of British theatrical activity. Firstly, the

> abolition of the institution of theatre censorship, practised since
> the eighteenth century by the Lord Chamberlain. The most
> obviously irksome manifestation of censorship applied to sex
> (the writer Joe Orton suffering particularly and amusingly)
> but political censorship was also involved and the very bureaucracy
> of script approval (which took several weeks) effectively
> pre-empted topical or improvised work. (Edgar, 1988:24-25)

Secondly, the gathering strength of the feminist movement as well as of the Gay Liberation Front. This was as a result of

> a climate of change in the organisation of family life
> and the liberalisation of laws on sexuality...
> the partial decriminalisation of male homosexuality in 1967.
> (Wandor, 1981:17)

Next, the repeated failure of the Labour government to bring about social change which bred feelings of disillusionment and discontent and naturally led to all kinds of, including theatrical, backlash at its ineffectiveness (Itzin, 1980:6). And finally, the direct and indirect influences of foreign theatre activities such as that of the Blue Blouses, Mayakovsky, Meyerhold, Piscator and above all Brecht and his Berliner Ensemble (all of which has been discussed at length in the previous chapter) and the visits of many foreign theatre companies.[3]

Given all these ingredients essential for a truly charged theatre, it is no surprise then that a number of alternative theatre groups sprung up at this time. Foremost among them was CAST (Cartoon Archetypal Slogan Theatre). CAST was originally formed in 1965 by two dropouts of Unity Theatre, Claire and Roland Mudoon, who were disillusioned by the Communist Party agenda which the Unity

stuck to insistently. CAST sought, literally, to cast the working class population and its method was striking in that it veered between agit prop and agit pop. In other words it definitely attempted to agitate its captive audience (found initially in pubs) but instead of adopting a solemn tone, they employed what Muldoon himself described as 'rock and roll theatre' (Itzin, 1980:14). The central character of their shows was a Muggins (appearing in different plays with a different first name)- a character who represented the 'mugging' or slogging working class. It was however, the play written by John Arden and Margaretta D'Arcy called Harold Muggins Is a Martyr which they performed in 1968 with CAST (quite a disaster as performances go from all accounts) which was a breakthrough in that it led to a kind of cultural confluence of politically awakened theatre activists.

Emerging head above shoulders over the ventures that were an outcome of this confluence was the Agit Prop Street Players (later renamed as Red Ladder),

> the name itself summing up its approach—which grew out
> of requests from tenants for 15 minute pieces dramatising rent
> strikes. (Davies, 1987:164)

This company while seeking to bring about greater class-consciousness steered clear of

words like 'capitalism', 'communism' or 'socialism in favour
of more concrete and direct images. (Davies, 1987:165)

The characteristic that distinguished the theatre of the Agit Prop Street Players
from other theatre was that there would always be a discussion after the play with the
audience—a very deliberate agit prop feature.

Another company that formed at this time was the Portable comprising of
university educated writers such as David Hare and Howard Brenton. The work of the
Portable which was inspired by the counter cultural ideologies of the late sixties (such as
that of the French Situationists) was 'violent, anarchic and destructive.' (Edgar, 1988:26).
Their political stance unlike that of the Agit Prop Street Players who believed deep down
in a workers revolution

> was seen as being much less about the organisation of the working class
> at the point of production, and much more about the description of
> bourgeois ideology at the point of consumption. The center of the
> revolution had shifted from the factory floor to the supermarket. (Edgar,
> 1988:26)

A little more must be said about the contribution of Ed Berman's Inter Action.
His aim behind the creation of the Ambiance Lunch Hour Theatre Club and the Almost
Free Theatre has been already mentioned in the previous pages. Inter Action actually
mothered a number of smaller theatrical enterprises that had a vast range of objectives
and target audiences. For example, there was a children's theatre company called Dogg's
Troupe that involved the local community of the housing estates through Game Plays; the
Fun Art Bus aimed at generating environment consciousness by performing plays and
using video screens on the boarding deck of a bus to the bus queues

> and TOC (The Other Company) which, under Naftali Yavin, examined
> sociological theories of role-playing and game theory in an attempt to
> break through the artificial barriers which exist not only between people
> but also between stage and audience. (Craig, 1980:23)

Another new theatrical venture whose aims were similar to Inter Action (i.e. the
betterment of the community) was the Brighton Combination which presented playlets
that dealt with localized community problems and 'fulfilled in a manner—which few

41

later political groups have done—the central function of agit prop: agitate, educate and organise.' (Craig, 1980:23)

Thus in that turbulent year of 1968 it was only natural that theatre responded to the politically high-wire situation and in the decade that followed, this theatrical drift towards politics became further entrenched.[4] 1969, the year that Neil Armstrong walked on the moon, saw a rightist coup in Cambodia with an escalation of conflict in Laos and South Vietnam; the secret visit of Dr. Kissinger to China in 1971 which paved the way for a summit between President Nixon and Mao Tse Tung in Peking (which Nixon visited in 1972). 1972 was more eventful in that there was the Stockholm Conference to prevent pollution; President Nixon visited the Soviet Union and signed the agreement on Strategic Arms Limitation Talks; and England entered the European Common Market. The next year saw Britain, Ireland and Denmark joining the European Economic Community; US withdrawal of troops from Vietnam and the signing of the peace settlement at Paris; military coup in Chile with the overthrow of the Marxist President, Salvador Allende; and the October War where the Arab States attacked Israel and ceasefire was imposed after 5-weeks of fighting. 1974 brought in the resignation of President Nixon after the Watergate scandal. A year later, there were communist victories in Cambodia and the end of the Vietnam War with South Vietnam surrendering to North Vietnam; and a 3-day Helsinki Summit of 35 nations. 1976 was again, a packed year what with race riots erupting in South Africa; Angola becoming the new center of power rivalry; Palestinian right to independent Statehood being voted by USA; Khmer Rouge taking control of Cambodia; America celebrating the bicentenary of its independence and electing Jimmy Carter as President; and the death of Mao Tse Tung. In 1978 there were border clashes between Vietnam and Cambodia; and the USA agreed to diplomatic relations with China and severing its ties with Taiwan.

This was the general political scenario at the International front; perhaps it is more necessary to have a closer look at the British political scene from 1968 to 1978.[5] It has been mentioned in the previous paragraph that Britain entered the European Common Market but part of the entry fee was an inevitable rise in food prices. An Industrial Relations Act in 1971 was bitterly resented and resisted by the Labour Party and the

Unions. As unemployment and prices rose, Edward Heath (the Conservative leader whose successful negotiations had made Britain's entry into the Common Market possible) fell back on a statutory Prices and Incomes Policy (Phase I, 1972; Phase II, 1973). By late 1973, industrial unrest had reached a new peak. In response to stoppages and overtime bans by electricity supply workers, train drivers and miners, Heath announced a state of Emergency and eventually a 3-day working week in all offices, shops and factories. This was to conserve fuel, which was in unusually short supply because of the Arab-Israeli War of 1973 and the OPEC decision to double the price of crude oil. In 1974, the General Election concluded with the resignation of Heath and the formation of a Labour Party government headed by Wilson who stayed in power till 1976 to be followed by Callaghan till 1979.

One of the major problems that Britain was faced with was the reappearance of the 'Irish Question' with the renewed activities of the Irish Republican Army (IRA) in the late 1950s. In 1969, Wilson sent British troops to Northern Ireland to enforce law and order. The Royal Ulster Constabulary (R.U.C) was disarmed, the B specials were disbanded and the Catholics welcomed what they initially viewed as impartial protection. By 1971, distrust and violence had escalated again and in January 1972 British soldiers shot thirteen people in a Catholic demonstration in London Derry. In 1973 a 'power sharing' executive of moderate Catholics and Protestants was formed in the Sunningdale Agreement of December 1973 and it seemed that a liberal solution acceptable to Westminster, Dublin and Belfast had been found. However the General Election of 1974 where 11 out 12 anti Sunningdale candidates were successful and the all out strike by the Protestant Ulster Workers Union in May destroyed whatever hope there was for this 'power sharing' executive. A new Constitutional Convention in 1975-76 failed to hammer out an acceptable political formula. The subsequent political violence was so intense that it led to a Peace Movement initiated by two Belfast women, Betty Williams (a Protestant) and Mairead Corrigan (a Catholic) to restore political sanity and trust between members of different religions sects. Though they were given the Nobel Peace Prize in 1977, the Catholic extremists were not stirred enough by their message. In 1978 and 1979, Provisional IRA prisoners seeking special political (as opposed to criminal) status in gaol devised the 'dirty' protest where they refused to use any of the clothing, washing and lavatory facilities of the prison but remained in stinking squalor for months. Whatever sympathy this action may have won for them was more than destroyed by the cold blooded murder of Lord Mountbatten and two of his family in August 1979 and in a separate incident on the same day, the murder by remote controlled explosions of 18 British soldiers at Warren Point.

Apart from these governmental machinations, a movement that had started gathering momentum in the late sixties and became loudly public in the early seventies was the feminist movement. The first major public statement was made in 1970 during the twentieth Miss World Contest where suddenly a group of women interrupted the spectacle in full media viewing with

> flour, smoke and stink bombs, blew whistles, waved rattles and
> distributed leaflets to members of the audience, protesting against
> the objectification of women in beauty contest ...The women were
> arrested, Bob Hope cracked a few defensive jokes and the show
> continued. (Wander, 1981:36)

It was perhaps this movement that attempted to negate gender biases that inspired the formation of professional theatre companies such as the Women's Theatre Group (1974), Monstrous Regiment (1975-76) and Gay Sweatshop (1976). Initially the feminist theatre groups (with which the Gay theatre movement invariably joined hands) worked collectively and their plays used overtly agit prop and music hall elements. By the mid seventies however, though this tendency continued, the convoluted nature of feminist/ gay issues began to be taken up and plays by individuals rather than groups began to find their way on stage. It was not just the specifically feminists/gay theatre companies alone that dealt with these 'gender bender' subjects but also other agit prop theatre companies like the Agit Prop Street Players (Red Ladder) whose Strike While the Iron is Hot (1974) later re-titled as A Woman's work is never done (the title is self explanatory) remained effective for more than two years. Among other alternative theatre companies who took up gender issues were the Theatre-in-Education Companies (such as the Bolton Octagon

TIE Company's <u>Sweetie Pie</u> in 1972) where students and teachers lent their sense of heightened gender consciousness into the making of feminist plays.

But the larger political tensions also provided ample scope to theatre companies who were prompt in their theatrical response:

> Older groups received new life, new ones were formed such as the General Will in Bradford and the Broadside Company put together by two former members of Red Ladder. Their Sketches retained the simplicity and bluntness of agit prop...Unlike the Workers Theatre Movement or Unity, these groups were not identified with any single political organisation. (Davies, 1987:166)

In July 1971, John McGrath formed 7:84 as a popular political touring company which two years later separated to form the English and Scottish branches. In her article 'Good Nights Out: Activating the Audience with 7:84 (England)' Nadine Holdsworth described the origins of this Company such:

> 7:84 emerged from a period of national and international socio-political and counter–cultural events which initiated the politicisation of a new generation of theatre workers, and heralded a burgeoning enclave of left wing political theatre, which included Red Ladder, Foco Novo and General Will. (Holdsworth, 1997:29)

In the same article, Holdsworth continues that 7:84 (England) had open connections with the Labour Movement. Sometimes the relationship would entail financial backing, as with the <u>Six Men of Dorset</u> production in 1984. At other times individual performances were organized through a trade Union, local Labour Party or trades council.

> This alliance functioned as both a rhetorical and authenticating convention through which audiences were initially attracted and could subsequently read the performance event.
> (Holdsworth, 1997:31-32)

North West Spanner, a small scale touring Company based at Manchester since 1971 specialised in creating shows with immediate relevance to a working class audience and taking them out to non-theatrical venues like factory canteens and trade union clubs. In its early days it was part of Inroads, a community arts project aimed at children and based in York, where Inroads was dedicated to education through play and used a Pied

Piper form of street theatre to recruit their customers. By 1979 North West Spanner was a shop floor theatre company—performing at building sites, dry docks, workers canteens and factory gates as well as in evenings to audiences attracted from the workplace. Most of their early plays had generic titles, for example The Rents Play of 1972 or the Nurses Play of 1973. Commenting on Spanner's play Partisans, Richard Drain says:

> What distinguishes Partisans from other shows attempting his kind of subject is its readiness to credit its characters with an imaginative life alongside their working life—an imaginative life so uninhibited that it can turn inside out the realistic format in which the play is cast...It takes Spanner to show that serious political intentions can leave room for zaniness...The group that Spanner came closest to is the Combination...(Drain, 1979:14)

Yet another company that sprung up in 1973 and sought to entertain with material and forms that were articulate, progressive and created from the viewpoint of working and oppressed people was the Belt and Braces Road show. A significant characteristic of this Company was its use of rock music and its incorporation of productions of socialist theatre companies on the mainland of Europe; especially well known has been their production of Dario Fos' Accidental Death of an Anarchist.

> Another response to the changed political climate was simply: so what? Some groups such as Broadside continued to produce plays which covered topics in a direct manner: its The Lump was written together with the building workers themselves who formed its subject. And if there was not enough suitable material to hand then 'history' was to be raided for examples of 'socialist revivalism'. Foco Novo for instance produced the Arthur Horner Show about the Welsh miners' leader and also The Nine Days and Saltely Gates which linked the General strike of 1926 with the miners' striker of 1972. (Davies, 1987:168)

The Foco Novo Theatre Company was essentially the brainchild of one determined individual called Roland Rees who along with David Aukin and Bernard Pomerance co-founded the Company in 1972. In keeping with the meaning of the name which in Portugese reads as 'a new focus on starting point' it supported new writing not just by established playwrights but also by new dramatists such as Mustapha Matura and

Tunde Ikoli. The main characteristic of Foco Novo's work 'stylistically has been what might be described as a form of heightened realism.' (Hay, 1985)

Choosing to produce plays that veered between 'socialist inclined 'art' theatre and that of a localized community theatre with distinctively populist leanings was the Half Moon Theatre Company.' (Craig, 1980, p41). Their production of <u>George Davis is Innocent OK</u> contributed largely to the successful campaign to free George Davies from his wrongful arrest and thus proved the powerful impact of theatre on society.

It is perhaps pertinent to mention the fact that the seventies also saw the growth of Asian, Black, Polish, Cypriot and other 'ethnic' and 'community' theatre. While this thesis aims at analyzing 'English' theatre companies specifically, it is important to note the immigrant and 'minority' voice gradually asserting its presence through a cultural/artistic medium.[6]

If the decade starting 1968 saw agit prop theatre in Britain flourishing, the election of Margaret Thatcher as the first woman Prime Minister and thus the return of the Conservative Party to power in 1979 dramatically changed the theatre environment in Britain.

In 1981 Ronald Reagan became the President of the USA while in France, the Socialist Party Chief Francois Mitterand was elected President (co-incidentally Thatcher, Reagan and Mitterand all came in for a second term starting '83, '84 and '88 respectively); the House of Commons passed Britain's controversial new Nationality Bill.

After four centuries, Britain and the Vatican resumed full diplomatic relations in 1982 and in the same year, Argentina surrendered to Britain in the Falklands; the Soviet President Brezhnev died and Yuri Andropov succeeded him; a new constitution for Canada came into force and Switzerland decided to join the UN. 1983 saw the Caribbean's Island of St Kittis and Nevis becoming the world's newest nation. The year that Indira Gandhi was assassinated i.e. 1984, had North and South Koreans opening borders for the first time since 1945; China and Britain signed an agreement to transfer Hong Kong to China in 1997; the Soviet President Yuri Andropov died and Konstantin Chernekov became the new Soviet Communist Party Chief. A year later Chernekov died and Mikhail Gorbachev was elected the General Secretary of the Communist Party while

Andrei Gromyko was elected the President of the Soviet Union; Reagan and Gorbachev met at Geneva, the first superpower summit in six years.

In 1986, Queen Elizabeth II gave her formal assent to the Australian Act, abolishing all remaining legislative, judicial and executive links of the country with Britain; Gorbachev was reelected General Secretary of the Soviet Communist Party for 5 years and Reagan and Gorbachev met at Reykjavik for their second summit. Margaret Thatcher made history in 1987 when she won the third term in the elections; more history was made that year when Reagan and Gorbachev signed a treaty in Washington to scrap intermediate nuclear weapons; China witnessed campus demonstrations for greater democracy and the Chinese Communist Party General Secretary, Hu Yaobang resigned, succeeded by Prime Minister Zhao Aiyang. Whilst Salman Rushdies controversial novel The Satanic Verses was making waves and awarded the Whitbred Prize for fiction.

1988 also saw the signing of the Geneva accord for Afghan peace; the withdrawal of Soviet troops from Afghanistan; the opening of the five day Kremlin Summit by Gorbachev and Reagan; the dropping of President Gromyko and four other top figures from the Kremlin leadership so that Gorbachev emerged as the most powerful; the election of George Bush as President of the US; and the celebration of 40 years of unanimous adoption of the Universal Declaration of Human Rights. The next year Margaret Thatcher completed ten years as British Prime Minister; tens of thousands of Chinese students in Beijing demonstrated for democratic rights so that martial law was imposed resulting in soldiers storming Tianamen Square and crushing the month old students pro democracy campaign killing hundreds and injuring many more; France celebrated two hundred years of the French Revolution, Hungary became a democratic republic putting an end to the era of communism; the Berlin Wall, a symbol of animosity between East and West Germany was broken up at various places; East Germany appointed its first non-communist Head of State—Manfred Gerlach; in Czechoslovakia, the first government without a communist majority in 41years headed by a Communist Prime Minister Marian Calfa and President Vaclav Havel was sworn in.

1990 finally saw the end of the Thatcherite era when Thatcher faced a crisis as Geoffrey Howe resigned over differences with her approach to European Economic and

Monetary Union—she later announced her decision to step down as also her intention not to run for the second round in the leadership election; in the election, John Major who was the Chancellor of the Exchequer in the Thatcher cabinet took over as the Prime Minister; the South African leader Nelson Mandela was freed after twenty eight years in prison; Gorbachev took oath as the first Soviet Executive President; East Germans voted for the unification of both Germanys; non communists on the Hungary election; Boris Yeltsin was elected President of Russian Federation; US President George Bush and USSR President Mikhail Gorbachev agreed on ending the Cold War; the Soviet Parliament passed a key law giving private business the same legal status as state enterprise; the Soviet Union granted freedom of the press and journalist rights, abandoned censorship and allowed anyone who so desired, to publish a newspaper (all steps towards the dissolution of the USSR and the formation of the CIS).

Even a casual glance at the long narration of selective events in the Western World is indicative of a definite movement away from Communism as the ideal form of the political being of a state. While this does not therefore imply that it was necessarily to be replaced by extreme right wing politics, it surely spells out that communism was an unattainable ideal and thus the socialist ground was shaky indeed:

> The fall of communist government and the embracing of a free
> market economy by much admired people such as Vaclav Havel
> was more than most idealism could withstand. (Shank, 1994:15)

According to playwright David Edgar, 'Conservatism was not planned by a conservative woman Prime Minister in a blue dress. It was an ideological movement...There was disillusionment throughout the world with ideals of egalitarianism and collective emancipation.' (Lustig, 1991:10)

In Britain under Thatcher, the pervasive right wing ideology meant a climate of sheer repression. As Nadine Holdsworth says that those theatre companies that had evolved from a world

> which had to do with class consciousness, ideological resistance and
> the recognition of a plurality of cultural activity, had virtually
> disappeared, displaced by the promotion of individualism initiated by
> Thatcherism, contained under Majorism, and embraced by New
> Labour. (Holdsworth, 1997:38)

All through the eighties, the Right Wing government concerned itself with smashing individuals and groups that attempted to dismantle hierarchical structures. Whether in economics terms where traditional working class communities were shattered by their disempowerment due to the decline of traditional industry and the suppression of trade union activity; or in the cultural sphere where, for example, theatre companies that had based their activities on the belief that the class struggle must be fought and will be won, there was no room for a resistant ideology. As McGrath admitted: "So there was I, basing my whole artistic practice on the concept of 'class consciousness', and there was the leader of my country telling me it didn't exist." (Holdworth, 1997:38)

Any registration of protest that critiqued the high handedness of the State by theatre companies was as severely dealt with as was the miner's strike of 1984-95 that voiced the economic and social strife of the people.[7] State intervention in the cultural domain took the tangible form of withdrawal of state subsidy, using the Arts Council as its agent. Thus a number of oppositional theatre companies in the mid eighties such as CAST, Joint Stock, Monstrous Regiment and Foco Novo found their funding cut off. Consequently, agit prop theatre companies had to now find other sponsors so that their business activity began to take precedence over their theatrical progress. This also involved a lot of change/compromise for some companies who had to either shift their aims/subject matter or their target audiences; as with Red Ladder who from 1985 increasingly began distancing themselves from the radical theatre movement and performed primarily for college going youth.

Broadly speaking the oppressive Thatcherite era saw four trends emerging at the theatrical front. In the first place, theatre practitioners learnt to speak what Jenny Topper, Artistic Director of the Hampstead Theatre in 1991 called 'shitespeak' i.e. the language used in the courting of sponsors. As David Edgar commented on the increased commodification of theatre:

> You'll have noticed how British Rail now imitates the airlines, with their chief steward's announcements and their 'situated towards the rear of the train.' The same thing has happened in the theatre. Its begun to take on the language of the cinema with words like 'package' and 'product' and with the

> rise of the producer. It is ironic that at a time of restricted
> finding the theatre should use the language of commercial
> production. (Lustig, 1991:12)

Continuing on the same subject Edgar believed that

> 'corporate sponsorship has redefined the theatrical
> experience. It's like going to a right club. It has created
> a two-tier experience with special bars for sponsors
> and made the whole thing into a passive experience.
> (Lustig, 1991:12)

Art sponsorship accelerated under Thatcher but ironically it must be noted, the Association for Business Sponsorship of the Arts (ABSA) was founded in 1976 under a Labour government.[8]

The second significant aspect was the sense of unease that theatre activists had in dealing with the ideology of the time. Even bold playwrights like David Hare and Howard Brenton revealed an uncertainty as to how to respond to Thatcherism in an atmosphere where political protest of any nature was choked (for example, Tumbledown, the Falkland Faction directed by Richard Eyre for television caused a furore in high places).[9] One way of responding to Thatcherism was to do it obliquely as David Edgar's key play about Thatcherism, Maydays did; it was about how important defection was and how important people were who came to the New Conservatism from the Left. An inevitable outcome of the almost obsessive concern with and perception of Margaret Thatcher was that she was often accorded a quasi mythic status in stage representations, becoming almost an icon for both, her admirers and her detractors; she invaded even the classics.

> Perhaps it could be argued that attacking Thatcher head on,
> impersonating either her or her most oppressed victims on
> stage is an action of those who wish to prove their radical
> credentials while the Davids and Howards of the playwriting
> community felt no need to do this. (Lustig, 1991:13)

Another way of responding to Thatcherism was the building up of nostalgia or the 'heritage industry' as David Edgar has called it where images of 'Merrie England' and tradition were deified; where, with the exception of the expansion into Europe, the repertoire was narrowed such that popular Shakespeares and Chekovs were staged interminably.[10]

Coming to the third and really grave aspect for theatre development was the fact that Thatcherism worked its own ideological terms very well. It ensured that it was difficult to put the collective idea across. Political energy became colossally fragmented, both in the theatre and in politics; the women's theatre movement and the ethnic theatre movement for example, were politically and culturally important. But they lacked the force and motivation to come together in a wider common purpose and thus failed to bring about unifying action. Younger theatre groups immediately started off thinking about individual sponsorship using contemporary machinery and language rather than actually addressing themselves to what they were trying to say and to whom.

Thus, the fourth emergent trend by the nineties was that though some of the agit prop theatre companies that were rooted in the socially committed tradition continued to exist, their work was on a smaller scale and under constant threat.[11] Performance practice in the nineties thus saw aesthetic experimentation attaining greater significance as against the importance of the audience. Though the new theatre companies did provide unconventional and dynamic ways of intervention and interpretation of social, political and personal identities they appeared to be distanced from the larger political structures. And certainly did not attempt to directly activate the audience. Perhaps it would be relevant to observe what kind of agenda this 'new generation of 'Thatcher's children'' has been developing as their 'responses to contemporary society' for 'the cultural impetus faced by companies like 7:84 (England) has been consigned to history.' (Holdworth, 1997:40)

The term 'Thatcher's children' has been used for these companies not because they were born in the Thatcher years but rather because, at a time when the drastic cuts in arts funding resulted in the demise of numerous fringe companies, the innovative work of companies like The People Show, The Welfare State Company, Lumiere and Son, Hesitate and Demonstrate, Forced Entertainment, Alternative
Cabaret, Dogs in Honey, DVB Physical Theatre and Station House Opera, continued to flourish.

52

The People Show was created in 1966 by sculptor and Jazz pianist Jeff Nuttall who brought together a group of visual artists to stage a 'happening' in the basement of Better Books at Charing Cross Road. This involved motor bikes, fishing nets and very fat women in Nothing Hill Gate, London. The goal of the People Show was not to preach any particular political or theatrical ideology but to explore situations that allowed the creative spirit to reign supremely free, In their early days, The People Show attempted to stage performances which 'involved found spaces and objects subtly transformed into anarchic compositions which challenged the members of the audience to devise their own interpretation of the images.' (Shank, 1994:92). Gradually however, by the mid-seventies, the 'happenings' style was dropped by the group who then took to a kind of Dadaist style creating images that were dreamlike and irreverent. The Company never appoints a director but works as a collective, taking up each participating individuals current preoccupation be it an idea, an object of interest, a desirable action, an obsession, interesting art work or themes worth studying. Though the narration is loose, an aesthetic unity develops from the intertwining of both imagistic and ideological themes. Images such as the bacon sandwiches consumed by The People Show participants and the glittering ball are supposed to represent the lower lasses; while the upper classes are symbolized by such images as people on the top of a scaffolding or a gentleman sitting in the throne room and playing with a model of the set. Of late the company has introduced more text and such skills as acrobatics into their shows.

The Welfare State Company was founded in 1968 by John Fox and Sue Gill and based in Ulverston South Cumbia, (though their network spreads throughout Britain as also some parts of Europe and Canada). The company was also known as Engineers of the Imagination, Civil Magicians and Guardians of the unpredictable. The Company's use of visual images whether for miniature or gigantic pieces is an attempt to recreate Britain as it might have been in the Dark Ages. For this, they use costumes, props, lanterns, masks, giant puppets, ice sculptures, fireworks and all the other devices employed by the mummers or music hall or carnival traditions. Thus, an almost festive spirit invades the productions and the interactive nature of the performers invariably concludes with performance and participants dancing together.

Lumiere and Son began in 1973 under the artistic leadership of director Hilary Westlake and writer David Gale. The company inquires into abnormalities of the human mind be they obsessions, fixations, illness, habits, rituals, jokes and exaggerations and thus their images are akin to dream and myth rather than 'documentary reality'. The humour in their productions therefore is a black humour. The distinctive feature about Lumiere and Son's productions is that the text and the visual score operate as separate but equal entities with each conveying its own independent meaning; the emphasis is on discovering new stylistic solutions to the subconscious workings of the human psyche. According to Gale:

> Our work is not about a gothic inclination of an artist to dignify the 'backwaters' of his or her psyche, but to try to find points of contact between these 'backwaters' and those of the audience. We aim to challenge people's complacency and expose the complicated motivations for the things we do. (Shank, 1994:99)

Quite similar to the 'happenings' format followed by The People Show was that of the 'events' performed in public spaces by Hesitate and Demonstrate, a Company founded in 1975 by Geraldine Pilgrim and Janet Goddard (which functioned till 1986 when it closed due to financial reasons). The 'event' lasted for a brief while in a public place even while the normal routine of the chosen site continued as always. The name of the company arose from a principle of movement where, influenced by Edward Muybridge's photographs of human movement, the performers would hesitate a little before carrying out a movement as if deliberately demonstrating it to the audience. The use of sound tapes with not just classical and popular music but also various sound effects was as striking an aspect as the origins of the Company's name; these sound tapes were often self sufficient narratives in themselves. The productions focused on a surrealistic sequence of events which though not in linear order, concluded with a theatrical climax.

Alternative Cabaret developed from the fringe theatre of the seventies as a collective with half of comedians and half musicians who performed regularly at the Comedy Store at Soho. The idea behind its formation by Toni Allen, Alexei Sayle as well as Jim Barclay, Andy de la Tour and Maggie Steed was to provide theatre to not just coterie audiences but to a

> real cross section of seedy show biz people who come out of the strip club below, real reactionaries who don't know what they are going to see.[12]

Their shows were actually stand-up comedies where the audience decided how much they'd had of a certain comedian. Though most of the members of Alternative Cabaret came from Left backgrounds, their shows did not have a singled out politically motivated approach. Rather they attempted to show people the humorous side of the Left and thus challenged Left Wing prejudices as much as other types. Instead of theorizing their personal politics and arriving at common ground, they preferred to individually tackle their audience in their different ways; whether it was a conscious undermining or support of Left Wing ideas or straight political satire about current affairs. As Andy de la Tour put it:

> Alternative Cabaret is not just a comedy version of a fringe theatre company. In fact it's the difference that makes Alternative Cabaret such a good thing. In fringe theatre there's all the hassle of grants, then justifying the grant-doing the gigs and the tours. Alternative Cabaret is just a group of people who vaguely agree on general things about entertainment and politics. We're loose organizationally and it's a big plus that we're not a company.[13]

Experimenting with the physical in theatre are such companies as DV8 Physical Theatre, Forced Entertainment, Dogs in Honey and Station House Opera, all formed in the eighties. Of these DV8 is an extremely well known and widely traveled company centering its attention upon physical movement, both harsh as well as gentle. The objective of this Company is 'taking risk, breaking down the barriers between dance, theatre and personal politics and above all, about communicating new ideas directly, dearly and unpretentiously. Dances struggle with an unknown force to gain control of their bodies; one falls, another seeks to fly. Each player struggles to find a voice so as to be heard but their words remain soundless'. (Shank, 1994:9)

The works of Forced Entertainment, Dogs in Honey and Station House Opera draw their inspiration from TV culture where each fragment or episode (as in a serial) becomes 'a unit of informational exchange.' (Shank, 1994:111). The notion of a linear narrative is replaced by disconnected images and scenes and film is referred to at some level be it image, design, lighting, sound track source or stage set. Somewhere is the underlying principle that our own psyche and lives are actually a series of fragments put together in some sort of order rather than being an unbroken experience.

Such a description of theatre companies that grew in the Thatcher years, even if superficial, points out clearly that pure agit prop could not and would not work, for socialism as a political ideology was surely only a concept and not a reachable ideal. However, there can be no denying that the drive to create new forms and structures which is a secondary aim of agit prop theatre performances has perhaps opened the doors for novel ways of understanding the individual in a community and intervening meaningfully in society. How successful they may be in creating a new version of agit prop theatre remains to be seen.

This chapter would remain incomplete without the inclusion of playwrights like Trevor Griffiths, David Edgar, Howard Barker, Howard Brenton, David Edgar, Howard Barker, Howard Brenton, David Hare, Snoo Wilson and Heathecote Williams (apart from John Arden and John McGrath who have featured in the course of events discussed so far). The contribution of these playwrights to the cause of agit prop theatre has been immense and most of them have been associated with one or the other agit prop theatre companies. Trevor Griffiths for instance has written for 7:84 and amongst his well known plays, Occupations (1970), a 'quasi–documentary account of 1920s revolutionary politics in Italy', The Party (1973), Sam, Sam (1971), Comedians (1975) and Through the Night (1975) stand out. The distinctive quality of Griffith's work is his linking of

> personal and political lives, the everyday with the illusory...
> There is a genuine sense...that new alignments are
> taking place in contemporary British politics, that a traditional
> commitment to the Labour party's view of cultural change
> has proved inadequate. (Ansorge, 1975:66)

Comedians for example, is about a conflict regarding the comedians role with two competing views of comedy offered to the students. The external examiner, Bert Challenor, believes that comedy should exploit, but not challenge established values; the teacher of the class, Eddie Waters, believes that comedy should steadily subvert those same values. (Zeifman and Zimmerman, 1993:248)

David Edgar's plays have found a platform in The General Will Company.

His work with the General Will showed him to be an effective lampoonist, a talent most perfectly attuned to his 1969 mock pantomime Tedderella in which Mr. Heath takes the country to the Common Market ball. (Ansorge, 1975:58)

A reporter initially by profession Edgar's keen desire to strip a subject off its mysteries and reveal clear evidence can be seen in a play like Excuses Excuses (1971) which deals with the motives of a factory arsonist. Destiny (written originally in 1973; produced in 1976) is a landmark in Edgar's playwriting career; for rather than being rabidly leftist, this complex play shows the attraction of right wing politics. Thus it is a sensitive handling of the issue of political choices made by people. It also "represents an important development in contemporary theatre insofar as it marks the 'promotion' of radical theatre to suitably large and prestigious settings." (Craig, 1980:138)

Howard Barker 'is in many ways the Peter Pan of his generation. While other writers have toned down their early sense of moral outrage and class hatred, Barker's plays continue to carry an intense, emotional impact and a deep and often unfocused series of political and sexual antagonism.' (Craig, 1980:139). His better known plays are Cheek (1970), Alpha Alpha, Claw, Stripwell (1975), That Good Between Us (1977), the Hang of the Gaol (1978), Fair Slaughter (1978) and The Love of a Good Man (1980).

Howard Brenton and David Hare, like Trevor Griffiths and David Edgar learned almost their entire craft from the fringe theatre of the 60s—on stages in colleges, art centers and village halls – and till about 1973, made fervent claims for the fringe as a weapon in a repressive society. However with time, Brenton and Hare moved from the Portable to more established and mainstream theatre revealing their fears about the future of the fringe. But their plays did not diminish in terms of political content. While not necessarily containing a strident Marxist note, their plays deal with the fears and hopes of their contemporaries and the call for mercy and strength in crisis. Thus they have all the potential for bringing about social change.

Brenton's <u>Magnificence</u> (1973) and <u>The Saliva Milkshake</u> (1975) deal with urban terrorism. <u>Weapons of Happiness</u> (1976) 'juxtaposes the sufferings of a former Czech Communist leader, Joseph Frank, imprisoned, tortured and tried in the 1952 Slansky show trials (and in realty hanged) with the fumblings and sometimes ludicrous groupings towards political awareness of a group of South London factory workers.' (Craig, 1980, p120). An earlier play, <u>Hitler Dances</u> (1972) is antiwar propaganda which Brenton addresses by showing the various ways in which we identify with and participate in war. <u>The Churchill Play</u> (1974) dares to portray Churchill as an eccentric and is a bleak vision of the future, set as it is in an internment camp in 1984, headed by a coalition government and supported by the military.

> Brenton was and remains the figurehead of his generation. It was
> he who initiated the most immediate response to Margaret Thatcher's
> fist election victory in 1979 by collaborating with Tony Howard on
> <u>A Short Sharp Shock</u> a savagely satirical attack the original title of
> which, "Ditch the Bitch," neatly summarises its aims. (Zeifman and
> Zimmerman, 1993:327)

<u>The Romans in Britain</u> (1980), <u>Thirteenth Night</u> (1981), <u>The Genius</u> (1983), <u>Bloody Poetry</u> (1984) and <u>Greenland</u> (1988) are some of his other memorable plays.

In a lecture delivered at King's College, Cambridge in 1978, David Hare said that theatre had drifted to politics because it was in a position to reveal

> an age in which men's ideals and men's practice bear
> no relation to each other; in which the public profession
> of, for example, socialism has often been reduced by the
> passage of history to wearing personal fetish, or even
> chronic personality disorder. The theatre is the best way
> of showing the gap between what it said and what is seen
> to be done, and that is why, ragged and gaptoothed as it
> is, it has still a far healthier potential than some of
> the other, poorer, abandoned arts. (Bigsby, 1981:41)

He himself writes:

> about politics because the challenge of communism,

in however debased and ugly a form, is to ask
whether the criteria by which we have [been] brought
up are right, whether what each of us experiences
uniquely really is what makes us valuable. (Bigsby, 1981:42)

While vividly depicting the personalities of his characters, David Hare also showcases the socio-politico-cultural environment that is responsible for their personality traits. He began his career in 1968 with the comedy How Brophy was made moving to contemporary theatre in right earnest with Knuckle in 1974 in which he expresses his feeling that English society at that time

the society of property millionaires and political
accommodation—was morally corrosive, the more so because
it was willful. (Bigsby, 1981:44)

Fanshen (1975) is about a Chinese village in the aftermath of revolution. Plays like Slag (1970) The Great Exhibition (1972) and Teeth 'n' Smiles (1975) are all about the gradual crumbling of relationships/organisations/institutions. Licking Hitler (1978), Plenty (1978) and Dreams of Leaving (1980) again, deal with the shattering of those myths that bind a society—with no attempt at retrieving those myths. And the 1974 collaboration between Hare and Brenton, Brassneck 'spans the years between 1945 and 1973, covering the history of three grafting generations of a Midlands commercial dynasty' and is 'inspired by the revelations of corruption in the early 1970s.' (Craig, 1980:126-127)

Stephen Poliakov and Barrie Keefe are two other playwrights whose plays expose a world of unrealised dreams and hopes similar to Hare's; but there is no truly Marxist perspective in spite of the revelations made about the nature of Capitalism. Poliakov's Hitting Town (1975), American Days (1979), Bloody Kids (1980) and Keefe's Gimme Shelter (1975-77) and Frozen Assets (1978) adequately exemplify this aspect.

Preferring to write plays that are akin to those produced by Lumiere and Son and The People Show is Snoo Wilson who is the youngest of the Portable trio. His vision incorporates the bizarre in the mundane and thus he is able to write on a vast range of themes be it Feminism, Irish republicanism (for example A Greenish Man, 1978), ecology, apartheid or confronting the Anti Christ. This last theme can be found in his The Glad Hand (1978). Soul of the White Ant (1975), Pignight, Blowjob, Vampire, The Beast and The Pleasure Principle are some of his other plays which are filled with diverse images and ideas.

Bearing a striking resemblance to Snoo Wilson is Heathcote Williams who however is known best for his play AC/DC in 1969 which 'embodies both in its form and content many of the neuroses, terrors, joys and fashions of the acid age.' (Craig, 1980, p131)

Theatre, like any other art form, evolves. Agit prop theatre too has grown in its dimensions as this history of its birth and maturity in England proves. And though most critics consider it deceased, I would like to regard this as just another stage in its evolution. For the volcanic potential of agit prop theatre still exists albeit in a changed mode—and perhaps, the very fact that it has changed is evidence enough of its progressiveness.

Notes

[1] Almost all the critics referred to be it Itzin, Craig, Bigsby, Peter Ansorge, Nadine Holdsworth, Davies, Lynn Sobieski, David Edgar etc, in this Chapter, have at some point outlined all the events that declare the significance of 1968

[2] From Chapter 22, 'Performance, Community, Culture' by Baz Kershaw in Goodman and Gay, 2000, p.141

[3] 'The Living Theatre, La Mama, Bread and Puppet, the San Francisco Mime Troupe...Luis Valdez's El Teatro Campesino, Joseph Chaikin's Open Theatre, Jerome Savary's Grand Magic Circus, Ariane Mnouchkine's Theatre du Soleil, Grotowskis' Theatre Laboratory. (Itzin, 1980, p6)

[4] The book A Dictionary of Dates and Events ed Dr A N Kapoor and V P Gupta, Ambe Book, Delhi, 1995 has been of immense help to this Chapter.

[5] The book A History of the Modern World by Richard Poulton, Oxford University Press, Oxford, 1981 was among the many books consulted and gave a clear, concise picture of Britain and the rest of the world till the eighties.

[6] Chapter Four entitled 'The Public-going Theatre Community and Ethnic Theatre' by Naseem Khan in Sandy Craig's Dreams and Deconstructions is a good starting point on this subject.

[7] Pam Brighton in an NTQ symposium entitled 'Theatre in Thatcher's Britain: Organizing the Opposition' says acidly "Thatcher is firing on all bloody guns; one has a working class that's entirely bloody vulnerable, and becoming daily more vulnerable as every piece of legislation that's passed further erodes its freedoms, its possibilities, and its ability to eat; and one talks about Serious Money being a political play. What politics are we talking about?" in NTQ New Theatre Quarterly Vol V No 18 May 1989, p121

[8] While discussing the problems faced by theatre companies in the Thatcher years, Rob Ritchie says, "I

think you have to talk about the economic because its obsessed a lot of people working in the theatre in the last eight or nine years. That's to say, much of their time has gone into devising clever ways to ensure they can raise the funds to keep going. Because of that there's been a silence about discussing the work and the kind of practices that companies are operating." NTQ, New Theatre Quarterly Vol.V No.18 May 1989, P113

[9] To quote Pam Brighton again who dwells on this aspect: "…There is a plan for ideologically dense and very difficult plays; people always scoff at playing to the converted, but the converted want entertainment and stimulation as much as anybody else. One's other brief is what it's always been: to find the audience which will never enter the institutions which have been redundant since they were created. The critical question is not just one of theatre and Thatcher, but of one's own politics under Thatcher" p.114 and further on "…you have to site a political theatre company where it's actually going to do ideological battle with Thatcherism, because those glimpses of political change are going to occur less and less: and when they do occur, they will be more ruthlessly repressed." NTQ New Theatre Quarterly Vol V No 18 May 1989, p119

[10] Pam Brighton is vitriolic about this aspect when she says "…we are taking about a country that is in a state of political crisis, where interpreting the bloody Tempest three times as season is a complete irrelevance" NTQ Vol V No 18 May 1989, p121

[11] Andrew Davies discusses this aspect in some detail in Chap 11, especially pp 183-184 in Davies, 1987.

[12] From 'Alternative Cabaret Comedy of Social Comment' in Platform New Perspectives on Theatre Today Summer 1980, p2

[13] ibid, p3

RED LADDER: THE FIRST RUNG

To recall the outline of Red Ladder Theatre Company as described in Chapter Two, originally Red Ladder was simply called The Agit Prop Street Players—a name that clearly spelt out the aim/venue/methodology of the company—and it emerged when a group from a socialist information service performed a play at the Trafalgar Square Festival of 1968. Prior to <u>A Woman's Work is Never Done</u> which was the first really full length play produced by Red Ladder, we learn from a 1972-73 leaflet that the earlier plays were actually small units that took

> as their subjects vital issues such as unemployment, rents, the Industrial Relations Act ... that are the immediate concern of the audiences involved. The plays are designed to lead into a discussion of the issues raised; they aim not just to provide a forum in which experienced Trade Unionists can air their views, but to provoke even the most reticent members of an audience into participating.

Under the heading 'How do you use the Plays?', the leaflet describes the plays as

> short, about 30 minutes each which 'can be shown together, separately, or in twos, depending on the time available. A typical 'evening' would consist of the Housing Play, followed by a discussion, followed by the Women's Play ... and another discussion ... and so on.

It continues that though at that time there were only a limited range of plays to choose from (namely the ones on the pamphlet), future times would see plays on 'Collective Bargaining'; Ireland; Apprenticeship and Racialism'. The leaflet also points at the kind of stage setting required when it informs that the plays could be performed in a hall or large room without a special stage or curtains, 'only a floor 20x20 and a ceiling height of 15 ft.' Apart from these indoor plays, the leaflet adds the availability of Outdoor plays

> 'Designed—unlike the indoor plays—for specific performance outdoors—on demonstration, picket lines, factory gates, etc. As well as dealing with crucial issues they add pageant and spectacle to outdoor events.'

Gradually the basis of the work broadened and plays that fed directly into particular struggles and issues developed such as <u>The Big Con</u> against the Industrial Relations Act and <u>The Cake Play</u> against productivity bargaining. By 1971 the name Red Ladder evolved after a much loved and used prop. There also evolved a policy of taking theatre to 'working class' audiences in places where working class people usually find their entertainment which now included trade union clubs. By 1973 the commitment of the Company was recognized with an Arts Council grant of four thousand pounds and in 1976, the Company moved from London to Leeds, Yorkshire; and it is still located in the city although it continues to tour on a national basis.

Whilst early Red Ladder plays from 1968-73 fed directly into political disputes of the time, 1974 onwards, the work of the Company diversified as did its Artistic Policies. It would be convenient if one were to have a bird's eye view of the 1970s production list of the Company. Between 1974-75, Red Ladder produced A Woman's Work is Never Done (also known as Strike While the Iron is Hot), published by the Journeyman Press, which dealt with the role of women at work and home and their growing political awareness. It Makes You Sick by Frances McNeill was produced between 1975-76 and it was a club show about the National Health Service (NHS) written and devised in close collaboration with National Union Public Employees (NUPE). Steve Trafford's Anybody Sweating followed in 1976-77, a club show about unemployment, highrise flats and Britain in 1976. It became known as 'Would Jubileev it' and was Red Ladder's contribution to the celebrations in 1977. A watershed in Red Ladder's Artistic development was the 1978 production of Taking Our Time by Steve Trafford and Glen Parkes published by Pluto Press; this created a more analytical approach to story telling as opposed to the simple solutions of Agit Prop. It was a play with music about the industrialization of the weaving industry in Yorkshire and the rise of Chartism. The play was massively successful and attracted a wide, popular audience throughout Yorkshire and the north, supported by the Union of Dyers and Bleachers. In 1979, Nerves of Steel by Steve Trafford and Chris Rawlence was produced which explored the impact that overtime and shift working had on family life. A reworking of the Faust legend around the subject of nuclear power and arms was Steve Trafford's Power Mad which was produced in 1979-80.[1]

The earliest play that the Red Ladder Theatre archives could yield turned out to be a worn out typed script with inked notes a May 1975 version of the Cake Play (the original was performed around 1968-69).[2] This short skeletal frame of a play is pure agit prop, condensing almost the entire history of the post-fifties crisis in Britain and incorporating actual political figures such as Harold Wilson (who became Labour leader in 1963), Edward Heath (the Conservative leader who propounded 'new conservatism') and Denis Healey (the then Chancellor of the Exchequer). Thus its contemporariness at the time of its performance could not have been made more abundantly clear. Clear too is the fact that the play functions palpably as a Ritual text for in critiquing social reality, engendering protest and urging collective action on the part of the audience (as the analysis will illustrate), the Cake Play could not have served as a more fitting example of a Ritual Text. In brief, the play deals with the growing defensive solidarity among the workers at the time when employers sought wage cuts due to poor trade and it also grapples with possible solutions provided by authoritarian figures as well as showing the loopholes in such solutions.

Indeed, the entire Cake Play reads like a Nebentext with the Haupttext being actual/lived/meta political reality existing in the here and now wherein the play was scripted; in fact, the point when the momentum breaks to discuss 'The International Crisis' spells out clearly that the play is only an agent to foreground the complex issues involved in the struggle between the interests of Labour and Capital. So at various moments, the text of the Cake Play seems to have accorded itself a certain hortatory function crystallized in particular rituals of empowerment by which it comes to give itself the power of social interrogation and regeneration. However, just as we begin to conclude that the text has not only appropriated the garb of but also internalized (the coerciveness of) a dominant order, it distances itself from such a conclusion. This it does by filling the social totality it has created with an alternative set of values, where power belongs to the people. How this happens will be the focus of analysis in subsequent sections.

When Marx wrote on a military escapade in Spain, he did not write 'a history of Spain' but he thought it necessary to think Spain historically. Politics, besides being seen as an aspect of the social whole obviously has a strong historical dimension. The knowledge acquired through studying this historical background helps one to think the 'present crisis' (in the context of the plays, 'present' refers to the early 70s) historically, helps one to quarry the pattern of development through time by using new concepts and asking different questions. The <u>Cake Play</u> literally begs for a reading of its historical background not merely to observe the machinations of various political leaders like Wilson and Heath but also to interpret the contemporary struggle of the British people. If one examines the vocabulary of the Cake Play the key terms around which the play appears to revolve are 'Inflation', 'Pay', 'Profit', 'Wages', 'Price Controls', 'Rent Freeze', 'Depression', 'Slump', 'Doom', 'Social Contract', 'IRA', 'Tax Concessions', 'Income Policy' among others of a similar vein. Mapping history through these terms is no easy task. For it is difficult to shrink time, especially politically active time as one tends to overlook many of the complex twists and turns of politics which are all significant in their own way. One thing that these terms make transparent, however, is that the history of struggle in Britain from 1960 onwards was primarily a struggle between the interests of labour and capital. The political system was shaped by the needs of capital in its effort to constrain, deflect or absorb the political power of the working class.[3]

In the years after 1900, British industrial weakness led to crises that was social and political as well as economic: a crisis of defence strategy; a crisis of order in industrial relations; a challenge to the authority of the elected government by the right wing in the House of Lords, and in the officer corps of the army, over the issue of Home Rule for Ireland; and a challenge to its legitimacy by the direct-action wing of the suffragette movement. This accumulating crisis was suspended by the outbreak of war in 1914. The war and inter war years saw a series of adjustments and compromises which gave a new lease of life to the old system. But by 1960 when the rest of the world had altered radically, in Britain nothing essential seemed to have changed at all. In fact by the end of the 70s virtually all industrialised economies were experiencing reduced growth rates, rising unemployment and inflation. What distinguished the British experience however and underlined more clearly than anything else its endogenous nature was that in Britain the crisis had already begun in the 60s. The almost derisive fidelity with which history was repeating itself bespoke of something systemic, a kind of syndrome towards which the whole society was periodically driven by the pattern of forces at work within it. Hence, whether it was Labour leader Harold Wilson's comprehensive reforms that were designed to modernize the structure of the state; or Conservative leader, Edward Heath's dismantling of the apparatus of state economic intervention created during the Wilson's years—no initiative whatsoever changed the situation in Britain. Thus appropriate ingredients were available to Red ladder for the remaking of the <u>Cake Play</u>; when WI says about the 'Boss'

> We've had this bugger on our backs for the last 200 years,
> and its time we got him off

he is thus in effect spelling out this recurrent historical crisis riding on Britain's back while also declaring that it was high time the cause (here, the Boss—a symbol of capitalist forces) was summarily dealt with.

At the time when this version of the Cake Play was scripted i.e. May 1975, Harold Wilson and Edward Heath (one an active and the other a passive, protagonist within the play) had both served their term in heading the government; Heath had been replaced as recently as February of the same year by Margaret Thatcher as leader of the Conservative party. Wilson had however retained his leadership of the Labour Party and had decided to use the 'Social Contract' to repair his image and strengthen his hold on the Party. What was this 'Social Contract' which the <u>Cake Play</u> too refers to as "the only hope that all of us have got" and as "Harold's solution to the bosses problem?"

Responding to the industrial militancy of the rank and file of the party and unions, the 1971 Labour Party conference had adopted a more far-reaching programme than anything it had entertained since 1945, including a 'socialist plan of production, based on public ownership, with minimum compensation, of the commanding heights of the economy'. (Leys, 1986:84). At Wilson's insistence this was later watered down by the National Executive, although the tone of party statements remained radical. The 1974 manifesto pledged 'a fundamental and irreversible shift in the balance of power and wealth in favour of working people and their families'. (Leys, 1986:84). When Wilson took office in February 1974, the government was a minority one with Liberal and nationalist Party support. It was also a government confronted with a catastrophic balance of payments deficit, inflation accelerating towards 20 per cent and the pent-up frustration of a labour movement more mobilized than ever before—but not, for the most part, any more committed than before to fundamental social and economic change. Wilson, for his part, was as committed as ever to the view that the only realistic goal for Labour was to find an agreed basis for reviving the ailing capitalist economy. He now made Labour's special ability to repair the governments' relationship with the unions the cornerstone of his policy and of his electoral appeal.

The key phrase in this exercise was the 'social contract', adopted by the party and the TUC to denote the set of understandings between the state, capital and labour on the basis of which the state could look for the Trade Union cooperation with its policies, and which Heath was charged with having destroyed. Wilson undertook to repair the 'social contract' so that the voluntary support of the unions could then be obtained for a new incomes policy. This background serves to explain part of Wilson's longish speech in the Cake Play when he attempts to pacify the workers:

'Now I've got a perfectly ordinary flag here…(Puts flag over boot)
Here we are in times of trouble
Inflation soars and prices double
Heath policy of confrontation
Has made us a divided nation.
Now Britain's riding stormy weather
We must all work hard and pull together.
…[illegible typescript] lets get busy…social contract. (boot again)
Yes we'll remove all pay legislation.
If you'll ask for wages in moderation?

By the end of 1974 however, the rate of inflation was 23 per cent, and over the twelve months from July 1974 to July 1975 it rose to more than 26 per cent. Over the same period earnings rose nearly 28 per cent. Meanwhile, the current balance of payments deficit for 1974 was no less than 3.6 billion pounds. The deficit was covered partly by the inflow of funds for investment by foreign companies in the North Sea oilfields, and partly by short-term foreign loans. (Leys, 1986: 86). So by May 1975, it was clear that a final crisis was not far off. Labour's claim to be able to deliver union cooperation in stabilising the economy was now to be tested. Obviously, The Cake Play as we have it before us was well timed. The justifiable resentment at Wilson's social contract and the inability of the Labour Party to deliver is voiced by the workers at the end of the play:

So that's the social contract Harolds solution

to the bosses problem. The promises are broken.
Prices soar, and still Harold and TUC tell us to
Cut our wage demands.
But we've got a right to a living wage.
We build the cake…But they own it.
We don't need them up there, we've got the skills
and strength to run things for ourselves.
Until we do our wages will go on chasing their prices
If you want to get rid of inflation, you have to get
Rid of the boss…we don't just want more cake we
want the bloody bakery.

By demonstrating to the audience a shared political reality (that it is shared is prominently clear when at one point the script includes the audiences' apparently positive response to the rallying cry of the workers), the text proves that its effectiveness was contingent upon the agreement between spectator and performer at the principles being illustrated. The text does not stop here: it also urges the audience to appreciate their own 'skills' and capabilities; it initiates the audience into a recognition and an assertion of their rights to "own the bakery" by ejecting the bosses—"You have to get rid of the boss"; and it thus, thrusts the onus of collective action, of empowerment, upon the audience. Thus <u>The Cake Play</u> navigates its way through political factuality within its text to negotiate strategies of action with its audience. If, as has been discussed earlier, a Ritual text seeks to generate mass consciousness and direct it towards a concerted collective action, then <u>The Cake Play</u> surely functions as one, helped no doubt by the fact that it is entirely seeped in the historical reality that it critiques.

At the broad thematic level then it is easy enough to see how <u>The Cake Play</u> functions successfully as a Ritual Text—contemporary reality is held up as a backdrop and criticized so as to engender protest. The presence of personae such as Wilson and Healy (and that of the invisible but present Heath) and the language of the play ground it firmly in the current situation. But there are other agents that facilitate the realization of the purpose behind its performance. These include the use of meaningful symbols

Ritualisation entails the repetitive use of emotionally charged symbols in
symbolically significant locations at symbolically appropriate times. New
symbols need not be introduced in rites in order to get people to change their
political beliefs. The American flag can be as valuable to the civil rights marchers
as to the Ku Klux Klan in defining what is good for the community. The trick is to

introduce dramatic variations on these powerful symbols, to change their meaning by changing their context. (Kertzer, 1998:92)

That the play is named <u>The Cake Play</u> is in itself symbolic and within the text, the ritual creation of one tier upon another of cake augments the symbolism of the title. This symbolism is elementary. Situationally the 'play' is between workers and owners for a larger share of the 'cake' which is spatially, being 'baked' by the workers in a location metaphorically called a 'bakery'; simply speaking, the cake refers to the output that will earn (a) profits for the owners and (b) wages for the workers while the bakery serves as a symbol of all the forces of production. The 'play' is for a just distribution of the cake. The two sides i.e. owners and workers are marked by their characteristic attitudes: on the one side there is every effort, mostly foul, to ensure that the profits remain within the ambit of the minority class and on the other, the sheer resentment at the underhand means of the opposing faction generates fierce resistance. As each layer of cake gets erected, so does the distance between the labourers and the capitalists—symptomatic of the class struggle in the class hierarchy. Thus the 'play' (also a synonym for 'performance') is for the benefit of an audience that has obviously allied itself with the working class and aims to usher in far reaching changes through joint effort. Hence this is not idle play or pastime but a deliberate activity that hopes to be consequential. In fact the two instances within the text which indicate the liminality of the performance site are (a) when the Nebentext says 'At this point the International crisis should be dealt with' and (b) when the audience response is evoked during the performance. This deliberate breaking of spatial boundaries demarcating actors from audience only reaffirms the propagandist nature of the play.

The text includes other 'paraphernalia of ritual' as Blumer terms it by which he means such vehicles as slogans, songs, cheers, expressive gestures and uniforms, which within a ritual activity 'acquires a sentimental significance symbolizing the common feelings about the movement, their use serves as a constant reliving and re-enforcement of these mutual feelings'. (Kertzer, 1988:72). In <u>The Cake Play</u> the Profit bag and the flag hat worn by the Boss (who sits symbolically on the shoulders of the worker—also the narrator—WI) and the coat worn by the workers mark out the different modes of dressing typical to a class/profession. At one point a worker is shown to desire the hat which obviously earmarks a higher social structure or a successful material condition and as he reaches for the hat, he significantly sheds his working coat. Thus attire infuses a sense of self importance and provides one of the means by which people see themselves as playing certain roles. It also makes an individual semiotically identifiable.

The use of the megaphone and press card by 'MM' records the role of the National Press in aiding and abetting the capitalist classes. The megaphone through which MM speaks is redolent of sensational headlines; the same MM corrects the Boss when the latter wails:

O my God!! What am I going to do? I can't pay them
any more. It's bad for my cake.

MM is quick to alert him: 'Don't be silly. It's bad for the national cake.' What could be a more telling example of the way the Press manipulates language to suit its own purpose, to serve its own assumed ideological stance and to befuddle the common man?

But the working class too is equipped—with drums and cymbals—that are resonant of a militant position and that reverberate through the atmosphere to drown down the sound of the megaphone. In one instance this militancy is augmented by the song—only one line of which is available in the play but which is enough to declare the purport and message behind it: 'Let's all pull together' is obviously a rousing song to enlist support and build cohesiveness amongst the workers.

The working class also uses a down to earth prosaic language while speaking and this is far more effective compared to the frequent use of rhyme by the Boss and his coterie. This is unlike earlier literary paradigms where the nobility spoke in verse form, their poetic language adding to their grand stature. Here, the verse form is mere scurrilous rhyming which points out that, under the surface of their authoritative images, those in power are rogues who have no compunctions in using the most devious underhand means to retain their power. Their language reads almost like a spoof of the heroic verse form. Underlining the agit prop mode of the play and reinforcing the theme of class struggle are the use of the red ladder, the flag, and signboards with significant words like 'Inflation', 'Profit', etc that are propped up at apt moments. The colour red for the ladder (and of the song 'red flag' played by WI on the trumpet) is obviously a symbolic vehicle bearing an alternative understanding of political reality, an alternative basis of social solidarity—i.e., a communist ideal. That the expropriation of symbols can undermine strength (a strength that grows through time) is seen by the way in which all kinds of schemers find shelter under the national flag; traditionally a flag is not simply a decorated cloth but the embodiment of a nation. It arouses feelings of pride and fervour. In The Cake Play this aspect is satirized, for the national flag is literally treated like a coloured cloth (umbrella like) that will protect or cloak all kinds of corruption—representing then, a nation gone to the dogs.

In evolving into a complex ritual complete with attempts at generating mass participation, in deploying complex symbolism including iconism, the text presents itself as a viable option to the metatextual. This empowerment occurs because all these facets of rituals form an alternative matrix of potent conventions/signifiers. To repeat an earlier comment, the text however does not accord itself the status of the dominant order—it seeks, through its alternative signifiers, to suggest that power belongs to the people as a whole. Again, to reiterate, it seeks to erase the spatial boundaries of the performance area, thus

> demystifying the gap between performer and audience and making
> the political consciousness raising which followed a performance
> something which was also shared, thus helping to politicise the theatre-
> going process itself.[4]

Red Ladder's Strike While the Iron is Hot alternatively called A Woman's Work is Never Done first performed on March 11, 1974 begins with that most vital element of agit prop, a song. Entitled 'Don't Get married, Girls', this incredibly tongue-in-cheek song by Leon Rosselson only too honestly describes the different ways in which women allow themselves to be trapped into playing the myriad roles that their male counterparts expect of them. It is a simple song but it succinctly describes the unresisting construction of female identity and suggests a contestation of this formation. Though the tone of the song is half mocking, its very subversiveness makes it effective. This is not the only meaningful song in the play. Songs dominate the play and are a potent means of engaging the audience emotionally. Victor Turner describes how in ritual, 'the dominant symbol brings the ethical and jural norms of society into close contact with emotional stimuli'. He says:

> In the action situation of ritual, with its social excitement and direct physiological stimuli, such as music, singing, dancing, alcohol, incense, and bizarre modes of dress, the ritual symbol…effects an interchange of qualities between its poles of meaning. Norms and values, on the one hand become saturated with emotion, while the gross and basic emotions become ennobled through contact with social values. (Kertzer, 1988:40)

Thus the songs precisely because they are simply writ, are also a strong means of uniting symbols of social reality with the emotions that the performance intends to stir; the songs do not lull one into an atmosphere of stability but aid in exciting angst at a male dominated, gendered world. The use of placards with slogans, subversive wit and humour as the tone of the play and limited, functional props on stage are the other typical agit prop characteristics that the play endorses.

The process of scripting this play, indeed its very conception, evolution and reception by different audiences has been outlined by Red Ladder actor-member Chris Lawrence in the Note to the Play of this edition. It makes for a telling reading for several reasons. One reason is that it reveals the schism between the ideals of a 'collective' and what actually happens. Working as a collective "implies a challenge to authoritarianism and the rigid division of labour which help perpetuate oppressive relations, and stifle creativity and contributions from performers". (Introduction:9). Chris Rawlence's account of the functioning of Red Ladder as a collective while drafting Strike While the Iron is Hot reveals that beneath the umbrella of 'collective' writing, there exist not only different ratios of involvement with a particular theme but also conflicting opinions amongst the members. Strike While the Iron is Hot brings out engrained male chauvinism in the process of cultural production and therefore the continued non-posteriorization of, for and by women in this process. The story as Chris Rawlence tells it goes thus that at first it was decided that the play would be one of many units i.e. theatre pieces that dealt with subjects as wide ranging as technology, housing, Ireland, racism, etc. Depending on the need of the target audience, a relevant theatre piece would be performed but along with it, the Women's Play (as Strike While the Iron is Hot is addressed) could also be enacted to widen the scope for discussion, post performance. Hence, Chris Lawrence says:

> Predictably we couldn't keep the unit length down to fifteen minutes. The first two—on the Housing Finance Act and the implications of new technology for white collar workers—ran to thirty and forty minutes respectively and were only ever twice performed in the same evening. The third of these new units was the Women's Play. That it should have been relegated to third place was pointed to by the women in Red Ladder as symptomatic of its priority by Red Ladder men (Note;17)

Not just in terms of prioritizing the theme, but even in terms of ideological commitments, varying perspectives emerged. Chris Lawrence speaks of the two factions: one, under the banner of Marx, Lenin and dialectical materialism, felt that womens' oppression could end by ending exploitation of the working classes by the bourgeoisie; the other, influenced by such like Shulamith Firestone, believed that the patriarchal stranglehold upon women was of greater importance than the class struggle.

Of course these oppositions within the "collective" were resolved eventually. The Womens' Play was drafted into a single unit entitled <u>Strike While the Iron is Hot</u> by Autumn 1973 thus allowing the theme to come into its own. And ideological differences too were sorted at by the use of "two banners which appeared simultaneously at the end of the play. They read 'women will never be free while workers are in chains' and 'workers will never be free while women are in chains.'" (Note;18)

However this collective experience of writing <u>Strike While the Iron is Hot</u> was a learning experience for the three women and one man who undertook to write the play. Collating the material from different sources led to a closer look at the multifaceted nature of the theme. It also instilled a desire to be politically correct in viewing women— thus one of the scenes in an early draft of the play included a stylized History of the Family which attempted to show the changing nature of the family from prehistoric times to the present day. Though dropped for its didacticism, the very conception of this scene showed a deeper understanding of and a growing familiarity with women's issues on the Company's part. Nonetheless, the interweaving of the class struggle with that of the women illustrates that 'Red Ladder's political base line was a socialist approach which

73

was then influenced by feminism'. (Introduction,:10). In a nutshell, the play centers around a young married couple, Helen and Dave, both of whom are part of their unions in their work place. While collectively the women in the union at Helen's workplace learn to fight for their rights, Helen simultaneously introduces changes in the division of labour at her homefront. Initially Dave resists but with Helen's changing situation, his consciousness as a man and a husband undergoes changes as well. 'Although the main emphasis in the play is on the women's self activity, the end suggests the possibility of an alliance between men and women, in which the divide and rule ideology of bourgeois social relations has been exposed.' (Introduction:13)

This synopsis of the play suggests a kind of processual structuring which fits neatly into the phases into which Victor Turner groups the public action constituting social drama. The first of these phases is:

> 'breach of regular norm governed social relations made publicly
> visible by the infraction of a rule ordinarily held to be binding, and
> which is itself a symbol of the maintenance of some major relationships
> between persons, statuses, or subgroups held to be a key link in the
> integrality of the widest community recognized to be a cultural envelope
> of solidary sentiments. (Turner, 1986:34)

Scene One of the play depicts a traditional wedding with the usual revelry, clichetic speeches full of nostalgia and attempts at witticism, and the elation of the bride, the groom and their respective mothers. The optimism about the marriage stems from all kinds of conventional reasons—the bride is sure about her choice and appears to be delighted that she is close to attaining her hearts' desires, i.e. marrying Dave and bearing his children; the groom is satisfied with Helen because she qualifies not just in terms of looks and intelligence to be his wife but also because of her submissiveness; and the mothers of each are so happy about the ceremony and the gifts that any qualms they have about Helen being able to manage a home are forgotten. An aspect worth noting in the first section of this scene is the advice doled out by the mothers: both proffer advice that ensure the groom's contentment; obviously they represent a generation not impacted by feminist ideals, a generation that corroborated with and furthered patriarchal norms and conditions. The placards with the slogans 'And they lived happily ever after' and 'The

End' are ironically meant to imply the kind of 'end' that the performance would like to give to the farcical, stereotypical familial relations that exist in society. Thus these slogans are immediately offset by the song of the chorus that lists out all the tedious chores that Helen needs to complete. It is this choric song that strikes a note of discord in what should have been an idyllic post-marital set up; it thus serves to create a 'breach' in what is presumed to lead to a well ordered life.

For we see that Helen does not take her restrictive life style, the stifling drudgery of routine domesticity too well. Though she masks her discontentment in Dave's presence, things do not augur well for him because Helen has started showing the first signs of not being the meek housewife he would like her to be; she has started grumbling. Scene Two carries over Helen's resentment which now spills over in her resolution to pick up a job in order to break her desultory existence and her financial dependence. The second stage following the 'breach' in domesticity, has been reached. This stage, Turner calls 'crisis'

> when people take sides, or rather, are in the process of being induced,
> seduced, cajoled, nudged, or threatened to take sides by those who confront
> one another across the revealed breach as prime antagonists. As Durkhiem
> and Rene Girard have argued and my observations confirm: crisis is contagious.
> When antagonisms become overt, ancient rancours, rivalries, and unresolved
> vendettas are revived. Non-rational considerations prevail: temperamental
> dislikes, unconscious desires and aggressions, reanimated infantile anxieties,
> as well as the conscious envies and jealousies which break loose when a
> major normative knot is cut. (Turner, 1986:34)

Thus Dave, fed up with Helen's taunts about the way he spends his leisure time and money, challenges her to work in a factory like himself. By doing this, however, he opens the door to new avenues for Helen little realising the advantage that is now on her side and the price he would have to pay if Helen is to take him on. Which, of course, she does.

Since the play moves across two spaces—domestic and the workplace—similar structures appear in both.

> Deconstruction, which I rely on…for my critique of community,
> shows that a desire for unity or wholeness in discourse generates
> borders, dichotomies and exclusions. I suggest that the desire for

> mutual identification in social relations generates exclusions in a
> similar way. A woman in a feminist group that seeks to affirm mutual
> identification will feel and be doubly excluded if by virtue of her being
> different in race, class, culture, or sexuality she does not identify with
> the others nor they with her.[5]

In 'The Sweatshop' where Helen works as seamstress, the 'breach' occurs due to the attitude of the manageress (which filters down to the foreman who acts as per her orders). Due to her higher class status and her role as an owner rather than a worker of production, the manageress stands outside the feminist community that Helen and her colleagues build up; in fact the construction of the feminist collective is a direct consequence of the intolerant stance adopted by the manageress. When Sheila, a co-worker, returns after a few days leave (her absence was because she stayed home to nurse her youngest child suffering from chicken pox), instead of sympathising with her or appreciating her effort in making suitable arrangements for her son's care, thus allowing her to resume work—the Foreman orders her to quit. Thinking that the manageress, because 'Well, she's a woman, she should understand' (Act I, sc.3a, p.31), Helen decides to take up the cudgels on Sheila's behalf. But, as noted earlier, the manageress stands at a different social level in terms of her class position and not only does she completely rebuff Helen, she is outraged by Helen's audacity in questioning her. It is the realization that the boss may be a woman, but is also the boss, and an unrelenting one at that, and the fact that her job depended on the whims of this boss that makes Helen recall the union at her husband's workplace which worked towards preventing injustice to employees. Ironically, earlier it is this same Union that Helen had suspected as being responsible for Dave's absence from home during evenings. In the alternative scene written for the NUPE on Tyneside, the workplace is represented by a school kitchen (NUPE organize school meal workers). Here matters come to a head when under the garb of a bonus scheme, the workers while slaving for a bit of extra money, are faced with the most inclement of work conditions; so much so that Helen first slips on the cramped floor and then cuts her finger while peeling potatoes. Mrs Edward, the school meals manageress and quite like the Sweatshop manageress insists that Helen's cut be unattended and work go on. At this, Doris, Helen's colleague immediately calls for a meeting of the 'union' and their joint efforts not only result in Helen receiving first aid at once but also acquiring an extra hand at work, thus easing overall work pressure. Helen, who for long, has been sceptical about the functionality of a Union is converted into believing in its efficacy. The manageresses, in both instances, refuse to stand up for the cause of the sex to which they belong. They allow the mantle of their class positioning to war with their gender role. This breach of confidence or, in other words, betrayal of same gender concern is what initiates the development of a feminist collective.

The formation of this collective is an uneven one. For not everyone joins it without hesitation. Helen's own initial misgivings aside, noticeable dissent/abstinence comes from young Chrissie who is unsure about joining the strike that the Union decides to stage. And her reasons are gendertypical: she is afraid of losing her boyfriend whose male ego cannot tolerate the idea of her earning more than him in case of the womens' strike succeeding. She doesn't know whether she will gain more by being on the side of the Womens' Union or on the side of her boyfriend. Of course, the other women, with a knowledge born from age and experience do their best to persuade her to join the Union; Helen's comment at Chrissie's dependence upon her boyfriend's decision is

> Look, love, when I first got married I used to let my husband make all the decisions. After a while you begin to feel like half a person. You've got to start making up your own mind. (Act I, sc.8;55)

It is the presence of differences between the women themselves that prevents the easy formation of a Womens' Union;

> The ideal of community presumes subjects can understand one another as they understand themselves. It thus denies the difference between subjects. (Nicholson, ed., 1990:302)

In order to bridge this difference and enlist more members into the Womens' Union, the line adopted by its stalwarts is that joining the union would promote the development of each woman's individuality.

This problematic taking of sides or the stage of 'crisis' in Turner's phraseology is discernible more obviously in the case of the men supporting the women. In Scene Five which is ushered in by the placard 'The Disputed Pint' it is again the 'difference' between equal parity and equal pay between men and women that is cause for dispute. The men want equal pay amongst them for equivalent work; the women's cause merits little concern on their part for though not averse to the idea of the women getting a raise, the possibility of this raise being equal to their payscales does not even occur to them. The basic premise operating here is that men consider womens' work inherently lower than theirs. The women naturally consider this a fallacious perception and their demand is for equal parity between men and women as well as equal pay for the same kind of labour. In this scene Mary, the wife of Helen's colleague, George, lists out the vast quantity of unpaid labour that she undertakes everyday. Her husband laughs it off by saying that she is repaid in the form of his 'undying love and affection' for her. However, this skirting of a justifiable issue of angst amongst women is symptomatic of

> ...a gender based division of human activities and hence the existence
> of socially constructed sets of gender arrangements and the (peculiar
> and in need of explanation) salience of gender itself.[6]

Thus activities like childrearing and in Scene Four, the abortion scene, even decisions related to bearing a child (or not) are left entirely to women as things of their domain.

> 'The third phase that Victor Turner demarcates in the action of social drama is
> the application of redressive or remedial procedures. These range
> from personal advice and informal mediation or arbitration to formal
> jural and legal machinery and, to resolve certain kinds of crises or
> legitimate other modes of conflict-resolution, to the performance of
> public ritual. This phase is perhaps the most reflexive of the social drama.
> The community, acting through its representatives, bends, even throws
> itself back upon itself, to measure what some of its members have done,
> and how they have conducted themselves with reference to its own standards.
> Sometimes this phase too is initially violent...But the violence is here
> conceptualised as being an instrument of a value-bearing group's solidarity
> and continuity, not as serving sectional or personal needs. (Turner, 1986:35)

This phase is followed by the fourth phase and 'consists either of the reintegration of the disturbed social group or of the recognition and legitimation of irreparable schism between the contending parties.' (Turner, 1986;35). This fourth phase seems to mark a kind of closure or end of the social drama, of the 'action'. But in actuality, since each human being has

> his/her 'individual cognitive, evaluative, and affective mappings of the
> structure of events and classes of events', 'a culture has its distributive
> existence as the set of personalities of the members of a population' thus
> allowing for negotiation and dispute over what should be authoritative or
> legitimate in that culture, in other words, for social dramatic action. (Turner,
> 1986:36)

So, the completion of the four phases in the development of action in social drama demands *shared* understandings and experiences in the lives of members of the *same* sociocultural field.

In terms of the class struggle (i.e. between labour versus employers) Scene Six of Strike While the Iron is Hot seems to herald the start of remedial measures in that the parity issue between the men (equal pay for equal parity) seems finally to be reaching a climax. This occurs when the Director directs the Management representative, Johnson, to settle the issue and end the five weeks long strike. He is however, also firm that the answer to the women's demand for equal pay is to 'on no account give way to that. It will set a precedent for the whole corporation and cost us a fortune.' (Act I, sc.6:43) The only step he is willing to make is that 'If the worst comes to the worst we'll offer them a job evaluation and try to get round it that way.' (Act I, sc.6:43) The remaining scene captures the farcical nature of the redressive measures employed. While the men (John and George) argue with Johnson about settling their claim regarding parity between employees of the male sex, and finally agree to his proposal that parity would come about but only in stages i.e., only in late 1975; the issue about parity with women and equal pay for them as well is completely sidelined. George in fact, initially even forgets to mention their case to Johnson and needs to be reminded by John to do so. This, considering that the women on whose behalf they are to speak are their own colleagues, is a comment on the gendered nature of the class struggle. The accord between the men, whether of the management or of the work force is visible when it comes to their getting together and cracking jokes at the expense of the women. At this moment disparity of any kind between the men seems to be non-existent and their bonding makes a mockery of the seriousness of the women's demands. This aspect is evidenced further when the so called Time and Motion Man or Job Evaluator comes along to evaluate the nature of the jobs undertaken by the women and decide whether their pay scale be equal to that of the men. Obviously, aware of the instructions of the Director, the Job Evaluator brazenly cheats the women by placing them a grade below the men. Thinking that the antagonism of the women can be easily contained by deterring them with the threat of shutting down the whole place, the Director appears to be completely unconcerned with the women work force and their needs.

The play does not end with Scene Six however and, so, if the womens' Question is shown to be neglected thus far, the subsequent scenes illustrate that evasion cannot remain unnoticed. In Scene Eight when the women display aggression (a form of the Violence that Turner speaks of, as quoted earlier) the remedial measures seem finally closer to being achieved. The placard heralding the scene ironically says 'The way to a man's heart is through his stomach' and as usual the scene following the placard, plays out its subversive nature. Using a subject of much 'joking', i.e. the means to capture a man's heart, the women actually turn the tables on the men to prove that it is no laughing matter. For when the Canteen is shut down and it is clear that the women have no intention of being subordinated to the needs of the men, their power in terms of the dependability of the men upon them is clear. The helplessness of the men is revealed by their almost childish rage and protest at this insubordination of the women, at this movement away from their gender role. When it is obvious that the women are unwilling to budge an inch until their demands for equal parity and pay with men are fully supported by the men; when all the assertions of the men are met with rejoinder after counter rejoinder, the men are left groping for a way out. Trapped, they submit to the demands of the women and thus ironically prove the strength of the slogan to their own detriment. This strategic manipulation is what Judith Butler emphasises:

… The critical task for feminism is not to establish a point of view outside of constructed identities; that conceit is the construction of an epistemological model that would disavow its own cultural location and, hence, promote itself as a global subject, a position that deploys precisely the imperialist strategies that feminism ought to criticize. The critical task is, rather, to locate strategies of subversive repetition enabled by those constructions, to affirm the local possibilities of intervention through participating in precisely those practices of repetition that constitute identity and therefore, present the immanent possibility of contesting them. (My emphasis) (Butler, 1990:147)

Hence the redressive measures lead to a breaking down of gender roles which serves as a kind of compromise binding these contesting factions. It also implies that it is this integration that creates a collective workforce which is now equipped with enough power to contend with the dictates of the management. True that the drama is incomplete in that the play does not progress to actually show whether this collective workforce succeeds in beating the management at their own game. But there is definitely a plausible contention in depicting that it is not impossible to create a union of working men and women capable of confronting the owners of production. That in itself is no easy task as the play showcases all along.

At the familial level too, Scene Seven 'Parity begins at Home' and Scene Nine 'Strike While the Iron is Hot' (incidentally, this entitling of each scene underlines the implied 'message' of the play) posit the gradual gender role interchanges. In Scene Seven, Helen, exhausted after a days hard work both at her workplace and at home, cannot respond to Dave's sexual overtures thus irking him no end. She responds to his wrath not by weakly surrendering but by drawing his attention to his comparatively easier life i.e., one bereft of domestic responsibilities for example, as against her own, burdened with 'two—one in the factory and one here.' His suggestion that she give up her job, is unacceptable to her because

> I'm not going back to asking you every time I want a bob or two
> for something. Oh, look, Dave. Work's not that marvelous, but
> for the first time I've got a life of my own outside these four walls.
> I've got friends of my own at work. And with this closure threat,
> we've got a real fight on our hands.

She concludes with the directive

> So, you're just going to have to start helping at home,
> You can—start with the ironing. (Act I, sc.7:51)

The scene ends with the song 'The Maintenance Engineer' which is a biting attack upon the slavish existence of a housewife. What is significant about the song is that the apparent guilt of the men and their desire to fight for women's rights is curiously slapped down by the working wife. It is suspected that such support is motivated by a desire to keep the woman in a restricted and restrictive place. The woman would rather be helped out in such a way that if 'you did your share at home, then I might have some time to fight some battles of my own' (Act I, sc. 7: 52-53)

The liminal space wherein the man is forced to enter by the woman in this scene is resolved into a virtual reality in Scene Nine where Dave is actually involved in completing domestic chores while Helen is out. But is this enough? Not for Helen who dreams of more, of 'a world where women really are men's equals, not just with equal pay—that's just equal exploitation—but a world with no exploitation. This means big changes and only you and I can make them. But if they're needed, can you say we're asking too much?' (Act I, sc.9:62)

Marvin Carlson writes that in performance:

> The audience's expected 'role' changes from a passive hermeneutic
> process of decoding the performer's articulation, embodiment, or
> challenge of particular cultural material, to becoming something
> much more active, entering into a praxis, a context in which meanings
> are not so much communicated as created, questioned, or negotiated.
> The 'audience' is invited and expected to operate as a co-creator of
> whatever meanings and experience the event generates. (Striff, ed., 2003: p8)

In questioning the audience, in a pointed conjoining of the 'you' with the 'I' and thus making the audience a party to the intended action behind the performance, Strike While the Iron is Hot ceases to be merely a play to be watched. Instead it becomes a ritual text that has served its purpose in mediating between the performers and the audience to demonstrate that it is not always clear where a performance begins and ends: If drama is all about, etymologically speaking, 'doing', then the conversion of an audience into 'doers' is a sure measure of ensuring the longevity of the dramatic text.[7]

It has been seen that The Cake Play was seeped in contemporary history; Taking Our Time[8] performed by Red Ladder first in 1978 was

> ... based on past events in the West Riding ... with the intention of
> reconnecting our audiences with that past ... the period we chose
> needed to have specific resonances with the contemporary experience
> of our audiences if it was to be of more than passing interest to them ...

82

> ... Putting the year 1842 in the spotlight, we hoped to identify what
> 'qualities of life' were lost in this transition with a view to suggesting
> what parts of it might be regained in a socialist future. (page ix of the Text)

Located within the mid-nineteenth century Chartist Movement in the industrial north of Britain, Taking Our Time showcased the split between the old handloom weavers and the new generation of mill workers through the experiences of a single family. Red Ladder aimed to make the audience question themselves that if in an earlier era, a mass movement like the Chartist Movement that was 'determined in its actions to bring about a people's parliament and a democratically controlled economy and at times it looked as though they might achieve it' (p.xii of the Text), could be generated; then why the apathy in terms of reviving the socio-eco-politico structures in the current scenario?

While the collective drafting of Strike While The Iron is Hot revealed differences of opinion among the individuals that put it together, the 'collective' writing of Taking Our Time resulted in a further development. This was the inclusion of credits, something that Red Ladder had been avoiding but the necessity for which arose because 'some company members felt they wanted individual credit as a form of reference, should the need arise to seek work elsewhere' (Note preceding play). Already then, though still functioning as a collective, we observe that a subtle change had taken place: there was more 'professionalism' in the attitude towards the production. This does not imply that the commitment to the ideology of the collective had diminished but the consciousness of individual scope in a larger world, one beyond Red Ladder; the consciousness that social activism was but one dimension of a larger relationship with theatre, had increased. However unlike the usual crediting system that one is accustomed to where 'It is all too common to find directors, writers and stars in bold print and at top of lists; whereas wardrobe, technicians and administrators are relegated to the bottom, in small print, if indeed they appear at all' (Note preceding play), Red Ladder reversed the order with Costume Design and Costume Production leading the Credit List. This may appear to be a small change but it is resonant of Red Ladder's persistent efforts to foreground the marginalized in every possible sphere of activity.

The analyses of the two plays taken up earlier were significant in terms of their themes: The Cake Play in questioning socialist solutions to contemporary problems; Strike While The Iron is Hot as a strong social drama that transformed, in a strategically structured manner, a passive female community into a socially committed active collective. Though the plays were thematically linked in that both propagated the concept of equality between classes and between genders (to an extent, all the plays are correlated as they, in different ways, further the Company's ideology) the difference was visible in the stylistic devices involved in presenting the theme/s. While The Cake Play was undiluted agit prop with an apology of a plot, Strike While The Iron is Hot evolved a more well knit form using polarities such as home versus workplace, working men versus working women, as the base upon which to build a super-narrative. With Taking Our Time one finds a tightening in the plot construction and a subtler, but not less powerful weaving in of ritual agit prop devices.

The depiction of an unavailable, existing historicity which formed the Haupttext or Metatext of the Cake Play was an all engulfing principle of the play; in Taking Our Time the metatext becomes not just the presentation of a historically turbulent period of time but also the modus operandi of Red Ladder (as representative of all agit prop) Theatre Company. In other words on sees an intersection of two discourses within the play (a) a discourse on ideology and (b) a discourse on theatre modes. The Nebentext right at the beginning of the play elucidates this aspect at once:

> Sunday, eight August, eighteen forty-two. An ale house in Halifax.
> Woolcombers and weavers of calderdale gathered for a social. There
> Is a banner in the ale house reading: 'WITHOUT VOTES WE ARE
> SLAVES. GIVE US THE CHARTER.' Most are Chartists. As audience
> enter, a medley of traditional songs is being sung, some political, some
> of love. The auditorium becomes the ale house. Some songs sung
> communally. Blackout. (Act I, sc.1:1)

In effect, this Nebentext (1) spells out the political message of the play (and therefore the aspirations and leanings of the Theatre Company) through such specifications as the date, the kind of people gathered, the slogan on the banner and the political songs being sung; (2) by extending its boundaries ('The auditorium becomes the ale house'), converts the theatre site into a performative space—thus engaging the presumably like-minded audience almost immediately (like minded for else how can 'some songs [be] sung communally'?)

Having extended the limits of the original performance area, let us call it P1, outwards into P2, as the Nebentext in effect informs, we find the Haupttext now entering a different zone with the setting up of another play within the larger text i.e., Taking Our Time, entitled 'St George and the Dragon.' This process of first enlisting and then distancing i.e., a combination of the Alienation and mise-en-abyme techniques[9] is a tactical move to initiate a co-operative audience into recognising that their presence as spectators is only a phase in preparing to become actors in a drama beyond the bounds of the auditorium. The play itself, 'St George and the Dragon' is more along the lines of a Morality play, its outstanding features being its use of verse and symbolically named characters: so, 'Hard Working' is a mill worker; 'Machinio' is the dragon of the title; 'Mill Grind' is the mill owner and the 'St George' who in the kernel story slays the dragon, is a Chartist. The action follows a cyclical pattern of order-disorder-presumed reorder. Hardworking and Machinio work together harmoniously until one day, with an eye on profit, Millgrind steals Machinio away and monopolises its services, reducing Hardworking to penury. When Hardworking expresses distress, Millgrind is willing to allow Hardworking to tend to Machinio's needs, but only for a pittance. Hence Millgrind is out to eke the maximum profit from both, Machinio and Hardworking. Then along comes St George, the Chartist who points out that only by wresting Machinio out of Millgrind's control could fairplay become possible—but for this Hardworking would have to contribute her own bit by joining the strike. The play ends not by revealing whether the action plan succeeds or not but on the note that 'the answer to the problem is up to me and you.' (Act I, sc.1, p.4) After the play is over, Peter, who has been one of its narrators makes a little speech where he calls upon those acting as spectators in P1 to actively participate in the election of the delegate representing the Calderwike and District Chartist Society for the National Convention in Manchester. In a few words, Peter charts out the Chartist vision of securing a People's Parliament in the years to come.

In a nutshell, 'St George and the Dragon' serves as a discourse on the procedures of agit prop theatre because it functions like one:

> Discourses structure both our sense of reality and our notion of our own identity ... enables us to consider ways in which subjects can come to a position of disidentification, whereby we not only locate and isolate the ways in which we as subjects have been constructed and subjected, but we also map out for ourselves new terrains in which we can construct different and potentially more liberating ways in which we can exist. (Mills, 1997:15)

Consequently, though choosing to stage a play within a play may well have been due to the contingencies of the plot, it has a dual role as it also succeeds in reminding the (non alehouse) larger audience that spectacles ought to catalyse a series of actions in much the same way as 'St George and the Dragon' intended to achieve with its own particular audience.

That the play 'St George and the Dragon' as discourse does not 'exist in a vacuum' but is 'in conflict with other discourses and social practices which inform them over questions of truth and authority' is what the rest of the Haupttext of <u>Taking Our Time</u> unfolds. What then are these different and differing discourses? The Chartist discourse which the play 'St George and the Dragon' projects is undertaken outside it (i.e., within P1) by the majority of the cast including John, Mary, Jenny and Elsie. The key principles underlying this discourse are: (1) a Right to a People's Parliament (i.e., the right to vote); (2) a Right to the implementation of the Charter; (3) a Right to shorter, more convenient working hours (and not the regimented timings of the mill) and (4) an equal distribution of profits. [These last two rights for which the Chartist movement fought were actually an attempt to regain the freedom of lifestyle which the mills and machines had robbed the people off]. In total opposition to the Chartist ideology is the dissenting voice of William who is completely appropriated into the mill owner Akroyd's discourse on the power of Machines and a bright future for the Mills. This pro-machine/mill discourse is not the only anti-Chartist discourse: the orthodox Methodist preacher uses religion to malign Chartism and the revolutionary zeal of the Chartists. Torn between these discourses is Sarah who would like to be persuaded into William's ways of thinking but here, it would be relevant to note that William also uses the discourse of love in eliciting Sarah's support. While both, William and the preacher practice an anti-Chartist discourse it must be observed that their reasons vary. William genuinely believes that 'steam power has come for good. You can't stand in the way of progress', that 'machines'll make the future' (Act I, sc.1, p.5) and that 'Akroyd brought work to this valley, and new power looms'll mean even more.' (Act I, sc. 1:6) He sees the machine age thus as heralding a promising future for youth like himself. The Preacher's concerns however are with the spirit of Chartism; he regards their fervour as an ominous sign of rebelliousness against leading a disciplined life and thus against the strict, rigid rules of government that Methodism believed each individual ought to adhere to.

Using these divergent discourses the plot is constructed such as to show which will emerge the most effective and successful. When John, Mary and Peter under the guidance of Tom Tinker, the clown, manage to steal the lead (needed to repair John's pan) from the church roof right under the Preacher's nose, they use the language of religious discourse subversively and by fooling the Preacher reveal the inherent weakness of such discourse. Thus the Preacher stands on shaky ground indeed in using religion as the backbone of his anti-Chartist discourse. It is interesting to note that, at one level, his discourse and that of John's meet—this is with regard to their views on morality: John regards the Mill as an evil place where immorality reigns and women cultivate bad habits; the Preacher considers the alehouses, which is where the Chartists generally meet to discuss their course of action as a 'contagion' and sees 'death in these honeyed pots of pleasure.' (Act I, sc.1:7) Morality then, is the underbelly of their argument and that they are both privy to partly fallacious and partly correct logic is proved, in John's case, by Jenny's song. In this song, Jenny while acknowledging the preponderance of sexual overtures made to her in the Mill, also speaks of the contingencies that have driven her to work in the Mill, her dodging of the physical passes made at her and the secret dreams she cherishes (of freedom?). By her repugnance for the advances of the men in the mill and by underlining that it was financial necessity and not desire for illicit sexual relations that drove her to work, Jenny, if she can be seen as spokesperson for numerous other young women like her working in the Mills, puts John's views to test. As for the Preacher, his harangues on morality are consistently debunked by the Clown's sarcastically witty rejoinders; his excessively religious rhetoric is pompous and patronising and results in his becoming a laughing stock.

Amidst these discourses, is that of the Clown. The construction of a character like Tom Tinker, the clown, is in itself part of the political agenda of the play, as the Introduction admits:

> We wanted to show when and why the destruction of this popular
> culture took place; and we used the conflict between the preacher
> and the clown to describe it. Tom Tinker is based on traveling tinkers
> of the time who used clowning to ply their trade; a clown called Old
> Crafty is recorded as being active at fairs around Slaithwaite in those
> years. Tom embodies the dying of a popular culture. For the orthodox
> Methodist preacher he is the devil incarnate. Because Tom encourages
> fun and enjoyment: a fullness of life that is anathema to both the stoic
> requirements of Methodism and the disciplinary requirements of Akroyd's
> new mills. Tom is not the only cultural target of church and employer.
> Our play within a play ... and such goings on come under heavy attack
> as well. (px)

Apart from illustrating this objective of Red Ladder, the Clown as narrator cum commentator cum actor (a choric figure, in fact) is extremely important in that he shows the flip side of everything. Hs words before the knocker upper song indicate that it is his task to awaken the people. He therefore reinforces the ideological perspectives of Red Ladder and can be viewed as the voice of Red Ladder's political discourse in the play.

Though the plot concludes with Akroyd's victory through using the police force (the clown's comment on the semantics of the 'police force' is a pertinent diversion about the ironies of linguistic usage), the final song 'Great Expectations' suggests that such a conclusion to social action can be avoided. It depended upon the arousal of the spectators from their apathy and an active involvement in reconstructing socio-eco-politico-culturo structures to bring about a different end.

> Since the mid-nineteenth century a country's music has become
> a political ideology by stressing national characteristics, appearing
> as a representative of the nation, and everywhere confirming the
> national principle ... Yet music, more than any other artistic medium,
> expresses the national principle's antinomics as well. (T.W. Adorno)[10]

Within Performance Studies it is important to remember that a written text is not always a superior form of communication; to that extent, songs (i.e., music) can be used as an effective weapon, to assert or to overthrow or to protect authority. Taking Our Time is full of songs and they do all of these as well as provide us with knowledge about the characters, the situations and the ideological intent of both, and to a great length urge us to either perceive hitherto unperceived things or perceive them differently. The immense emotional power of music in a ritual act/text is an acknowledged fact and it is not difficult then, to comprehend agit prop theatre's use of it for its own ends.

The play in fact, as has been discussed earlier, begins with songs, initially sung by actors and later, after the audience enters, communally. This instantaneous bonding between the actors and the audience through songs is a ritual device of initiation used by agit prop theatre to create a feeling of unity. Soon after is the Clown's song where he lists out his duties, and the key lines of his song

> I see a new world that's hidden from view and if you look hard
> enough you'll see it, too. I turn the world upside down. I am your
> traveling clown. (Act I, sc. 1:7)

are meaningful not just for the reasons cited earlier, i.e., in terms of voicing Red Ladder's ideology; the fact that he is a 'travelling' clown, in other words the whole idea of mobility (physical as well as a mental) of unrestricted movement, as being the source of his keener understanding is a noteworthy notion. If we extend the category of mobility further, we observe in the concluding sections of the play, the mass movement of the working populace from different parts of Britain to emerge as a strong and threatening force to contend with. Also relevant at this point are William's comments on the construction of the Railway track in Act II scene 10 where he sees this as making the world smaller and opening new opportunities for all. The anti-technology stance of the Chartists, then, though justifiable must be balanced by looking at the positive side of technological advance—conquering topographical boundaries is after all only the first step in ushering bigger changes. Thus the mobility of the traveling clown can be studied as a trope for a larger mobility that is required of the people if they are to achieve freedom from the oppressive Mill and machine forces. Prior to the knocker upper song, the Clown's words

> But most people never wake up. They sleep with their eyes open.
> All their lives, fast asleep. My job is to wake them up.
> Before they get knocked up. (Act I, sc.4:13)

are consistent with his sustained efforts at arousing people from their blindness to a deteriorating situation. In fact his efforts are unflagging right till the end, i.e. even after his 'death', with the 'Great Expectations' song which concludes the play with the words:

> They'll say that you're a clown, a fool to try
> But take your time and live before you die.
> Wake up from the dream
> Wake up from the dream.
> Great expectations
> Your time is here.
> Great expectations
> Before the time of your life disappears. (Act II, sc.13:51-52)

In stark contrast to the kind and motivating words of the Clown's songs is the knocker upper song which is cruel in its mocking of people's dreams and reminding people that 'the man with the big stick's gonna knock you up? This song and Akroyd's song entitled 'The Song of the Self made Man' are similar in that they belong to a discourse that would deny any humane considerations and look only towards material gain. But contesting this discourse are such songs as the 'St. Monday Song' (sung during the Fair) and the title 'Taking Our Time' song sung by John and Mary both of which express a desire for regaining traditional values and a past world that had all the freedom of which people were now bereft. The opposing themes of the songs, then, augment the contrasting discourses within the play.

The two other songs in the play, 'Jenny's song' and 'Sarah's grief song' are different from the rest of the songs in that they express personal angst (of course Jenny's song also describes the appalling conditions that young girls face in the factories) and are both poignant. Jenny's nurturing of secret desires, which her song expresses, makes her death in the factory she abhors a greater tragedy. Sarah's grief song lamenting the loss of her sister Jenny marks that crisis in her life where she makes a leap of faith; in wanting to avenge Jenny's death, Sarah's song inadvertently joins the discourse of that very camp that she has been rebelling against. Hence her song of grief is also an indication of her conversion to Chartism, and a change in her identity.

Apart from the discursive structures that the songs outline, the power of officialese or official discourse and of agitational rhetoric are also clearly spelt out in the play. The first is evidenced by the Coroner's report read out by the Clown where the official language of the report is a complete distortion of the truth behind the accident leading to Jenny's death; the officiousness is the disguise with which responsibility is avoided by the powers that be. Inverting the potency of official discourse is the agitational rhetoric employed by John and Mary who are passionate in their goal to achieve the Charter and are prepared to use violent means, if the need arises, as Mary so forcibly puts it just before the march to Akroyd's Mill:

> ... There could be trouble. Don't be provoked.
> They've had troops saddled and ready in Leeds
> for two weeks now. But I say we have been
> saddled by the masters and their lapdog parliament
> all our lives and it is time for us to throw them off.
> We will have the Charter, peaceably if we may, but
> forcibly if we must. (Act II, sc.13:47)

If, following a Focauldian frame of reference,

> literature, as well as being the means whereby
> a sense of national culture is established, is also
> the means whereby a shared culture can be contested. (Mills, 1997:20)

Then the ensemble of conflicting discourses within the text of Taking Our Time does precisely the latter. In the final analysis it is through the power generated by its discourse that the meaning as well as the success of a Ritual text can be decided. Taking Our Time can hence in this light be seen as a sample of the discourse used by agit prop theatre.

From the Cake Play to Taking Our Time, marks a decade of practicing agit prop theatre and already one observes that a major paradigm of this theatre, the subordination of form to content/ideology, was undergoing a subtle but steady change. There is a tightening of the plot structure and the development of a linear story line; the feminist perspective was gaining ground, even with Taking Our Time, set in 1842, the gender issue was given prominence; and hints of the changes that were to happen with Red Ladder as a collective, can be sensed with the introduction of accreditation. However such changes only augured well for the future of Red Ladder Theatre Company as this study will further elucidate.

Notes

[1] Information from the Red Ladder archives

[2] Unpublished typed script sent by Red Ladder

[3] Politics in Britain: An Introduction by Colin Leys (first published by Heinemann Educational Books, 1983), Verso, London, 1986 provides an excellent political background (henceforth, Colin Leys, 1986).

[4] Introduction to Strike While The Iron is Hot. Three plays on sexual politics edited and introduced by Michelene Wandor, The Journeyman Press, London and West Nyack, 1980: 10

[5] From Iris Marion Young's Essay on 'The Ideal of Community and the Politics of Diference' in Nicholson, ed., 1990:301

[6] Essay entitled 'Postmodernism and Gender relations in Feminist Theory' by Jane Flax in Nicholson (ed), 1990:47)

[7] Though Strike While The Iron is Hot was first performed in 1974, since the version analysed in this section is a 1980 edition, it has been examined after The Cake Play

[8] Taking Our Time by Red Ladder, Pluto Press, London, 1979

[9] Mise-en-abyme is the narrative technique of setting up of a mirror within a mirror or reflexive mirrors where a hierarchy of reflections/refractions are set up. [Alienation or Verfremdung, a Brechtian notion has been discussed in Chapter I]

[10] Cited by Paul Gilroy in his essay entitled 'Jewels Brought From Bondage': Black Music and the Politics of Authenticity' in Striff, ed., 2003:137

CLIMBING TO THE EIGHTIES

The early 1980s became another watershed for Red Ladder Theatre Company as it made the Company consider the role and practice of political theatre in the 80s, a very different environment from that of the sixties and seventies. It led to a year of experimentation with new ideas, building on the experience of the past, which was perhaps easier due to the financial assistance provided by such bodies as Arts Council of Great Britain, Greater London Arts, North West Arts, West Midland Arts, East Midland Arts, Yorkshire Arts and South Yorkshire Metropolitan County Council (such assistance was acknowledged by Red Ladder in the policy information that appeared in programmes produced for the 80s plays, for example, Circus).

This period saw many 'firsts'. In 1981, the Company produced its first extant script, The Blind Goddess by Ernst Troller which was translated by Michelene Wandor and was about socialism in a fascist state, the position of women and the hypocrisy of justice; the Company's first writing commission from the Northern playwright Paul Goetz with the 1983 production of Preparations by Paul Goetz and Pat Winslow—this piece looked at the response of both, the individuals and the authorities, to the threat of the holocaust; and with the 1984 production of This Story of Yours by John Hopkins, the Company took a new path as the play was aimed exclusively at Theatre venues. This play explored male violence and sexuality from a highly charged position: the main narrative was about a policeman being accused of murdering a suspected child abuser during an interrogation.

Apart from these ventures, in 1980 Red Ladder produced Ladders to the Moon, an account of a strike in 1893 at Featherstone Pit in Yorkshire which resulted in the army shooting and killing several miners. Circus by Rony Robinson produced in 1981, was an allegory in which the state of Britain in 1981 was likened to an ailing circus of the 1930s where the owner deceives the workers who have no real control over their work. 1982 saw two productions, Playing Apart and The Best of British 'whose country is it anyway? The first was a club show about life in post-war Britain from the 'never had it so good' fifties, through the 'swinging sixties' and the 'cynical' seventies. A show that did not

93

achieve much success was the 1983 production of <u>Bring Out Your Dead</u> by Peter Cox. This looked at Britain in 1988 after another term of Tory government and had Big Mac from America running the privatized health service. Put together at very short notice following cancellations of <u>Bring Out Your Dead</u> in 1983/84 was <u>Dumb Blonde</u> by Peter Masters and Geraldine Griffins, a Busby Berkley style musical with music by Mc Govan/Dougall which took a light hearted look at women at work. Besides <u>This Story of Yours</u> mentioned earlier, 1984 saw three other productions: <u>Happy Jack</u> by John Godber (an extant script) charted the history of a coal miner and his wife through six decades of living on a pauper's wage; a commissioned work from South Yorkshire writer, Rony Robinson, <u>The Beano</u>, was a sensitive but hilarious account of a brewery workers' day trip to Scarborough in 1914: the revelers frolicked on their one day out while clouds of war were gathering in Europe; and <u>The Danderhall Red Beano</u>. This was not a show at all, but a week long festival mounted by Red Ladder in conjunction with Mid Lothian District Council in the mining village of Danderhall, near Edinburgh—it marked a return to the true spirit and ethos of the Edinburgh fringe. A double bill, <u>Stitchin' the Blues</u> and <u>Mixing it</u> by Maggie Lane, was produced in 1985: the former was a one woman show based on the Lee jeans occupation of 1981 while the latter took a look at what happened when an unemployed CND activist got a job building a nuclear power station. The year also saw the production of <u>Safe With Us</u> by Frances McNeill, a play commissioned by the Confederation of Health Service Employees Union for their 75th Anniversary celebrations. This fast moving play used comedy and music to look at current issues within the Health Service.

1985/86 radically changed the shape of the Company from a collective to a Hierarchy with the appointment of a Board of Directors who in turn appointed an Artistic Director—Rachel Feldburg. A new policy was developed with a commitment to Equal Opportunities informing all areas of the Company's work. At this point, it is relevant to not to paraphrase and instead to quote in Red Ladder's language, its aims as well as Artistic and Audience Developments.

The Company's aims were as follows:
- To create an artistically exciting socialist feminist theatre

- To take this work to audiences who would not normally see theatre, young people 14-25 and the adults who work with them. To perform on their own grounds, in Youth Clubs and places where they normally meet, rather than in theatre venues.
- To make our work accessible to all young people and in particular to reach young people for whom there is little or inadequate provision; young disabled people, Black young people (within which we include Asian and African Caribbean teenagers), young people in inner cities and isolated rural areas.
- To offer theatre of the highest possible standard which is exciting and challenging both for the audience and performers and which uses a wide variety of forms and which seeks to develop the vocabulary of this form of theatre by offering young people 'the best'.
- To base this work on issues of concern to our audience and to develop the ways in which theatre can be used with parallel groups and professions (for instance Youth Workers). To encourage these workers to use theatre as part of their work with associated training, preparation and follow up.
- To continue to implement and develop the Company's Equal Opportunities Policy (including our Anti-racist Strategy and Action Plan on Disability) placing it at the core of our work and seeking to achieve a fully integrated Company at all levels.
- To raise the profile of this area of work amongst other Companies, funding bodies and professional workers and to encourage Regional Arts Boards and Local Authorities/Youth Services to work in partnership.

Artistic and Audience Developments

- An innovative tri-part programme for Asian girls to include parallel projects in India and the North of England, coupled with development of a new, long term, Asian women's theatre project based in the North.
- A consistent development of the Company's work for disabled teenagers through a series of experimental projects—using sign theatre, dance and an environmental installation.
- A continued development of the Company's work with disabled performers, pursuing adequate funding for their support.
- A continued exploration of work with teenagers in unusual and artistically challenging environments through a promenade piece and a mobile performance space for isolated rural areas.
- An emphasis on work which draws on different artistic and cultural forms. 'Bilingual' work will be a focus of the three small-scale 'work in progress' projects.
- An extension of the Company's role encouraging new writing from under represented groups through the creation of an annual 'work in progress' slot backed by dramaturg attachment.

Keeping these aims in mind, the next decade or so with Rachel Feldburg at the helm of affairs in Red Ladder saw the production of plays that targeted specific groups and had clearer cut storylines. State Agent by Rachel Feldburg and Ruth Mackenzie in 1985 was a new play for youth clubs about young people and homelessness, exploring what happened to young people who lost their benefit in the now forgotten (but then notorious) 'bed and breakfast laws' (Bed and Breakfast was a method of tax avoidance whereby shares were sold one day and bought back the next day to avoid capital gains tax.[Referring to the temporary nature of the transactions as if it were bed and breakfast accommodation]). 1986 saw two productions: Back to the Walls by Jane Thornton, a new play based on young peoples' experience of Youth Training Schemes which targeted young people 15+, unemployed people and school leavers and On the Line devised by the Company is Beat Box Britain which countered the myth that Britain was a country where "there is no such thing as a racist attack" and looked at the origins of racism—where did it come from, who profited and most important—what was to be done about it? Written for youth clubs, the play tackled a difficult issue in a lively and accessible manner (Beat Box is a way of speaking by using your voice /breath as a drum. It was popular in the eighties with the African Carribean communities).

An interesting change that appears in the production list following the last two plays mentioned is that the productions are now seasonally dated which seems to imply a more structured and planned calendar year of activities for the Company. Thus, the spring of 1987 saw the production of Winners by Rona Munro which was specially written for young women exploring gender issues while the Autumn of the same year saw the production of Empire Made by Paul Swift, a play for senior youth groups which dealt with racism and police attitudes. In winter 1988 Red Ladder produced One of Us by Jacqui Shaprio and Meera Syal which targeted Asian girls groups and was a comedy about Nishi's life as she grapples with her expectations and the realities of the world around her. Off the Road by Rona Munro followed in spring 1988, a show that compared rural and city life and toured to girls groups while autumn 1988 saw Mike Kenny's The Best, a play that explored issues of young deaf people. Bhangra Girls by Nandita Ghose, the first commissioned work touring to young Asian girls groups was produced in spring

1989; in the autumn came Philip Osment's <u>Who's Breaking</u>, a play for mixed senior youth clubs focusing on HIV/AIDS issues, integrating British Sign Language (BSL).

A letter to Peter Mair, the Drama Officer in the Arts Council of Great Britain dated 5 March 1980 by Stephanie Munro of Red Ladder, retrieved from the Red Ladder archives, spells out that all was not well with the Company when the eighties started. Munro's letter is a response to Mair's letter of 21 February 1980 (unfortunately, this letter is unavailable) and it is evident from Munro's words that Mair had expressed his misgivings regarding (1) a fall in the number of people attending Red ladder shows that year as against previous years and (2) inability of the Company to meet the estimated number of performances. In spite of Munro's persuasive defence of Red Ladder and optimism about the Company's future, what remains visible is that the artistic climate was not favourable towards the kind of agenda that Theatre Companies like Red Ladder had. This disfavour was expressed vocally and in writing, neither conducive to raising the Company's morale; but it was also expressed in the more damaging form of funding cuts or at least threats to do so. In fact, available correspondence reveals that a large part of the early eighties was literally a fight for survival and attempts at protecting the subsidy on which the Company's existence depended. Of course, apart from these additional hurdles, the perennial hazards continued, i.e., primarily the heavy workload due to constant touring of one night stands leading to strain and exhaustion and performers taking ill.

As if such impediments were not enough, 1983 saw the staging of a disastrous production by Red Ladder, <u>Bring Out Your Dead</u> by Peter Cox. This play and its production can surely be cited as an example of unsuccessful agit prop theatre and the three show reports available in the archives certainly do not mince words in completely denouncing not just the production but also, unfortunately, Red Ladder as a Company.[1] What were the charges levelled against this play? Some of course concentrated on technical details with comments like 'lighting was abysmal', 'sound was excruciatingly bad',[2] 'the direction (Richard Stone) non existent, the performances...amateur and the technical side weak'.[3] In one instance, the venue picked by Red Ladder, i.e., the Skipton Town Hall, was inappropriate as the production could not function as the club show that it was intended to be. To sum it up in the words of another critic, 'one of the worst productions I ever had the misfortune to witness.'[4] As far as such comments go, this thesis must trust the show reports. But there were other shortcomings mentioned in these reports that could be examined, such as a 'thin, weak and politically naïve' script[5] and, similarly a comment that 'the material was poor, the script...was shapeless and badly constructed'.[6] In fact the structuring of the script has been acidly commented on:

> Only the bravest or most naïve, inexpert or foolish of companies would include a musical number entitled 'I'm Bored' just before the interval. In doing just that and conforming to the latter attributes Red Ladder consistently held to the same dismal level throughout the long and depressing evening.[7]

To any theatre going person conversant with agit prop plays, such complaints may seem all too familiar. It is indeed an inherent weakness of all ritual forms including performance that no matter how responsive a ritual/performance is to the needs of a community, it will cease to be an effective agency if it lacks the requisite emotional quotient and the dramatic quality that will bond with the audience. It must be remembered that the process of a Dramatic Text moving to a Theatre Text is a series of encodings and decodings where the final decoding is done by the spectator who works upon and is worked upon by the visual dimension as an integral aspect of the reception procedure.[8] Hence no matter how loaded a play may be in terms of its ideological content it will cease to matter if the spectator is unmoved by it. In the concluding section of the previous chapter, one had begun to see a recognition on Red Ladder's part of the unfortunate fallacy engrained as an agit prop theatre dictum, i.e., the subordination of artistic form to ideology, and thus a slight moving away from such a principle by Red Ladder. With Bring Out Your Dead this step forward seems to have been retracted and the play is unable to sustain the message that it seeks to communicate.

What is the play all about, i.e., what are the issues that the play engages with? Virtually everything it would seem from the NHS (National Health Service), employment problems, corruption of political leaders, gender issues, to America's Big Daddy strategies, the manipulativeness of the media and the foul play of Life Insurance Companies in their Get Rich Quickly tactics. As for the plot, the five characters in the play recreate their individual experiences (within their entangled lives). Helen, a freelance journalist, narrates the abject failure of her marriage and a non-happening career, both due to her inability to fight against aggression. Saa Saa who is made of sterner stuff than Helen and is part of Saa Saa and Tchi Tchi, the media managers of Big Mac, has an unpleasant personal life, being a single mother of two children: her dislike for her husband almost equals her indifference towards her children—she isn't even able to recall the name of one of her children. (SaaSaa and TchiTchi is based on Saatchi and Saatchi, the ad agency that calls itself 'an ideas company'. It has centers worldwide and is known for its award winning print and TV ads). Obviously ambition is the overriding factor in Saa Saa's life. Sandy Washbottoms as his surname suggests is the stereotypical subordinate beleaguered by his superiors (Big Mac and Saa Saa) and nurtures dreams of making it big. Nog, an ex-convict, is the 'lucky winner' of the 'Sponsor an Old Lag' scheme initiated by Big Mac which entitles him to a job with an annual monthly holiday, a weekly salary of 27.00 pounds and alternate Sundays off. Over and above these personae is 'The Ex Reverend Delabere Mac Rigour' or 'Mac', representative of the self-made man with the rags to riches story, but whose methods in reaching thus far are dubious to say the least. The lives of the five characters intertwine as Helen showcases the 'generosity' of Mac in sponsoring Nog, following the interview with Saa Saa and Sandy.

The ritual use of symbolical names as in Morality plays may have done the trick in <u>Taking Our Time</u> (which was discussed in Chapter Three), but in <u>Bring Out Your Dead</u> it fails to inspire anything beyond a recognition of its usage and an awareness of the implications. So when Saa Saa speaks of Nog as "a tax reclaimable item" and says, "Just put him under miscellaneous" (p 36), she only confirms the fact that his name 'Nog' is an apt one. For if a nog is "a wooden block built into a masonry wall to hold nails that support joinery structures",[9] then understandably Nog becomes the peg upon whom Mac hangs his image of a kindly soul. The irony is that Nog is an ex-convict and yet, an apparently good citizen like Mac needs to be parasitic and depend on him—the world of crime and the 'good' world thus have dubious boundaries. 'The Ex Reverend Delabere Mac Rigour' is the name given to the man who is, according to the Nebentext, 'a cross between McEnroe, Elvis. A Preacher and MacGregor. He sings Elvis style in his

American accent' (p.12). The name is as redolent of facetiousness as the persona himself who comes across as a performer so steeped in the many roles he 'plays' that he ceases to be believable and is reduced to the ridiculous. Washbottoms, of course, is just that, an unhappy office subordinate literally (in slang) washing the bottoms of his superiors with the hope that something will come of it some day. When it comes to Helen and Saa Saa, their characterization too is typical: Helen may have the beauty but Saa Saa is sassy and has the brains. The contrast between the two women: one a weak vulnerable failure, and the other, a hardened successful businesswoman is drawn with thick strokes.

Why these symbolically named characters fail to rise above their symbolism is because the script allows them only a watered down subversion of their circumstances. They remain from beginning to end the cardboard characters that they are created as. Nog's brief encounter with Mac in the lift, when his narration of activities while in prison scares Mac silly, does expose him as a possible threat to contend with and it also reveals the cowardice behind Mac's apparent bravado, but the fact is that the situation remains much the same. Even if the play had ended with Nog killing Mac, such a resolution might have been theatrically dramatic, but to an audience looking for that something more, some kind of a realistic answer, it is no wonder then that the script appeared to be 'politically naïve'. The flatness of the characters, then, is offset by the flatness of the plot; there is no sense of denouement, no climax, no alternative offered: in other words, nothing really happens. Before analyzing this aspect further, it must be mentioned that the repetitiveness of the language, again a familiar agit prop device to drive home a point, while doing so creates an atmosphere of bleak and vicious circularity, one that would be difficult to break. This may be thematically well matched but, as a catalysing agent, its effects are dismal. One example right at the beginning is when Helen says: "1983 Heads you win tails I lose" (p.3) a sentence she repeats with only the year changing till she arrives at 1988 where she stops to be overtaken by Sandy who is more expository. But his exposition continues the unchangeability of time that Helen emphasizes for he reveals that 1988 had not changed his luck. The chorus of the song preceding these lines contain the same words. Two things are clear then. One, that conditions of life even with the passage of time have remained the same and two, that they have remained the same across genders (though within the same class). Sandy, Helen, the chorus, all voice like feelings. As reader audience (and most certainly therefore as viewer audience) the message could not have been linguistically more self-evident. But as a special (reader/viewer) audience, i.e., as one groping for more than merely this cognisance from an Agit Prop Theatre Company purporting to different agendas, is this enough? The audience that watched this play obviously thought not.

That some material (issues) may be more relevant for drama and others less so is an old debate that, for example, Una Ellis Fermor in <u>Frontiers of Drama</u> has elucidated.[10] To extend this point further, in terms of agit prop drama, is it possible to question the legitimacy of the 'material', i.e., whether some situations make for better agit prop drama and some less so? It is tempting to leave the onus, Pirandello like, upon a good author, i.e., where the power of a play would rest upon the merits of the author's skills, but it would be more meaningful to actually see whether <u>Bring Out Your Dead</u> does have a case in point in terms of strong dramatic content. The source would obviously have to be the contemporary political situation in England.

The primary concern of the play, to restate an earlier point, is the NHS and the anomalies in its practices under the Conservative Government. In the UK, the NHS is part of the social welfare policy. This policy refers to the use of the state as an income transfer mechanism to provide services and monetary supplements to sectors of the population deemed by the government to deserve such assistance through their social circumstances and to provide basic social services for all citizens. Some of these services, such as those offered by the NHS are provided to all of the public, and others, such as the public (or state run) educational system and government provided pensions, are provided to almost all of the population in a particular age group. A third category of social welfare, exemplified by programmes such as those for unemployment insurance, public (council) housing, child benefit, and the Supplementary Benefit (formerly called National Assistance), is more selectively implemented, usually requiring what the British call a means test to qualify for benefits. Nevertheless, all these programmes involve the state use of material resources gathered principally through taxes to relieve social needs by distributing funds and services to some groups of people. While there are obviously economic implications for all social welfare programmes, i.e., they cost money, it is not the economic aspects but the desirability of their social goals, their target population and their likelihood of success that dominate discussion.[11] The arrival of Thatcherism meant the abandoning of the welfare state as swiftly as electoral considerations allowed and the campaigning of such ideas as "hard work versus welfare scroungers" in keeping with Thatcher's subscription to the individualistic, anti-state, anti-union, anti-egalitarian views of her party's right wing.[12] Consequently, while private medical care was encouraged, charges for services under NHS were increased. Hence, Helen says in the opening song:

> Thought I'd put myself to sleep with something fats and painless
> Looked around for something cheap 'cos I couldn't afford the NHS (p.1)

While the basic health care provision of the NHS remained strong, was popularly supported, and UK ranked well on most comparative indicators of health care provision such as infant mortality rates and life expectancy, the government's reluctance to invest in the NHS made it subject to criticism. Furthermore, despite the central financing and regulation of the NHS, health outcomes were still class related in line with the 'class-war politics' as Thatcher's opponents described the Conservative government's redistribution of class power in a wide variety of spheres, from industrial relations to education and health services. The Conservatives advocated selectivity to concentrate resources on the poorest sections of society and efficiency in service delivery while Labour and to some degree the Liberal Democrats complained   of cutbacks in the basic social rights citizenship for all. In turn the Conservatives reiterated phrases such as "the National Health Service is safe in our hand" (a slogan that became the inspiration for Frances MacNeill's play Safe With Us produced by the Company in 1985) to fend off Labour accusations that the government was shortchanging social welfare services with a long term view to privatising them.

Obviously the sequence that best underscores the Thatcherite duplicity in handling the NHS is when Helen interviews Saa Saa and Sandy and her accusations at their mishandling of the 'institution' are completely wiped out by their glib talk sprinkled liberally with such jargon as 'reeconomising', 'redefining', and 'phasing out operation' and the justification on 'macro economic' grounds for keeping patients productive rather than occupied (the latter when Helen asks why the term 'Occupational Therapy' had been changed to 'Productive Therapy'). This is followed by the scene in which Helen showcases Nog as the recipient of the 'Sponsor a Lag' scheme initiated by Mac—the scene is almost farcical in the way it spoofs the whole notion of sponsorship stretched to bizarre limits.

The question that naggingly crops up after such ironic representations is that unlike in the Cake Play where similar depictions were followed by voices that demanded/asserted a certain intervention, that of workers' rights, this play stops at the spoofing. There is no attempt to resolve any of the existing problems; no direct interaction/involvement with the audience to agitate them or motivate them to think of possible resolutions. If the plot appears dismal and bleak, it is because it is an unresolved plot. It is one that fails to rise to the occasion and offer a way out of the hurdles of Conservative governance.

Yet another example of the 'awareness building' that the play seems to be aiming at can be seen in the depiction of the manipulativeness as well as the manipulatedness of the media as spoken about earlier. The search for demonstrable media effects has proven to be a difficult and controversial one due primarily to the fact that many people choose their source of media, especially their newspaper, because they already agree with its political positions, which limits the number of people who could potentially have their political choices affected by the media. Nonetheless the media serve as both, a major agent of political socialization and an intermediary institution in the political process. The media serve the double function of presenting information for mass and elite consumption and attempting to instruct both mass and elite audiences about how to interpret that information. In spite of the growth of alternative sources of information through international networks which may have reduced the power of the domestic British media to influence even the agendas of either the political elite or the masses, the potential power of the media remains important.[13]

When Helen interviews SaaSaa and Sandy, she is so browbeaten by the jargon they subject her to that she unwittingly adopts the same language while presenting a report of the interview on television (a classic case of conversion to the dominant discourse). Ironically, at the conclusion of her interview, SaaSaa's tongue in cheek comment "Surely you're experienced enough to know you shouldn't believe everything you read in the newspapers" (p.31) directly implicates Helen within the system and pointedly tells of the vulnerability of an institution like the media. Far from guiding people towards making the right choices, the media misguides; and what makes it more tragic is that it believes in what it propagates and is unable to perceive that it has itself been misled.

Traditionally the media in UK has been concerned with 'issues' but following trends in the US since the eighties, there is a growing tendency to emphasise the personalities of bigwigs and cull out those traits that are bound to win over people. This is the reason why in this play Big Mac is given such footage in television news worldwide and his campaigns blown out of proportion. When the 'Sponsor an Old Lag' scheme is highlighted, it is not Nog the recipient but Big Mac who hogs the limelight (Nog is in fact quite literally shut out from the spot lights). Political mileage is thus the name of the game and the power players miss no opportunity to gain it with the media's help. Helen's speech prior to Nog and Big Mac's appearance, is certainly, and discernibly, a dig at the numerous attempts of the ruling party to cut down expenditure on social welfare in the guise of so called 'noble' causes like 'Adopt a Granny' etc. But here again, the entire effort in exposing how the media is trapped by governmental machinations and cannot break free from the political stranglehold, while commendably dealt with, makes even the reader audience ask, 'So what is the way out? If the media falls prey to the cunning of those in power, what is the fate of the common man?' The plot offers no answers.

One returns then to the initial conclusion that while <u>Bring Out Your Dead</u> considers issues that are thematically appropriate for an agit prop play; while the linguistic and other methods such as spoofing/lampooning are suitable agit prop ritual devices that the play deploys, where it falls short is in the silence about answers. There is no effort made to stir up the characters (and in turn us, the audience) by the text to rebel against an overpowering and unjust system of governance.

The subtitle of the play reads 'a black comedy with songs.' The songs in Bring Out Your Dead received some appreciation attested by comments such as "The redeeming feature was the music: good numbers, well played and well put over especially by Robbie McGovan and Kathie Whitely". While there can be no denying that the songs are apt, some with artistic and emotional lyrics, it cannot be ignored either that they lack punch. They lack the rousing ability, the dynamism that songs in agit prop plays are habitually used for. In the last chapter Taking Our Time served as a good example to assert that songs are not just a powerful instrument to disseminate information but a means to incite spectators. No such attempt is made by the songs in Bring Out Your Dead.[14]

The distance between audience and actors, then, remains intact—a distance that Red Ladder has constitutionally always sought to erase. The play is reduced almost to a comedy of manners: one where we recognize the representativeness of the characters and happenings, the 'informativeness' of the play, but which does not provoke us to react as an engaged, actively involved audience. The move over from audience to activist, an aim that Red Ladder is firm on is certainly not achieved in this play through any of its dimensions.[15]

That Bring Out Your Dead had finally to be taken off the road following a van crash on the M1 seems to be a predictable end to a production doomed from the outset. But Red Ladder's troubles did not end with Bring Out Your Dead on the shelf and the comparative success of the next, hastily prepared play, Dumb Blonde. For the next two years Red Ladder struggled to remain standing on its feet and continue to receive the financial backing of the Arts Council; every production was geared to meet the mark and available correspondence shows their defensive stance in the face of fairly severe criticism.

Of these exchanges, one document that keeps cropping up at regular intervals is the weighty 'A Statement for the Eighties'.[16] This lengthy assessment and policy record clearly indicates the way that Red Ladder was circumscribed by the conflicting trends within and without the company. It is also recognition on Red Ladder's part of the need to change the nature of the Company. Some of the key aspects that the document highlights ought to be outlined. First, the political and artistic climate was severely affected by the election of the Tory government. In spite of Red Ladder's successes, the statement records "it has become sucked into the downturn that has affected the entire labour movement, and become shackled to outmoded concepts of political theatre".[17] Second, Red Ladder retained its political motivation: the desire to look for answers *with* an audience; the firm, long standing beliefs that (a) though theatre cannot change the world per se, it can affect the quality of perception, thinking and living of people, (b) that a live participatory theatre could be created even in non theatre venues, and (c) agit prop writing and performances were not inappropriate fare for a theatrically sophisticated company and audience nor was it a limiting factor. However, in spite of persevering with its ideological aims, Red Ladder was willing to acknowledge the contribution of mainstream theatre and the fact that a mass audience sought such theatre over participatory theatre—this audience needed to be tapped. Then, in terms of touring, the document reasserts its commitment to touring on a national scale and voices its concern "that funding bodies are moving towards a position where Labour and Trade Union clubs are not recognized as public performances."[18] As socialist and feminist entertainers, Red Ladder aimed to open up a wide range of venue (including theatre venues) "to bring people together to discuss political ideas and to discuss theatre; effectively to combat the isolation of so much of contemporary mass culture."[19] Next, reacting to the charge that Red Ladder was a Labour Movement Resource, the document declares its pride at this achievement but also states its realization that though more needed to be done than merely providing entertainment, its direct intervention could only be achieved informally: 'it is first and foremost a theatre company, comprised of skilled practitioners (albeit politically motivated in their work). This work is subsequently informed by the Company's collective politics, and this point is seen as central to the development and expansion of our audiences'.[20] While remaining committed to the principles of collectivism, the statement acknowledges that a number of structural changes would have to be introduced for the Company to function effectively in the eighties. The remaining sections of the document contain detailed descriptions of the artistic and ideological aims of the plays then under production such as Happy Jack, The Beano, This Story of Yours as well as other projects on the pipeline; the intention to pursue two long term objectives of (1) the pooling of the Company's political and creative ideas for the generation of writing and (2) funding for resident writers; a critical appraisal of the funding situation where the document expresses alarm at (a) "precedents such as the demands...to read scripts in advance and out of the context of the performance, and the trend to take control away from the Company's"[21] and records that, (b) "with the pending abolition of the Metropolitan County Councils...the funding issue is one of the most important political issues facing the arts today"[22] which has caused (c) "the divisive and competitive reality of campaigning for a slice of the cake, where one company is set against another".[23] The statement concludes on the note that confronting past failures and implementing crucial measures would surely help Red Ladder to remain one of the oldest surviving political theatres in the country.

The entire document testifies to the oppositions in every sphere within which Red Ladder was doing its balancing act. It can also be seen as striking a prophetic note in hinting at a possible outcome of this either/or situation; at the way the future course of action inside and outside the Company would shape its fate. In the light of the above account, it is hardly surprising that 1984 was not an easy smooth track for Red Ladder to tread upon and a review of this year serves to expose the twists and turns of Red Ladder's luck.

The year started with a production of a new play about a brewery worker outing to Scarborough in 1914, called The Beano, by a well-known Sheffield writer and broadcaster who previously wrote the successful 'Circus' for Red Ladder. The Beano toured until April and was extremely well received by audiences and organizers (particularly by older members of the audience, many of whom had not seen Red Ladder before). The success of The Beano led to the decision to tour the show again in autumn after a week in Scotland. Following The Beano, for the first time in many years, Red Ladder decided to tour an established piece of theatre. John Hopkins' This Story of Yours was a powerful drama that had been little performed and was perhaps better known for the film version The Offence. Unfortunately midway through the tour, the leading man, who played a mammoth part in which he never left the stage, seriously injured his back.

As a small touring Company unable to afford understudies, Red Ladder was forced to cancel the later part of their tour. Meanwhile plans for a fringe festival in Danderhall, Edinburgh were being drawn up with the help and encouragement of the Midlothian District Council. The week, which became fondly known as the Danderhall Red Beano, was a critical and artistic success, the audiences building up throughout the week. However, in financial terms, Red Ladder, which had funded the project made a loss due to the cost of travel, accommodation, and fees to guest artistes, etc. The Beano continued to tour until early November, to the Midlands, London and Wales. The later was an area of Britain that Red Ladder had long been trying to make inroads into and the reception was particularly pleasing. At the end of November rehearsals began for a double bill of Stitchin' the Blues, a one woman show written and directed by Maggie Lane, and Mixing It which was devised by the Company and scripted by William Tanner and Maggie Lane. As described earlier, the first play was based on the occupation at Lee Jeans in Greenock and the second play concerned the dilemma of two men forced by the lack of job opportunities into building a nuclear power station which neither men felt was right.[24]

These two plays broke the cycle of ill luck dogging Red Ladder's heels and the year ended on a high note. Audience reaction and critical acclaim increased local and national support for Red Ladder. Songs were used in a new way in the shows with backing tapes of music written and recorded by Red Ladder's musical director, Gordon Dougall. These were included in the shows without the use of microphones or elaborate technical equipment giving performers freedom of movement and never allowing the pace to drop; the whole effect being rather like watching a 'live film musical'. Yet in spite of the fair share of success in 1984, 1985 did not auger well for Red Ladder and it faced tremendous hostility from many directions, not the least from the media, evidenced by the press cutting entitled 'Exit Stage Left' in the Yorkshire Evening Post. This acerbic snippet questioned the Arts Council's funding of Red Ladder and suggested that the Council "depending on the size of the audiences, just might find it cheaper to buy a permanent venue for the Red Ladder lads and lasses as a one-off payment? Something about the size of a double garage perhaps?"[25]

Newspaper criticism only made public the ominous noises already being made by the Arts Council; letters recovered from the Red Ladder archives between Councillor BP Atha of the Leeds Playhouse and Dickon Reed, the Drama Director of the Arts Council and responsible therefore for the subsidies to the theatre companies, are proof enough of this. In February 1985, Councillor Atha appealed on behalf of a host of people to the Arts Council to rescue Red Ladder from the financial and artistic poverty into which it appeared to have fallen.[26] The suggestion was to run the current show till July, cease operations till late September, early October, in order to save incomes and to appoint an Artistic Director to maintain appropriate artistic standards. However no steps could be taken without the Arts Council's assurance of sanctioning the grant allocated for Red Ladder for the subsequent financial year. That the 'rescuers' of Red Ladder saw potential in the Company was clearly stated by Atha for he underlined that these members were willing to enter into the procedure for the creation of a Board of Directors, in spite of their considerable responsibilities only because they saw it as something very worthwhile achieving. Responding to Councillor Atha's plea, Dickon Reeds' sombre answer emphasized the Council's growing concern regarding (a) the deteriorating financial condition of Red Ladder, (b) changes in key personnel within the Company with no real clarity about the administrator, and (c) the lack of a discernible artistic director and policy on Red Ladder's part. Thus Reed made it clear that a financial grant to Red Ladder depended on its ability to explain how it would fill the lacunae pointed out by him and the evidence actual, sustained proof of such measures. He also asked for a plan of action and estimates.[27]

Councillor Atha's rather prompt reply contained the artistic policy of Red Ladder which is relevant to quote has:

> ...The Red Ladder would continue to provide theatrical performances of a nature and quality that it had always provided, in particular:
> 1. To present theatrical performances on radical themes to live audiences;
> 2. To provide performances of high artistic quality which by means of their content would be aimed at provoking discussion, argument and new ideas.
> 3. To achieve these objects by performances which will entertain.
> 4. To use new and established writers.
> 5. To develop differing musical styles in the context of different shows.
> 6. To take performances to the public who rarely, if ever, attend theatres.
> 7. To perform in non-theatre venues.

UNIVERSITY OF WINCHESTER LIBRARY

8. To develop a wider list of venues in the Yorkshire region.
9. To maintain a national touring commitment.[28]

The first change then that affected Red ladder and challenged the premise of the functioning of Red Ladder as a collective and completed its conversion into a hierarchical structure, at least in administrative terms (initial stages of this conversion were seen in Chapter Three), was the constitution of a formal Board of Directors. The Chairman of this Board was Councillor Atha and Ms Zibby Campbell was appointed Administrator. Soon after came the appointment of the Artistic Director, Rachel Feldburg (as has already been stated in the initial outline of this chapter). Other changes forecasted by the 'Statement of the Eighties' and supported by the Artistic policy drawn up in 1985 included the commissioning of plays (such as Nandita Ghosh's <u>Bhangra Girls</u> for example). But what is of utmost interest is the artistic trend of the plays, the target groups and the themes/issues of the plays, post Feldburg's appointment, that the Company foregrounded. In keeping with the current political scenario and the artistic needs of the times, Red Ladder displayed its maturity in understanding that the class and labour issues that its productions had been dealing with had largely become a hegemonic artistic discourse and appeared increasingly stereotypical. Red Ladder now began to explore in right earnest other avenues like the cultural differences between 'races', 'communities' alongside the 'gender' and 'class issues' within the lived 'multicultural' situation of Britain. These were rightly seen as appropriate contemporary resource material for the Red Ladder plays.

The four available plays that deal overwhelmingly with the whole question of ethnic identity and subjectivity are <u>On The Line</u> (1986), <u>Empire Made</u> (1987), <u>One of Us</u> (1988), and <u>Bhangra Girls</u> (1989) [brief outlines of these plays feature in the first section of this chapter]. These plays also recognise:

> that the central issues of race always appear historically in articulation, in a formation, with other categories and divisions and are constantly crossed and recrossed by the categories of class, of gender and ethnicity[29]

Thus the common meeting ground in the development of the power versus powerlessness nexus can be seen broadly in terms of race, ethnicity, class and gender (not necessarily all or in that order). It must be mentioned at this point that <u>Bhangra Girls</u>, while sharing these concerns, is specially tailored to meet the problems of young Asian women and so deserves separate reading though it will be referred to from time to time.

In the second sequence of <u>On The Line</u> when Fay and Mitch talk to each other about suntans and Fay wishes she could sport gorgeous brown skin to attract attention, Mitch is quick to undercut the desire with the words "Yeah and you'll get one fat greasy bloke who'd rush up to you and say 'Piss off wog back to where you come from.'" (p 6) What seems like an attractive proposition to Fay is completely the reverse experientially for Mitch who doesn't need the suntan, for, being Black is 'tanned' the year through and subjected to the most unwanted sort of attention. In a later sequence, Mitch describes how awkward it is to be the focus of indirect, shifty eyed glances—the curiosity of the White gaze that commodifies Black identity. A similar experience is narrated by Nishi in <u>One of Us</u> when she recalls how people coming towards her father's shop would change direction on observing who it was behind the counter. The 'otherness' of their origin as easily reflected by the colour of their skin and appearance prevents people like Mitch and Nishi from 'belonging'; making them out as distinct in the white gaze, pejoratively of course. Not just in their visual approach, linguistically too, whites have a definite (and demeaning) terminology for non-whites. In <u>Empire Made</u> Amarjeet and Paul react sharply to being called 'Paki' and 'Samba' respectively by Derek; the racist connotations surrounding such words being an established fact. Inversely, when Nishi in <u>One of Us</u> wears the prawn in her hat in the restaurant where she is a waitress, the obnoxious white male customer she has to serve thinks that he is complimenting her by commenting that with the right clothes on she could almost pass as "one of us". This kind of homogenising effect of appearance equally succeeds in undermining and negating the individual identity of the 'other'.

But markers such as skin colour, appearance et al, fade in comparison with the cultural myths regarding a community that are perpetuated with such ferocity that they completely appropriate societal psyche. Nishi's encounter with the old male customer just mentioned, on her very first day at the prawn restaurant, is a harrowing tale of the cheap advances she has to face because the white customer is under the impression that coming as she does from the land of the Kamasutra and of temples with gods and goddesses up to all kinds sexual tricks, it was inconceivable that Indian girls were innocent: their virginal reactions according to him cloaked their sexual precocity. Empire Made is more interesting because it shows different layers of response—Amarjeet versus Paul, Derek and Vicky versus Paul and Amarjeet (and vice versa), Amarjeet and Vicky versus Paul and Derek, Amarjeet versus Derek, etc. The umbrella term of 'Black' that whites apply to all non-white people overlooks the differences between ethnic communities and the fact that the 'Black' experience is not a singular, unified one. So, Amarjeet conscious of her 'Asianess' slips into the hegemonic white discourse, a discourse explicated by Jenny's words in On The Line

> You call one black person a criminal, and all blacks become criminals. It's how you give the blame out, anything wrong, blame the blacks. (p 41)

Thus Amarjeet accuses Paul:

> ...But you black kids aren't interested in hard work— ...All you care about is trouble. No wonder people are racist. You carry on like a load of animals and the rest of us have to suffer for it. (p 13)

The extent of the mythification is subversively represented in On The Line when the police deny the existence of a racial attack in which whites beat up blacks but are quick to accept crimes in which the opposite happens (i.e., blacks beating up or mugging whites). The play ironically portrays the tragic fact that the very pillars upon whom the meting out of justice, law and order depend, are weak, contained by and encouraging myths that allow discrimination and inequality. It is not insignificant that earlier in the same play, it is the police inspector (Fox) who suggests the idea of the race riot (as an ace he has up his sleeve) and then puts his plan into action at the incentive of a promotion; thus the police become a major force in propagating and perpetuating myths about non whites to suit their own vested interests.

In fact the police and its dubious modes of operating is depicted in a highly critical light in all three plays but most so in Empire Made. Derek, the policeman in Empire Made, is representative of everything ugly that one associates with the police force. He is violent, a violence stemming from an in-built sadism, a sexist, a racist and an egotist; in short, an archetypal representation of a corrupt and degenerate police force. All these qualities are evidenced by his cruelty towards Paul whom, as has been observed already, not only does he demeaningly call 'Samba' but whom he itches to hurt physically (and kills in the end) after handcuffing him and his chauvinistic attitude in delegating such tasks as the making of tea or cleaning up Paul to the women, Amarjeet and Vicky, at whom he passes many sexual remarks. That he cannot stomach the sight of blood and that he finds it necessary to keep Paul handcuffed even when Paul needs to relieve himself clearly unveil the essential cowardice that he disguises with his policeman stance and weapons.

Again, in <u>On The Line</u>, it is not just Inspector Fox's foxiness but the entire state of apathy pervading the police station that is mockingly recreated as one clearly perceives from the following telephonic conversation or rather, the callous responses, of Officer Jules:

> Sir...Hello...what...your being burgled...no, this is a police station, sorry, we can't help you...beg you pardon...no...we're very busy at the moment...they've broken what?...well you should sneak downstairs, do you have a gun in the house...no...well never mind...uhm...try the citizens advice bureau... (p 24)

Soon after when Neran comes to report the attack on his friend, a Black like himself, by White youths, the policemen refuse to co-operate and are instead hellbent on terrorizing him. They deny that such a racial attack can occur while, in their crowding in on Neran, they are unwittingly committing the same crime whose possibility they reject. They are only willing to consider a happening where Blacks mug Whites thus forcing Neran to change the truth in order to get them activated. This deliberate repudiation of actual events by a body of people supposedly engaged in maintaining law and order in the everyday functioning of the city reveals the process of the institutionalization of racism.

The police force is not the only institution or class of people that is targeted; the so-called aristocracy (in the form of Sir James) and rich industrialists such as CJ are also revealed as the scheming and completely heartless people that they are. When CJ discloses his company, CJ Multinationals, plans for launching a new product called Sniffo Soap Powder and pretends that this is his contribution in converting a miserable town for the better (a common practice of masking intentions reminiscent of the discourse of manipulative politicians), the falsehood of his words is made manifest by his actions thus:

113

CJ: Yes I'm going to give them something to live for. Pull
(They shoot Michelle)
SJ: Lazy Blighter anyway (p 4)

The callousness with which they dismiss their killing of the gardener (Michelle) proves exactly how little they value human life, especially of the lower classes. Apart from the elites, On the Line, akin to Bring Out Your Dead, lays bare the manipulatedness of the media. The media is shown to be completely moulded by political forces which enslave its integrity to do disservice to the general public (for whom it is supposed to be existing in the first place). So the race riot is cleverly crafted by the industrial scions in collaboration with the police force. Jenny's Black identity is deviously used by them and she is placed almost like a chess pawn on the scene of turmoil as a tactical move. Her reporter identity is created by these same schemers and though she reports the truth, what is printed in the papers is completely the reverse, for, as CJ states boldly later: "The truth belongs to those who can afford it." (p 40) The media is consequently up for grabs and plays the tune of the highest bidders. The question is, hemmed in by institutions that knowingly and purposely perpetuate racial myths, where does a Black/Asian, in other words, a non-white person seek equality in justice?

In Empire Made, Vicky is sympathetic towards Paul and one would imagine her standing by him in the end; her complete *volte face* and aiding Derek after he ruthlessly kills Paul comes as a surprise at first. Especially after one has had time to see that not much love is lost between Derek and Vicky. But on second thoughts, one can reason out how Vicky feels doubly duty bound to support Derek; doubly because (a) she is Derek's colleague after all and would like to be on an even keel with him if she is to survive in the male dominated profession she has chosen; she perhaps sees the favour she is doing to Derek as a means to making him feel obliged to her; and (b) analysed from the White versus Black equation, she must stand by Derek. This play painstakingly drives home the message that Empires may have territorially been dismantled but stay on in the mind. For complete decolonisation to take place, the white mind would have to rid itself off its assumptions of colonial superiority. The truth is that these psychological Empires, once created, are harder to erase than geographical ones.

While the operation of institutionalised instigation of racism is transparent, what works more insidiously and less visibly are those forces that colour the imagination of people. This arises either from a complete lack of information or from a twisted, invented and much circulated version of the cultural 'other'. When Mrs Bagnell tells Nishi in One of Us

> ...Have you got any of them cook in sauces? no? I didn't think you had you don't eat casseroles do you its something in your religion isn't it? And I'll have two slices of ham. Thin. I hope it's fresh. (p 5)

Nishi is stung into retorting (even if partly in her mind)

> Came in yesterday. Of course I'm sure. Yes its pork. Actually Mrs Bagnell, it's human meat. We're cannibals. We keep dead bodies in the cellar... (p 5)

That such false notions also lead whites to anticipate certain patterns of behaviour by non whites can be seen from the entire dialogue between Nishi and Babs is predicated upon such a happening. Babs' (familiar) notions of Indians as "spiritual non-materialistic" people, of Indian families "getting together for Sunday curries" (p 16) and of "yoga being an Indian way of life" (p 17), are all concepts that Nishi defies (thus reducing her 'exotic' value in Babs' eyes). That Babs is prey to an orientalist discourse that has created certain pictures of India which sell in the western world is only too clear. But what Nishi's repudiation of such impressions and her plaintive, "You've got to fit in, haven't you?" (p. 17) makes plain is the trauma of non-native English people located at the crossroads between cultures and pressurized by both, the native and the non-native, i.e., the home and the world.

This turmoil is felt at all levels, from modes of dressing to social interaction especially with the opposite sex, to choice of profession, way of living and social attitude. Jenny in On the Line may want a well paid job and fame but she cannot possibly live in isolation from her black family who feel that she has betrayed their community. Amarjeet in Empire Made has to run away from home because her parents refuse to let her marry her boyfriend on religious grounds—he is a Muslim. But her boldness belies her submissiveness to her boyfriend's wishes. When Vicky asks her what she intends doing after marriage, she replies: "Have kids. He says he wants a houseful." (p 18) Amarjeet is

115

conditioned by both, the modern forces of the outside world and her conservative domestic upbringing.

Again, Nishi in <u>One of Us</u> may rebel against the mythification of India and the Indianisms flung at her by her white counterparts but she equally rebels against the stranglehold of her rigidly patriarchal home where her mobility is restricted to the extent that her father literally locks her in if there's a man about, even if that man be only an electrician come to repair faulty wiring. In all cases, the only way out of such unease for these three young non-white women seems to be, leaving home, by choice and circumstances.

In Ritual discourse the space occupied by these personae would be called a liminal one with the individuals torn between different senses of belonging (i.e., to their native as well as their non-native environments). This liminal space is also one where rituals of oppression/terrorization/violence encounter rites of resistence. Thus ritual verbal/physical interrogation and attack by the police in <u>On the Line</u> and <u>One of Us</u> is countered by mob violence on the streets and factory strikes by the protestors; denial of freedom (whether it be in terms of profession or appearance or choice of friends) in the domestic set up in <u>Empire Made, One of Us</u> and <u>Bhangra Girls</u> is answered by a running away from home and then disobeying domestic dictums completely; sexual innuendos/passes ritually made by males in <u>Empire Made</u> and <u>One of Us</u> are answered in like manner by the women.

Cutting across the problems of race, whether of discrimination on its grounds or adjustment difficulties following clashes in cultures, is the whole issue of gender and the injustices arising out of gender biases. Take for example Derek's male chauvinism whereby he subjects Vicky to all kinds of sexual comments and jokes and also reduces her work as an able police officer to the making of tea or cleaning up Paul as if such acts are the only ones that Vicky, being female is fit for. Derek is not an exception in his psyche and behaviour but as Vicky's narrative reveals, it is the entire male majority of the police force who treat their lady officers in like manner. Vicky has to contain her feminity and her feelings of resistance towards the callous way her male counterparts treat women. In her own words:

116

> ...If I want to stay in this job, I have to be "one of the lads". I have to listen and smile while the "real men" talk about fighting and boozing and screwing women. I have to be a good sport, a good laugh, 'cos no matter how tough I am, or how good I am at the job, I'm not a real copper. I'm just a "plonk". That's what they call women police officers in the Met. "Plonks", which, according to my duty sergeant, "has an obscene origin and refers to the bit of you what sits down." And that's how they treat you. I spent my first week on station alone in a Panda car with PC Rawlinson, the "fastest truncheon in the Met", ho, ho. I've never met a bloke with so many hands. I had more finger marks on me than the A to Z. In the end I had to fight him off. I actually had to hit him to get him off me. "What's up with you?" he said, "Are you a lesbian?", "No", I said, "But I'm thinking about it!" They made my life hell after that. (p 24)

Vicky doesn't leave the police force on the grounds that she doesn't want to give her male colleagues the satisfaction of knowing that they could force her to leave—but it is a fact that all along, she has to constantly prove that she "might be a woman but…can be just as hard, just as tough as any of them." (p 24) If for the police force the us and them differentiates between enforcers of law and order and criminals, it also demarcates the 'us' of the lady police from the 'them' of the male police.

In One of Us, one sees Nishi's mother joining hands with other Asian women in picketing the factory where they work to protest against the disparity in wages—they are paid less than their white counterparts for the same work. In A Woman's Work is Never Done, it was observed in Chapter Three, the protest was for pay parity between sexes— One of Us complicates this further by exposing same gender pay disparities on the basis of race. Not just professionally, but even in personal relations, racial differences play a significant part. When Derek tells Amarjeet in Empire Made that he is more than good enough for her while attempting to molest her, he is in effect implying that he is superior to her not because he's a man but because he's white (thus of a higher order). He is not alone in his racist sexism: in One of Us when Nishi starts going out with her white friend, Erik, she narrates:

> ...he was nice. A bit slow but nice. Well, I say nice, but sometimes, well…he wasn't. It was alright when we were by ourselves, kissing and cuddling and all that, but when I went out with him it was like he had the Elephant Man on his arm. And when his friends came round, I felt like he would have liked to stick a paper bag over my head. It is not much fun I can tell you, walking down the road with your boyfriend, turning to whisper sweet nothings into his ear only to

117

discover that he's seen one of his friends coming and dived under a bloody bush. Well, I got pissed off with that so I left him didn't I?... (p 8)

Nishi's plight does not end with dumping Erik for she meets with the same responses to her Asianness when she works as a waitress in the restaurant. Her friend Carol may be casual about her misgivings at sexual advances made towards her by saying that all the waitresses had to put up with these but in Nishi's case, being an Indian adds insult to injury. The men might treat all the waitresses in a free and easy manner but with Nishi, her old white male client actually thinks that she is available as she comes from a barbaric land where there are no rules about sex. The most outrageous part of his speech is his concluding words:

> ...And what right do you have to be so choosy. Think anyone'd have you, do you? Lucky for you, I'm liberal-minded. Some wouldn't be as willing I can tell you. (p 12)

It is obvious that the client's mental make up is similar to that of Derek.

Amarjeet in <u>Empire Made</u> and Nishi in <u>One of Us</u> have it real bad not just because of the unfairness of attitudes towards them in the larger public world but also due to gender biases inherent within their own race and culture. Consequently, Amarjeet cannot marry her boyfriend because he is a Muslim and her strict father (the stern patriarch is a figure common to both plays) will not hear of such a religious deviation. Nishi cannot step out of the confines of her room when men are around because of her father's orthodox views regarding women's boundaries. Thus while gender prejudices govern the world over, Asian women in England suffer more due to the clash of their native cultures with the west. Recognising the problem of a multicultural situation,

> ...a recognition that we all speak from a particular place, out of a particular history, out of a particular experience, a particular culture, without being contained by that position...We are all in that sense ethnically located and our ethnic identities are crucial to our subjective sense of who we are. But there is also a recognition that this is not an ethnicity which is doomed to survive, as Englishness was, only by marginalizing, dispossessing, displacing and forgetting other ethnicities. This precisely is the politics of ethnicity predicated on difference and diversity.[30]

Red Ladder took a cue from the special place of Asian women in British society as emerged from these plays, and wrote and produced <u>Bhangra Girls</u> for Asian and other girls groups all over the country. Research for the play was carried out by Nandita Ghose (to whom the script is credited) and Kully Thiarai by visiting girls and in particular Asian girls groups, identifying their needs and the issues that should be raised. Like with other Red Ladder plays that were taken to young people where they were, in this instance, it was taken to young Asian women in their own territory. Written, directed, designed and performed by Asian women, <u>Bhangra Girls</u> shows the development of respect and understanding between four Asian girls, Suki, Jaz, Marie and Parveen, who form a Bhangra band as they share and face up to different challenges and problems, resolve conflicts and attempt to define their position as young Asian women in society. All four characters in the play have different 'problems' or situations which cross and overlap causing disagreements, arguments and emotional upsets but result in eventual acceptance and understanding. This develops through a realisation that they are not alone with the way they feel and that these things can be overcome through talking and sharing experiences.

Like other Red Ladder plays, <u>Bhangra Girls</u> did not provide any answers or come down on any one side, rather it attempted to show various ideas and attitudes and trigger off thoughts for follow up work. This took shape as usual in the workshops and discussions that followed every performance and gave the women the opportunity to talk with the performers and express their own opinions on the issues raised in the play. But the follow up did not stop at discussions alone for youth workers took away a comprehensive resource and information pack to develop the issues further within the club setting. For example <u>Bhangra Girls</u> was brought to Leicester as part of a six show package for the Leicestershire Youth Service on the invitation of Girls Work Youth Workers in the area who identified a need for a specific direct work with young Asian women. After the show, youth workers applied for funding for follow up work to take on and develop some of the issues raised in the play with young Asian women and workers in drama workshops in youth clubs and projects.

Using the subject of Bhangra as the focus of the play was bound to produce an instant identification for the audience with the performers, the Bhangra having its own cult status among young Asian people. The combination of traditional Punjabi music with a western style rock beat produced an interesting parallel alongside the problems faced by the characters in the play of being women and being Asian in a sexist and racist society. Parveen wears western style clothes and in the early stages dismisses the idea of the band playing Bhangra which raises the whole issue of image and pride in what we are and how we are categorised by race, culture and fashion. At one point in the play, Suki turns to Parveen and says "You should be proud of being Asian" to which the reply comes, "I'm not, I'm not anything, I'm just me." (p 22) But at the need of the play, Parveen identifies with her culture and her pride in being Asian.

If <u>Bhangra Girls</u> is analysed along the same lines as <u>A Woman Work is Never Done</u>, i.e., according to Victor Turner's structuring of social drama, then one observes that the first scene of the play contains all the right ingredients for 'breach' to take place.[31] Suki and Marie are off to a Bhangra with Marie wearing an Indian dress lent to her by Suki—it belongs to Suki's elder sister, Jaz. Just as they are about to leave, Jaz arrives striving to look cool as she smokes her cigarette in a pronouncedly sophisticated manner. She insists on accompanying the duo on the grounds of keeping an eye on them. Once they reach the disco they encounter Parveen who has come from London and seems bold especially in her attitude towards boys. Parveen's brother drops in unexpectedly into the disco forcing Parveen to leave after concealing herself with the Chunni (scarf) worn by Marie; as she departs, she fixes a time and venue ('Tomorrow, music room, after school') presumably to return the scarf. As things turn out this meeting would usher in new and exciting possibilities and effect a change in the course of their lives.

That Parveen for all her verbal bravado needs to hide from her brother or that Suki lies to Jaz initially about her and Marie's destination are signs that familial rules trespass upon sibling relationships no matter that the siblings may belong to the same age group. Parveen knows as does Suki that going to the (Bhangra) disco was against the rules and that by going for one on the sly they had breached the rules laid down by their families.

Breach aside, this first scene sets the plot rolling and introduces us immediately to aspects of the protagonist's personalities: Jaz is a typical 'elder' sister, domineering, interfering and slightly patronizing; Suki has all the resentment of a younger sibling and the desire to conceal things from her prying elder sister; Suki is also a music enthusiast and loves both listening to and playing the drums. Marie appears to have a more tentative nature and is carried along by Suki's drive while Parveen seems self-assured and aggressive, her bitterness about men hints at some unsavoury personal experience. More than the others, it is Parveen who comes across forcefully as fiercely desirous of freedom of action. Scene One also establishes through the slight skirmish between Jaz and Suki about the dress that Suki had borrowed off Jaz (without Jaz knowing) that, of the various cultural markers contributing to a person's identity, attire/dress codes play a definite role.

The departing words of Parveen in Scene One may not have indicated the nature of events to follow; Scene Two however is full of new developments at least for Suki, Marie and Parveen. When Suki and Marie meet Parveen in the music room after school as per Parveen's instructions, they find Parveen playing the guitar enthusiastically if not proficiently and with all the élan of a guitarist in a rock band. In the ensuing conversation the idea of the three of them getting together to form a band crops up. The fact that Suki and Parveen at least would have to keep this idea under cover confirms that joining such a band was in some way a breaching of a certain set of norms or codes whether of the family or of the community. However, the band does not form without coming to terms with individual problems and sorting them out. Suki is reluctant to lie to her parents about the band because though she may rebel against her parents strictures, she believes that they do know what they're about—thus she is torn between her personal urges and talents on the one hand and parental pressure on the other. Marie is keen initially though unsure about her own contribution to the band as a tambourine player but is certainly doubtful later at the idea of a 'Bhangra' band due to her experiences as a half Indian which has earned for her such terms as 'half caste' and 'chocolate drop' (p 23)—she doubts whether an ethnic band can attain success. As for Parveen, the notion of a 'Bhangra' band is totally unappealing as Parveen feels that no one listens to anything that is Asian/Indian. All three, then, face a crisis in terms of their ethnicity: Suki's ethnic community of which she is proud (therefore it is she who culls out a Bhangra tune and insists on the band being a Bhangra one in the first place) and which her parents are strong members of, cannot allow such happenings as an All Girls Band staying on after school to rehearse;

Marie being half Indian from her father's side has been subjected to such racist treatment that she fears the band, if Bhangra will fail; Parveen rejects anything ethnic because her own hybrid subjectivity is dismissive of all that is purely Indian. Interestingly however, Parveen displays her knowledge of the fact that ethnicity was at a premium at least in an institutional set up—so while personally rejecting ethnic markers she is not averse to using it as currency as when:

> …we can meet here. After school, fix it up with the teachers. They'll be alright—tell 'em it's ethnic or something. We'll have to practise everyday. (p 18)

Ultimately this first crisis is methodically resolved with Suki giving way to her own love for music on the fairly flimsy grounds that it would not be too much of a falsehood to say that she was taking music lessons after school; Marie is carried along by Suki and Parveen's fervour and Parveen submits to the Bhangra concept when she realizes that she might be missing out on a good chance of receiving some critical acclaim and is cajoled into believing that it would not be really too ethnic. The Bhangra Girls Band is formed at the end of Scene Two; that it must need be under crises is significant in foregrounding the nature of the so-called 'multicultural' situation of the UK. Within this theoretically multicultural setup, it is obvious that both, ethnic as well as non-ethnic cultures exercise different modes of authority and are differently as well as oppositionally hegemonic over individual identities.

Crisis however does not end with Scene Two. Scene Three continues the problems of intra-ethnicity. Suki's mother comes down heavily upon Suki and forbids her from staying on for her 'music lessons'. It is only when Jaz mediates and plays up the ethnic aspect of the band i.e., it being Bhangra and something intended for the school (not for the big lights as Parveen, Suki and Marie have dreams of), that the mother relents, thus proving the emotional and persuasive power of ethnic identity. Marie finds a photograph of her Indian father and as she talks to the photograph, it is clear that in her need to reach out to him, she is willing to play all the cards that she feels may win him over: so she speaks of Bhangra band and of her two friends in the band and emphasizes the Indianness of both. Her words, "I wish I was Indian. May be you wouldn't have left me then", (p 29), her keenness to embrace her ethnic origins in the hope of fostering kinship between herself and her father is a direct contrast to Parveen's shunning of her ethnicity. Parveen feels stifled both physiologically (as with the chunni, a part of her traditional attire) as well as psychologically, by her Indian origins. She cannot relate to her parents with whom she's on a word strike because of their clashing attitudes and ethical approaches. Among their many strictures, what Parveen dislikes the most is their interference in her social life—she envies Marie for not having parents who forbid her having boyfriends. Parveen blames what she sees as conservatism and narrow mindedness in her parents upon their ethnic roots. The problems of a sense of belonging generated by the ethnicity of young women with ethnic origin's brought up in the UK takes on different forms then, as Scene Three asserts: (i) a conflict between a liberal western outlook outside the home and the less liberal, traditional outlook of parochial parents within the bounds of the home, as exemplified by Suki and Parveen; the difference between them being that Suki deep down respects her parents and their ethnic ideals while Parveen is downright rebellious and anti-family; (ii) in Marie's case, the added complication of being discarded both by the father as well as by society—her ethnic identity being the big question in every instance and causing her thus to be at odds with it; she feels the pain of her partially ethnic subjectivity; she feels her father would not have left her had she been a pure Indian and as for society, she is relegated, to recall an earlier observation, to the category of half castes. Thus, the crises precipitated by ethnic complexities do not have easy solutions as Scene Three projects.

Scene Four carries these crises further. When Suki tells Parveen and Marie that she has not been allowed to stay back, Jaz intervenes with the information that Suki can participate on the condition that Jaz too be allowed to join in. Suki abhors the idea but finally gives in when Parveen assures her that she wouldn't allow Jaz to boss around and that the microphone used by Jaz could be doctored by them. However the practise session that follows is dismal as everyone appears to be distracted. Tempers are frayed and Marie is urged to bring out her poem to change the atmosphere; unfortunately matters become worse as Parveen completely misunderstands the poem. She reads it as a sentimental piece about boys (while Marie had actually intended it for her father) and spews venom about it. Marie runs out in distress and Suki rounds up Parveen. The rest of the scene contains a series of about turns by Parveen, Marie and Suki. Parveen reveals the secret of her relationship with a boy and how her suspicious parents insisted upon her leaving London for a place where she would be comparatively free from temptation and there would be many relatives to keep an eye on her. This story, after Parveen's haranguing about boys so far, is such an abrupt changeover, that it seems almost unbelievable. Marie too does an about turn in that she determines to ask her mother yet again about the true story behind her fathers' abandoning them, regardless of the consequences of her mother's response. And Suki, by the end of this scene, seems so totally besotted by Jaz that she is unable to see anything amiss in Jaz's behaviour. It is important to note that all these turnabouts involve the exposure of truth/half truths in some way. Parveen reveals her past, and though she does not come out with the full story, it is an admission of real happenings in her life. Marie's persistence in attempting to discover what went wrong between her parents shows how keen she is to know the truth and thus come to terms with it. Suki's blind support of Jaz and her refusal to accept that Jaz could possibly be breaking family rules by going out with a boy prove her inability to see the truth for what it is. It is impossible for Suki to believe that given their kind of upbringing, Jaz could possibly break family norms. It is an irony that Suki leaves the band at this stage, dragging Jaz with her simply because she is unable to understand that like her own self, Jaz too may have felt the need to deviate from the codes of the family, of the ethnic community. In fact Suki and Parveen almost come to blows because Suki's ethnic pride that surfaces at this point makes her champion the cause of Asian values and be indirectly critical of Parveen and Marie's dormant ethnicity, a criticism they resent.

Scene Four thus propels the crises in the formation of a Bhangra Girls Band to the peak. With Suki's departure, the tenuous nature of the affinity and friendship between Parveen, Marie and Suki comes to the fore. It is obvious that Suki has to return for the band to actually form. For this Suki's blinkered vision about Jaz will have to be corrected.

Scene Five initiates the redressive or remedial measures to achieve the goal, i.e., the creation of the Bhangra Band. In this scene, Suki's sexual innocence and curiosity is focused on through the leading questions she asks Jaz. Not only is she repulsed by her new found sexual knowledge, she is further aghast when she learns that Jaz does have a boyfriend as Parveen and Marie had suspected. But initial horror gives way to better understanding; Suki comes closer to Jaz after the disclosures Jaz makes and the positive outcome of their bonding is that they decide to go back to the band. Marie in this scene has asked her mother and finally has got to know that the only reason why her father dumped her mother was because he had a wife and kids in India and they had found out about his relationship—he did not think it worth the effort to return (especially, according to Marie, since she was a girl child). In burning her father's photograph and resolving to send him the ashes, Marie, through such a ritual act, literally cleanses her mind of all the thoughts bedevilling her. She begins to accept the reality of her racial origins with more practicality, even if it's tinged with bitterness. Parveens' is the happiest story in this scene. For Parveen receives a letter that makes her ecstatic. It is from her boyfriend and he wants her back. Thus the ritual journey or rites of passage of the trio, Parveen, Suki and Marie in getting together to form their band, though dotted with many obstructions seems to have a happy ending after all.

Or does it? Does the band really become rich and famous? Do the now comparatively happier Bhangra girls go on to accomplish great things? Scene Six is the final scene that shows not an integration of the band into society but rather legitimises the yawning irreparable schism between the Bhangra girls and society (conforming to Turner's pattern). And it takes only a single act to do this. In this instance, it is the man who snips off Parveen's long hair and in doing so is instrumental in closing down the band (which is hugely successful in its performance). Due to Parveen's lack of communication with her family and their conservatism, Parveen decides to run away from home for she is convinced that her parents will strictly confine her to the house after such an incident. Parveen rebels against such a notion:

> So we have to stay inside all our lives? Never leave our families' because of him. Because of people like him…(p.62)

Luckily for Parveen, her boyfriend's support seems to have arrived at an opportune moment and she can thus escape to him. But what then of the Bhangra Girls? Suki's and the play's concluding words "what's going to happen to all of us?" (p 66) labour the point that Parveen makes a little earlier "Maybe hell's better than here, better than this country where no one wants us but our parents." (p.62)

In the Artistic Policy of Red Ladder after Rachel Feldburg's appointment as Art Director, one of the key aims mentioned was to make the Company's work accessible to all young people for whom there were insufficient provisions including Black young people within which 'Asian and African Caribbean teenagers' were counted. The language of the policy is misleading for clubbing these different communities under the single label of 'Black people' may deny their specificities. It is to Red Ladder's credit that the Company was sensitive to such a fallacy. Thus <u>Bhangra Girls</u> may be about an Asian experience but it is not a singular homogenous one; the three completely different perspective, recognise the complexity of the Asian experience in the UK. In <u>Woman Skin Deep Feminism and the Post Colonial Condition</u>, Sara Suleri says:

> In seeking to dismantle the iconic status of post-colonial feminism, I will attempt here to address the following questions: within the tautological margins of such a discourse, which comes first, gender or race?[32]

The four plays analysed here may not have answered this question directly but the common thread between these plays point toward the towering significance of race or ethnic origins over and above ongoing gender based conflicts where the idea of 'multicultural' society actually masks racial assumptions, prejudices and oppression.

Engaging with the travails of ethnicity did not mean that Red ladder had stopped being concerned about other marginalized communities and their problems. Race may have become a new avenue for Red Ladder to explore and explode but its commitment towards other peripheral sections such as the jobless, the homeless, the elderly, the disabled and the sexually different remained unchanging. Nor were efforts spared to be innovative in terms of form and modes of performance so that multimedia and other techniques were adopted in many of the plays. Though performed in English, synopses of <u>Bhangra Girls</u> for example are available in more than one language, including Punjabi, Hindi, Urdu, Gujarati and Bengali to ensure that larger numbers of people would connect with the play. Osment's <u>Who's Breaking</u> and Kenny's <u>The Best</u> integrated British Sign Language (BSL) while Munro's <u>Winners</u> mixed screen images with stage presences to emphasis gender issues.

126

Red Ladder thus rose phoenix like from the doldrums of the mid-eighties by the changes it ushered into the content and form of the plays, the modes of performance and the administrative set up of the Company (transformed from a loose collectivity into a structured Hierarchy—but without losing the collective spirit and ideals). That it was successful in these measures is attested to not just by its survival but by the critical acclaim it received. In the May 1989 issue of 'Young People Now', Tim Burke's article on Red Ladder entitled 'Red Ladder Day' underlined that Red Ladder was the youth services only full time touring theatre company and one which tried to maximize benefits from each performance by developing a strong working relationship with each service. This meant that unlike other theatre companies, Red Ladder did not just descend on a club, perform and disappear but rather worked strategically as part of a planned process of social education. Burke asserted Red Ladder's success with the evidence of Bolsover, a mining area in Derbyshire which had taken all seven shows from Red Ladder in the past two years.

> This means that they can now work together in a structured cohesive fashion, which starts with workers attending a preview of each production. This not only gives feedback to the writers and performers at Red Ladder, but also provides an early indication of the issues that youth workers should start to raise in the club before the performance.
> The preview can also have benefits even before the Company arrives at the youth club. For example Red Ladder's decision to use sign language in their latest production, The Best, brought home to Bolsover youth workers the realization that they were doing no work with deaf young people. As a result they have been in contact with social services and a strategy for building relationships with deaf young people is being developed.[33]

Of course the article did not deny that Red Ladder had many obstacles on its track and that things could go wrong. For instance, when two performances of The Best were scheduled for consecutive nights in nearby clubs with a large crossover of membership, the result was a rapt audience of fifty on the first night and a considerably smaller and more fidgety number on the second. However these upsets faded when compared to the other spin offs of the Red Ladder productions; Burke quotes Steve Waterhouse, district resource worker in Bolsover,

> It's a great resource for issue-based work, and its' consumer-oriented: we know that our comments on each production will be listened to and acted upon.[34]

He says again that ideally every youth service ought to have its own theatre group as such a flexible resource could target local problems and the needs of specific groups.

From 1968 to 1998 Red Ladder had traversed a long way and altered a lot keeping pace with the demands of the time. But it had retained its status of a radical fringe theatre company, the most noteworthy asset being that it gave access to theatre to people traditionally denied it and was not ensured and "something that only goes on in that great big building down the road that none of them would ever go in."[35] Summarising the Red Ladder approach actress Kay Hepplewhite said:

> We want to entertain and be a catalyst to help youth workers raise issues. And we do that by doing the play in young people's own space, doing it in their language and within their frame of reference.[36]

Notes

[1] The three show reports are dated 8 September 1983 (from the Town Hall, Skipton production) 16 September 1983 and 19 September 1983 (from the Jackson's Lane Community Centre production).

[2] 19 September show report

[3] 8 September show report

[4] 16 September show report

[5] ibid

[6] 8 September show report

[7] ibid

[8] See Aston and Savona, 1991:142 where the spectator's reception of the visual dimension is seen as the final stage of a project involving four distinct phases.

[9] From Reader's Digest Universal Dictionary, The Reader's Digest Association Ltd, London, 1987: 1049

[10] See Chapter One entitled 'The Limitations of Drama' in The Frontiers of Drama by Una Ellis-Fermor, Methuen and Co. Ltd, Great Britain, 1964 (2nd Edition)

[11] See Great Britain Decline or Renewal? By Donley T. Studlar, Westview Press Inc., USA, 1996 : 165-166 (henceforth Studlar, 1996)

[12] Colin Leys, 1986: 91-92

[13] Studlar, 1996: 78-79

[14] Moloyashree Hashmi put it clearly in her conversation with Anjum Katyal published in Seagull Theatre Quarterly, Dec 97, issue 16 where she said 'Drama has to be created and crafted even on the streets; it involves a lot of hard work, trying new things'.

[15] Susan Bennet elaborates in Theatre Audiences, Routledge, London, 1990: 179 'Spectators are thus trained to be passive in their demonstrated behaviour during a theatrical performance, but to be active in their decoding of the sign systems made available.'

[16] The copy of the document used in this book is the one attached by Robbie McGovan with his letter dated December 30, 1983 to Dickon Reed, Drama Director of the Arts Council of Great Britain.

[17] p 1

[18] p 3

[19] ibid

[20] p 1

[21] p 7

[22] ibid

[23] ibid

[24] From Led Ladder archives; article entitled 'Review of 1984'

[25] From Red Ladder archives; this press clipping was attached with an Arts Council: Internal Memo dated 29 October 1985

[26] From Red Ladder archives: letter from Councillor Atha to Dickon Reed dated 18 Feb 1985

[27] From Red Ladder archives: Dickon Reed's response to Councillor Atha dated 1 March 1985

[28] From Red Ladder archives: Councillor Atha's letter dated 25 March 1985

[29] From 'New Ethnicities' by Stuart Hall in The Post-Colonial Studies Reader edited by Bill Ashcroft, Gareth Griffiths and Helen Tiffin, Routledge, London, 1995: 225 (henceforth Ashcroft, Griffiths and Tiffin, 1995)

[30] Ibid: 227

[31] For details about the various stages, Chapter 3 may be referred to.

[32] From 'Woman Skin Deep Feminism and the Post Colonial Condition' by Sara Suleri in Ashcroft, Griffiths and Tiffins, 1995: 273

[33] From Red Ladder archives; article entitled Red Ladder Day by Tim Burke in Young People Now, May 1989

[34] ibid

[35] ibid

[36] ibid

BETWEEN TWO CENTURIES: RED LADDER IN THE NINETIES

The examination of the plays performed by Red Ladder has been an integral part of the analysis of Red Ladder's career and achievements as a Theatre Company so far. That there can be no doubt about Red Ladder's perception in recognising that a strong script is essential for the propagation of an idea/ideological stance has been established in the preceding two chapters. This chapter too will continue to look at the plays but with a shift in attention towards the other dimensions that contribute significantly to the making of a successful agit prop production. This involves the psychological conditioning of the spectators as much through pre and post performance activities as through the play during performance time. Thus the handouts/leaflets/fanzines/ragazines, meetings with youth workers and/or members of the target audience prior to the production; follow up sessions (involving: discussion, inviting suggestions, solutions, criticism and comments; show reports, making the audience perform role plays and helping them to draw up a agenda for themselves); recording Red Ladder's achievements in forthcoming production advertisements, are all strategies used by the company. These are responsible for: (a) underlining the issues/themes of the play, (b) emphasising the status Red Ladder as a Theatre Company actively involved with such issues/themes, (c) locating the target audience that is affected by these ideas, and (d) the collective realisation of the play in terms of its success, both, as a performance and as an agency for suggesting viable solutions to the issues taken up within the play or put forward plans of action that the audience can explore. It is only appropriate therefore that this chapter focuses on such features over and above the plays themselves for a more complete knowledge of Red Ladder's mode of functioning.

The nineties began with the Bus Shelter Project by Lin Coghlan in the spring of 1990, a tour for young people meeting on the street, concentrating on homelessness and poverty. Kate O Reilly's Breaking the Silence written specially for disabled Asian and Girls groups using British Sign Language (BSL) was produced in Autumn 1990. In spring of the following year Judith Johnson's The Scrappie, about loss and separation, for mixed senior youth clubs, and in autumn, Consequences by Mary Cooper, a play touring to Asian girls groups were produced. Another play using BSL by Philip Osment, Listen, about a deaf young person and family relationships was produced in the winter of 1992; in spring came Though the Heavens Fall by Lin Coghlan about justice and law for senior youth club audiences while in autumn, Caught by Julie Wilkinson, a play for girls groups focusing on teenage pregnancy and integrating BSL were produced. A joint project between Kuffdem Theatre Company and Red Ladder, No Mean Street by Paul Boakye, was performed in spring 1993 exploring HIV/AIDS and targeting Black young people while in autumn, Philip Osment's Sleeping Dogs, a play for mixed senior youth clubs focusing on inter-communal strife in Eastern Europe, was staged.

1994 saw the appointment of Kully Thiarai, Red Ladder's first Artistic Director of Asian (Indian) origin and the chalking out of a new mission statement which read thus:

> Red Ladder, is a national touring company, recognizing that investment in young people is an investment in the future and is dedicated to:
> - Creating and providing artistically exciting high quality theatre for young people who have little or no access to, or experience of the theatre;
> - Touring new work nationally which, through exploring issues specifically designed for young people, is pure theatre;
> - Developing strategies which offer young people the opportunity to become involved in the artistic life of this country
> - Striving for artistic excellence in its performance and presentation in a way which is accessible and challenging to its audience
> - Developing new writing and other theatre skills.

With the stress now upon youth needs, new writing and pure theatre, one finds that in the next four years Red Ladder's plays dealt with issues that were of particular interest to the younger generation. In spring 1994 Mary Cooper's Mixed Blessings, a play for girls examining mixed race relationships between African Caribbean and white young people was produced. Gilly Fraser's The Wound, which emphasised domestic violence and toured senior mixed youth clubs followed in autumn 1994. Philip Osment's Sleeping Dogs was also retoured to Arts Centres and small-scale theatre venues. Set in Ireland and exploring issues of cultural identity, family and loss, Lin Coghlan's Waking was produced in spring 1995 and toured mixed senior youth clubs. The next year, 1996, came the first International Co-production with Red Ladder and Theatre Direct, Canada and the play produced was Noel Greig's End of Season which toured to youth club audiences and theatre goers and looked at tribalism, youth violence and cultural identity. This happened in the spring, and autumn brought in Roy William's <u>Josie's Boys</u>, a play about single parenting, leaving home and ambition that toured to youth club audiences. Maya Chowdhry's <u>Kaahani</u> which toured to youth club and theatre audiences for young people 14+ and was about gender, duty and kismet was produced in spring 1997. In autumn 1997 the company staged <u>Crush</u> by Rosie Fordham, a comedy about infatuation, fantasy and reality, men and women and Boybands—this was retoured in autumn the following year to Arts Centre and Youth Service. Spring 1998 saw a co-production with Theatre Centre in a play by Philip Osment, <u>Wise Guys</u>, which studied male identity and violence.

In 1998, Wendy Harris was appointed as the new Artistic Director; the Mission Statement and Artistic Policy however underwent only a little alteration:

Mission Statement

To commission and produce accomplished, innovative and relevant new plays that are artistically excellent in performance and tour them nationally to a youth audience who have little or no access to theatre.

Current Artistic Policy

- To create artistically exciting, challenging and pioneering theatre of the highest quality.
- To tour this work nationally targeting young people who have little or no access to theatre.
- To take artistic risks and explore new ways of working.
- To develop new writing that is high quality, imaginative, reflects cultural diversity and is challenging for our audience.
- To raise the profile of Red Ladder's work nationally and internationally as well as locally.
- To continue to pursue new ways to reach and develop our youth audience and to develop strategic new partnerships with art venues and other agencies that want to develop a youth audience.
- To offer excellent participatory ad residential programmes alongside the main programme of work and ensure the continued excellence of resource materials and follow up (in conjunction with productions).
- To undertake the above aims through strategies that enable us to implement our Equal Opportunities Policy within all aspects of Red Ladder's work.

With the significant inclusion of taking 'artistic risks' within the Artistic Policy of Red Ladder, one perceives not just a theatre catering to youth demands but a stylistically different and challenging theatre. Set on New Year's Eve of 1999, <u>Last Night</u> by John

Binnie, was produced in autumn 1999 and was the story of a pregnant teenager, an old man and a refugee. Red Ladder's millennium play, <u>After the End of the World</u> by Mike Kenny, was produced in spring 2000, a comedy that studied respect and morality where major characters who Stick, a teenage boy living with Chintz, his single parent mum, and Wrinkle, his disabled grandma. In autumn 2000, Noel Greig's <u>Picture Me</u>, an international story set in England and Mumbai exploring the emotional impact of HIV/AIDS on a British Asian teenager was produced.

It is evident even from this outline that the centre of attention in the nineties was the youth, their individual/societal identity and the factors responsible for the problems of recognition/misrecognition that accompany the making of these identities. As one of the fliers aptly put it 'Red Ladder believes investment in young people is an investment in the future.' Another area of special interest initiated in the eighties that Red Ladder focused on in the nineties was disabled/handicapped/special needs people. If traditional agit prop then could not be sustained in the eighties due to changing target groups and altered needs of the times, in the nineties it underwent almost a complete makeover. Red Ladder's work could now be seen as hand in glove with the work of youth clubs and social welfare organisations. The political agenda of Red Ladder now seemed limited to a concentrated effort to negotiate with the Arts Council for continued funding; quite a veering from the early sixties when Red Ladder's political programme was to protest against the malfunctioning of the government. Thus from the purely agit prop directly political theatre practiced during its inception to the strong theatre for social action or community theatre into which Red Ladder developed in the nineties, the shift was clearly visible and was an outcome of the demands of changing times.

In keeping with the nature of this target audience in the nineties, the leaflets/fanzines began to incorporate those features that would prove to be most instructive. Obviously the designing of these brochures, etc., had to be handled with skill so that they, both, caught the eye as well as provoked thought. The usual information about the Company i.e., its mission and goals; its staging requirements; quotes from reviews of plays previously performed; the acknowledgements section (mainly to funding agencies) and the credits, remained as before. But the information about the actors and the Company members involved with a particular production was now made more personal, almost as if on a one to one basis with the audience. Using humour, the actor's or Company members' revelations from his/her life and his/her perspectives about the theme of the play, was a deliberate attempt to erase performer-spectator distance and generate a spirit of collective understanding about a problem. Often, as with Philip Osment's Sleeping Dogs and Paul Boakye's No Mean Street, the programmes included the writer's intent and viewpoint, thus demystifying and making accessible the absent writer such as to connect authorial subjectivity with that of the audience. Both strategies of personalising the performing/production unit were tactical moves to lower any resistance offered by the largely youth audiences that the plays catered to: they desacralised the performance space. The question and answer stratagem employed earlier was further supplemented by the use of scores that placed the respondents in categories; such categorization aimed to generate within the respondent the desire to change (especially if the category was one with negative overtones).

A new characteristic of many nineties ragazines and fliers was the inscribing of the BSL on the handouts emphasising the need for more people to learn the language to enable greater and better communication with the hearing and speech impaired. Augmenting this proposition was the listing of helplines complete with addresses and phone numbers, providing handy options to be tapped during crises. The cartoons and other illustrations too seemed to be directed to making suggestions that would aid youth club workers and also every other individual to resolve difficulties. Given the increasing sophistication of the tools used by Red Ladder, the focus will shift from an analysis of the plays to an examination of the specific methodological rituals (especially resource kits) innovatively employed by Red Ladder in the nineties to ensure its continued effectiveness, as explained in the introductory paragraph of this chapter.

Performed throughout the UK in rural settings, large cities, to young offenders, in schools, community colleges, to young people with disabilities—in fact, anywhere a bus could be parked, Lin Coghlan's The Bus Shelter Show (1990) takes place inside a bus. The bus, on loan to the Company from Yorkshire Ryder Bus Company was converted so that the action happens around it, underneath it and inside it. The action focuses around the relationships between three young people, Se, Jan and Mikey with Rosie who left home and has lived on the streets since the mid-1950s. To escape from her court hearing and her mum's boyfriend, Jan thinks of the bus she has "nicked" and which only needs a starter motor to get it going. Se lives with and looks after his father and hates it when people call his Dad 'Paddy'. Mikey is Se's best friend and has the chance to join the army—he knows how to fit a new starter motor and they all know where to get one—the local bus depot. Rosie left home in the 1950s when she was 18 and lived in a hostel for 20 years; she sees the bus as her shelter, somewhere for her to live. Writer Lin Coghlan, chatted to young people hanging around the streets (as the programme informs one) and, based on the things they said, wrote this play to explore issues important to them.

The performance deals with many issues so that different aspects of the play affect young people in different ways, dependent on their own experiences, cultures and where they 'hang out'. For instance at one stage in the play the focus is on Mikey who has decided to join the Army, ostensibly to escape from the environment he lives in where he has little or no chance of securing employment. The issues involved in this are explored via his relationship with other characters. Neville Robinson who played the character of Mikey said that in reality this happened a lot, especially in rural areas or areas of high unemployment where they took the performance.[1] Young men did sign up for nine years just to escape their environment rather than from any real desire for a life in the armed forces. The performance tackles many other issues, including racism, homelessness, alcohol, and personal relationships which are all thrown up throughout the play (for follow up later in the discussions). The aim is to encourage young people to look again at what they are saying, thinking and doing and above all to ask why. Various one off lines from the play serve as starters for discussion which provides ideas and guidance for youth workers. When Mikey asks Rosie, 'Why do you live the way you do?' we are forced to question—is it Rosie's fault that she lives 'like that'? Do people make themselves homeless? Why isn't there anywhere for her to go? What is there for young people to go to if they leave home? Similarly, when Se asks his Dad not to let people call him Paddy anymore, we are faced with the issue of racism and stereotyping people.

When and why do people use abusive names for each other? Why does Se's Dad allow his friends to call him Paddy? Why do people put down Irish people, or black people?

The Bus Shelter Show reflects what young people deal with everyday and the questions youth workers always ask. Before the tour started Red Ladder held previews with workers and young people in each area to discuss the content and format of the play. As follow-up, the idea of a 'Fanzine' as a starter for discussion was used encouraging young people to write comments and ideas on it. The Company suggested that the contents were ideas for things to be done or things that young people had done locally and could include contacts for local information and events, help lines and support groups, comments about the local area—good things, bad things and those requiring change. Another method used in follow up work was drama or role play. The young people identified something that had happened to them or someone they knew who made them feel powerless—perhaps they kept being moved on from the town centre or were harassed about hanging around the bus shelter. They then decided who they wanted to meet to try to get the situation changed—it could be a policeman or a local councillor whose character they would then take on and create a role play for what would happen if they meet up with these young people. The idea was then to talk about how it felt and who had the power.

The potential of the bus was exploited to its full extent. Because one was 'inside the set' (at one stage the engine is actually started up) the dramatic distance between actors and audience was reduced. The tiny space, though posing considerable physical problems to the actors, added to the intensity. The play would go on all around the audience which created both a deep sense of involvement and a healthy lack of reverence for the performing space—the audience would start to comment and interact with the performers.[2] A remarkably simple idea for solving the problems of accessibility, the play proved especially useful in rural areas where young people had no building of their own. Not surprisingly, the play worked best and attracted most young people when the right preparation had been done, and when the performance took place at the right time and in the right place for its young audience. In Leicestershire for example, where the play was done mainly in school car parks, audience numbers were down because of the hot weather and the local industrial holiday fortnight.[3]

The Red Ladder Bus Shelter Tour proved that one didn't need a theatre or stage to produce good drama. The performance worked because it met young people where they generally while away freetime and focussed on and asked them to discuss the issues that concerned them. Intended specifically for young girls Kate O' Reilly's Breaking the Silence (1990) is about three teenage girls, Allannah (Ali), Jo and Damyanti (Damy) each with a different problem. Ali is partially deaf and this is the cause of quarrels between her parents: her father blames her mother, Bette, as Bette's mother too had been deaf. Bette is unable to handle a traumatised daughter and a bitter, frustrated husband and leaves home. But her love and concern for Ali keep bringing her back. Dami is Jo's friend at the beginning of the play, an unequal friendship since Jo never fails to remind her how she had stood by Dami when Dami had been made the butt of racist comments and acts. For this favour, Jo emotionally blackmails Dami into doing a lot of work for her. Dami, being Indian, is plagued by all kinds of demeaning racist attacks such as excreta put into her mailbox or nasty graffiti on the walls outside her house—Dami is outraged by such acts and would like to protect her simple mother from it all (a case of role reversal). Her brother Prakash, would rather she ignored it all. Jo's problem is that with her mother having walked out when she was much younger, she is completely dominated by the men in her house, her feminine identity kept well in check. She consistently quotes her brother, Paul, an aggressive and confused man himself. Matters come to a head when Paul along with his friend Neil (who has recently started dating Jo and getting sexually intimate with her) throw bricks at Dami's house with messages like 'Pakis go home', shattering the window panes. Jo follows them even if she does not participate in their actions. When Dami rounds up Jo for not stopping her brother, Jo's excuse is that she wanted to be accepted, especially by Neil. Meantime, Ali and Dami have become close, appreciate each other in spite of their so-called 'handicaps'; in fact learning the sign language proves to be a source of fun and bonding between them. Ali, however, hides her deafness from Jo because she sees Jo's hatred and mockery of what she calls the "loonies unit" (referring to the Partially Hearing Unit) and cannot bear to be subjected to such a treatment by Jo, herself.

The play brings to the fore the fact that the three girls are unhappy primarily because none of them know whom to turn to and share their pain. It also highlights the typically prejudiced attitudes that arise out of ignorance—thus Jo attributes the cause of all the problems with students in the PHU to their dimwittedness; to their being 'loony'; Jo's brother Paul and others of his ilk call Dami Paki (Jo too accuses Dami of speaking 'Paki language' whenever Dami lapses into Punjabi) unaware of/ignoring the actual origins of Dami. Such attitudes only serve to repress other identities and thus result in trauma.

The fanzine accompanying <u>Breaking The Silence</u> is loaded with leading questions. The very first page that starts off with drawings of the basic alphabet for BSL asks a vital question "But what happens if you don't speak English...or don't share the same culture?" This same page carries a quick quiz based on gender stereotypes with multiple options for answers, such as, "If a girl won't give a boy a birthday kiss, do you think (a) she's a spoilsport (b) she's just shy (c) she shouldn't kiss him if she doesn't want to." The next page continues the interrogation, the leading question being "How come it's girls that are kept in, when its boys that cause the trouble?" Again, notions popularly held in society are quoted and spectators asked to agree/disagree with such notions.

The third page features the desires of young women, disabled or otherwise and the obstacles that prevent the fulfillment of their desires. Among the desires listed are abseiling, mending cars, playing pool and the obstructions extend from "The magazines aren't in Braille" to "People don't understand what I'm saying" to "Other people don't give us a chance to try." It ends with the insistence "But we can" yet the confession "But sometimes we need help to get started..." and this is where the focus turns to the youth worker.

Not only do the questions make visible the general pattern of thinking in society, they are also intended to generate a certain sense of discomfort within each spectator in recognizing his/her own prejudices. In making the spectator answer these questions the effort is to draw the spectator as a participant into the central debates of the play.

While the first three pages asked questions, the next three, while not exactly answering them, provide clues to attain answers. Page Four actually gives evidence of concrete measures being taken to surmount gender and physical restrictions. Some of the examples given are worth quoting. "Deaf Teenagers have got together to make a minicom network"; "In Leeds youth workers and disabled girls got together to form the Get Away Girls. They organise trips and do all sorts of outdoor activities like wheelchair abseiling. Envious? How about starting one near you?" Again, "in Leeds Youth Workers met and talked to some young women on the streets. They've organised a weekend away together…and decided where to go and what to do…and fundraised the money…hired the equipment bought the food sorted out who was going and had a really good time." The box at the bottom shifts the focus from 'them' to 'you' to ask 'what about you?' thus directly implicating the audience in the process of shouldering responsibilities and changing situations.

But the entire burden is not placed upon the spectator alone who in the next page entitled 'Where to go to for advice' is drawn back to the play, where it is pointed out that by the end of the play Jo needed someone to talk to. Some of the suggestions made for Jo (and by extension the audience) include a trustworthy person like a teacher, youth worker or friend; useful numbers available especially in Thompsons directories, Directory enquiries and Libraries; local Samaritans who could be located in the phone book under S; organisations suggested by the local youth worker. In other words, the thrust is towards trying out 'local numbers first'. While the fifth page speaks generally of people and places where one can seek help, the next page is more specific in information and actually lists out national organisations with their addresses and numbers; such organisations can put a person in touch with local places if one is unable to find them any other way. From 'Alcoholics Anonymous' to 'Eating Disorders Association' to 'Lesbian and Gay Youth Movement' to 'Rape Crisis' and 'Keep Deaf Children Safe', the list is obviously well researched and comprehensive.

This page also includes quotes from people with physical disabilities—the quotes all highlight the fact that disabled people need to be treated like normal citizens with rights. They show a realisation of the fact that the cruel treatment handicapped people receive arises out of ignorance at the independence (and thus the 'normality') of the disabled. The last quote is almost an assertion of a disabled person's abilities: "Just because people see a person in a wheelchair or using a white stick, it doesn't necessarily mean that the person cannot walk and see. Just that to be able to walk and see they need wheels and sticks to make it a bit easier."

The last page is a copy of a photograph of all the Red Ladder people involved in the performance and a personal note about each; the note targets the past of each member to divulge the fact that the performing unit shared the same youth problems as the spectators. In taking up this personal angle, the obvious intension is to break down the barriers between performers and audience, thus underlining the mission and objectives of Red Ladder as a theatre company devoted to the task of community welfare through the medium of theatre. The photograph even has a dog belonging to Mandy Redvers-Higgins and good humouredly requests the audience not to feed Urma and spoil her concentration when she worked. The closeness of a family structure or of a well-bonded community comes through clearly from the photograph.

Incidentally, the fanzine has a number of cartoons/illustrations and a dog (representing Urma?) features as a character (a wise one too) in them. Hence the first page has a girl fending off a man who has taken her out for drinks and now presumes she should feel obliged to reciprocate his physical advances. The girl wards him off physically and the dog, an onlooker, comments sagely "Go halves next time—then he can't make you feel guilty?" An oblique way perhaps on Red Ladder's part to point out that even the underdog's voice ought not to go unheeded? Another thought-provoking illustration shows a girl on a wheelchair going across a tightrope while another girl hangs from the ropeway; the words being "Sorry, its wheelchair access only—but…we're not doing anything about it", thus a dig at the dismal state of the facilities available for disabled people.

No doubt Red Ladder's play may have acquired greater artistic merit but the very fact that the fanzine (a sophisticated development of the early propagandist leaflets accompanying a performance) contains every possible dimension for tackling social problems, and attempts to evolve measures that counter problems, is proof that Red Ladder, in an integrative rather than the earlier resistance mode retains its distinctly agit prop footing. In fact, the fanzine by itself often serves as valuable resource material even when the play is unavailable as with the summer 92 Fanzine supplementing the production of Lin Coghlan's Though the Heavens Fall. This fanzine is self-sufficient in that one doesn't necessarily have to watch the play to understand its thrust if one goes through the fanzine. It takes on issues of moral conscience in the form of a 'Scruples Quiz'; gives an opportunity for discussion through an agree/disagree section; informs about one's legal rights when dealing with the police or being put under arrest; initiates the idea of fighting for necessary prison reforms undertaken by such organizations as the Howard League for Penal Reforms and lists out addresses and phone numbers of those centers that provide legal aid to the young be they disabled, single parents, drug addicts, etc. Evidently the fanzines appear to follow a certain pattern—that of nudging the spectator into examining the issue in question in all its dimensions and then making constructive suggestions to tackle the issue. The tone of the fanzine is always a gentle though firm one seeking co-operation rather than inciting angst.

The Autumn 92 fanzine, part of the resource kit of the production Caught, a play by Julie Wilkinson, also follows the trend set by the earlier fanzines. The play revolves around thirteen year old Paulette, her baby daughter Cristal and her elder sister, Karon. The subtitle of the play is 'The Incredible Expanding Baby' and that is precisely what happens within the play where the baby Cristal's proportions increase to such dimensions (physically and metaphorically) that she makes living in the house impossible. Paulette refuses to reveal the name of Cristal's father; only much later are the facts uncovered and one comes to know that Cristal's father is non other than Karon's no good boyfriend Carl, who has just served a term in prison. Having had his way with Paulete, Carl has no compunctions in carrying on with Karon who of course leaves him on learning the truth. Meanwhile the baby is so huge that all kinds of forces—police, fire fighters—try to take her away from Paulette on the grounds that she is a menace (an example of the way state machinery ignores the humane element and operates coldly and autocratically). However, Karon who has been upset with Paulette does return to help her out. The story is narrated and performed in turns (except Paulette's role) by three characters suitably called Furies as they represent the gossip mongers who only spread venom through scandalous revelations.

In following the format of making spectators play the agree/disagree game, answer the quick quiz or the problem given, air their opinion; and in providing not just helpful information but also some clues as to how to handle problems of young, unwed mothers; of societal/governmental pressures; the fanzine works almost like an FIR. It is an immediate response to the issues of the play and it makes the spectators ideas/perspectives the centre of action. Thus the fanzine acts as a mediating agent between the performance and the follow up—it helps break the ice for the post-production interactive sessions. It allows for the immediate, direct and concrete involvement of the spectator.

Targeted for a mixed senior youth club audience, i.e., an audience comprising male and female adults belonging to different races of not more than sixty per performance, in the age group of thirteen to twenty-five, and of special interest to African Caribbean young people, the one hour performance of <u>No Mean Street</u> was written by the acclaimed Black writer Paul Boakye, after a period of research with young African Caribbean people. The production was a joint venture between Red Ladder and Kuffdem, a Leeds based African Carribean theatre company, who work with Black communities and groups throughout the country. The main protagonist, Arlington, does not make a decision to be tested for AIDS—he just goes to the hospital for a minor complaint. Diagnosed HIV positive, he discovers that he has no friends and is forced to change his street wise, lifestyle. The play explores the impact of HIV/AIDS on young African Caribbean people—the fear, isolation, prejudice and the dangers of living in a society which often refuses to acknowledge the realities of HIV; such feelings sharpened in a multicultural situation where racial prejudices, though cloaked, are certainly present.

The very act of collaborating with another theatre company, a first on Red Ladder's part, was tactically a sound move. Pitching resources under one banner helped in sharing not just artistic talent and expertise but also pooling knowledge as to how to tackle a tough subject. It also helped to establish the common interests of the two companies and by this connectedness, provided a live example of how different arts, different communities can work towards a particular goal. The ragazine (as explained earlier a magazine that literally put together 'rags' or scraps of information like a catalogue) complementing the play is, however, different in that it does not contain any of the usual games/quizzes, etc that are staple fare of the fanzines. Rather, it is packed with all kinds of information related to safe sex and AIDS, and how to handle such problems as AIDS and racism. There are sections devoted to African history, African presence in Britain and the Fight for Freedom; what AIDS and HIV are and how the virus is transmitted; what safer sex and condoms are, and notes differing attitudes to sex. There is also a poem addressing the concept of 'mules' entitled 'Excess luggage' by Remi, a performer in the play.[4] There are also sections that inform about the efforts of people in the Arts to warn against AIDS, as for example the video with pop stars speaking of the disease featuring a Salt and Pepa' sound track 'Let's talk about sex'; and the 'Red Hot and Rap' album featuring Arrested Development, LL Cool J, Gang Starr and the Disposable Heroes of Hiphoprisy where all the artists have contributed original tracks dealing with safe sex or intravenous drugs use theme.

Naturally the helplines section of this ragazine looks at organisations that are related to assisting Black people with AIDS, drugs and legal problems. In short, the ragazine encapsulates a tremendous amount of information in a crisp and easy manner. While not providing scope within the ragazine itself for spectators to express their viewpoints, the message of the play is conveyed clearly in the words, 'When you're dealin' with/the birds and the bees,/Don't shy away from/Dealin' with disease'. Thus the information loaded ragazine underlines the theme of the play to spark off debate and discussions post-performance.

Not just through ragazines, even direct statements made by Red Ladder declare their intent. The cover of the programme of Philip Osment's Sleeping Dogs states the purpose succinctly, "This programme has been designed to offer you more information about the Company and the work we do. Also, included are suggestions and ideas that can be used by you, once our touring team have moved on. We hope you will enjoy the play and take part in the discussion afterwards." Moving on from the purpose of the play to the intent behind the play's theme and facts about the people involved with the production, the next two pages contain briefs on the actors and the manager and a write up by Osment and a note on Red Ladder's work/the nature of the Company. The inclusion of the Osment's authorial statement within the programme, regarding his reasons for writing Sleeping Dogs asserts the deliberateness of the theme chosen (both, by the author, and in staging the play, by the Company). That Osment's words are followed by the note on Red Ladder which spells out that Red Ladder is a multiracial Company, with both disabled and non-disabled performers, catering to the needs of young people of all kinds; foregrounds the collective nature of the project undertaken. Red Ladder may not, as in the days of The Cake Play or Strike While the Iron is Hot, be functioning in the conservative sense of the word 'collective' when the plays were scripted jointly, but in making space for the author's voice and showing the similarity of interests, it is evident that in spirit, the Company remains a collective.[5]

The middle section of the programme features photographs and cartoons that amplify the question "Do we need conflict?" This question is followed by another on the next page asking "Do you see yourself as European or not?" Preceding this question is a quote by Mahatma Gandhi that speaks of individuality and assimilation; of tolerance: "I do not want my home to be walled in on all sides and its windows to be stuffed. I want cultures of all lands to be blown about my house as freely as possible. But I refuse to be blown off my feet by any." Above this quotation is a drawing of the globe with the heading 'Conflict' and the following...'Global', 'Community', 'Personal' and 'Cultural'—that conflict pervades all domains of life.

These early questions are only teasers to lead the spectators to a more concentrated and intense discussion of the key ideas/themes and issues in the play. The parameters for these are actually marked out on the penultimate page where a number of key terms are given to be used as stimulus for audience response—this list of terms is fairly exhaustive and in a sense, allows no room for deviation from the subject under consideration. While in the initial days Red Ladder's plays were so subject specific tangling as they did with a certain political moment, the nineties plays while continuing this particularity were artistically sophisticated as well. Again, this did not mean a toning down of the main objective of Red Ladder, that of agitating the audience about the issue/s enacted in the play and of propagating change. (Of course, the meaning of 'change' had altered by now from militant protest and resistance to community effort for welfare).

The analyses so far may have given the impression that all was well at the Red Ladder front in the nineties. Undoubtedly Red Ladder's continued presence in the theatre/arts world proved its success but the struggle continued. A document entitled 'Extending the Boundaries: 1995-1998', a Three Year Plan of the Company, actually contains an annual review of the years 1992-1995. What were the achievements and the failures that Red Ladder recorded in these years according to this document?

The main factor affecting the work in this period had been completely unforeseen. From the period of September 1992-January 1994, the Company did not have an Artistic Director in post. This was due to a number of factors including long-term sick leave, sabbatical leave, maternity leave and finally the decision of Rachel Feldburg to leave the Company. During this time, visiting freelance directors and artistes covered the duties of the post, whilst the Financial Administrator covered the overview in addition to her own duties. This put a tremendous strain on the programme of work as well as on any long term planning, resulting in a 'holding operation' by the remaining staff members. In spite of this situation, the Company's touring work in 1993 thrived and two extremely exciting, risk-taking pieces toured to universal acclaim.

To get down to facts, in 1992-93 Red Ladder commissioned and toured two pieces as planned to target groups: Though the Heavens Fall by Lin Coghlan and Caught by Julie Wilkinson which achieved the target number (one hundred and twenty seven) of performances. The use of Sign Language was developed by engaging an 'Actor Signer' for Caught. The first stage of joint production with Kuffdem Theatre Company which included the commissioning process/researching African Caribbean Writers resulted in the first commission for a new Black writer: a six month traineeship was offered to an

African Caribbean Administrator followed by an initial session for the same. The marketing strategy for the production commenced.

The Appraisal Recommendations of the Arts Council of Great Britain (ACGB) that were put into action included the three month sabbatical taken by the Artistic Director; an increase in all full time staff salaries in line with other Companies and engaging the services of a European Fundraising Consultant. The administrative and other achievements during this time were: the development of a Special Three Year Relationship with the Eastern Arts Board, the initiation of regionally based 'Training the Trainers' weekend as the first stage of new training strategy, completion of ten days of youth worker/young people training, and receiving 35 per cent upliftment in ACGB core funding.

However, this period also saw Red Ladder confronting numerous obstacles. The staffing levels, in particular the absence of an Artistic Director, affected the level of activity throughout the year. This had a direct effect on the following projects: the Asian Women tripartite programme was deferred as also the January/February 1993 'Work in Progress' project; without an Artistic Director, the Company was unable to conduct the 'Director's Workshops' as planned. Following the Appraisal recommendation that the 'Summer School' needed to be budgeted to make a profit, the Company undertook a feasibility study which found that Youth Services then were unable to meet realistic prices; with this in mind the project was abandoned and the issue of developing a 'Training Network' recommended. The original target audiences for Caught were disabled young men and women. Whilst researching the project, it became apparent that the Youth Services wanted a piece that would look at teenage girls and pregnancy. The show then toured to girls groups nationally but only reached 9.44 per cent deaf young women: this highlighted the importance of strategic targeting.

1993 toured two major productions that were hugely successful, the first being Paul Boakye's <u>No Mean Street</u>. To reiterate, this venture was Red Ladder's first successful co-production with a Black Theatre Company; it was also the first ever National tour of a piece designed specifically for young African Caribbean people in youth clubs and similar venues. The production involved the engagement of a Black freelance Director, a Black choreographer and a Black MD and the traineeship for the new Black Director. The original target to reach 40 per cent African Caribbean youth was exceeded and in fact Red Ladder achieved 50.9 per cent. The Administrative Traineeship for the African Caribbean administrator continued while a Youth Work training weekend focusing on No Mean Street was undertaken at Dudley.

The other 1993 play, Sleeping Dogs, written and directed by Philip Osment, achieved all its aims: the target number of sixty performances; the original brief to look at a small rural community which led to piece focusing on intercommunal strife; the target group, i.e., mixed senior youth club audiences in rural areas. This was a piece that was not issue led and should be seen as a major artistic development in the Company's work. The excellent feedback/response led to Company decision to retour Sleeping Dogs to Arts Centres in Autumn 1994. Also, two one day 'Introduction to Theatre in Youth Work' training days for Youth and Arts workers based in the Eastern Arts region were delivered.

In spite of the remarkable success of the two plays toured in 1993, the level of activity continued to remain affected by the staffing levels, particularly those projects which needed an Artistic Director at the helm: the summer project for Young People; the second New Writer's workshop; the 'work in progress project'; the summer school that was found to be financially unviable. Besides, No Mean Street achieved 56 performances instead of the anticipated 60. This was due to the pioneering nature of the project—targeting and finding groups of young African/Caribbean people.

January 1994 saw the appointment of a new Artistic Director, Kully Thiarai who ushered in a period of significant change. Building on Red Ladder's history and expertise in the field of Theatre in Youth Work, the Company, with Kully Thiarai at the helm, was keen to develop new work that took artistic risks (especially following the immense success of Sleeping Dogs, a play reminiscent of and inspired by Lorca) through form, content and style. In the 'Three Year Plan (1995-1998)' drawn up once Kully Thiarai took over, it was intended to actively debate and implement appropriate recommendations made by the Arts Council of Great Britain in its 1992 appraisal of the Company. While the artistic policy under Kully Thiarai has already been outlined earlier, some of the other characteristic features of the post '93 productions in accordance with the artistic policy need to be highlighted. The policy now prioritized new writing which was imaginative, challenging and accessible to youth audiences; a moving away from traditional issue based plays and a pursuit of a strong narrative form through which the issues and concerns of young people could be naturally addressed; a maintenance of commitment to new writing and pushing the quality of production scripts by engaging a dramaturg as part of the script development process; pioneering new projects through residency based work which actively sought/involved young people in the performing arts; taking along youth audience to theatre venues to empower them to become active participants and consumers of mainstream arts provision; and through the artistic process an exploration of the themes of internationalism and cultural diversity within Red Ladder's work. Training priorities included marketing Red Ladder's knowledge and expertise as a Training Agency in a way which generated additional income for the Company and undertaking and implementing the Asian Women's traineeship programme for Stage Managers and Administrators.

In keeping with the emphasis on new and challenging writing, one observes that a number of the projects lined up in the three year plan centred around 'Writing Policy', 'Resident Dramatist' and the 'Seeding/Workshop Programme' (whereby the Company would develop the skills and craft of young writers whom it was keen to work with but unable to offer a commission to at that stage). A document entitled " 'Creative Dialogue' Working With Writers", possibly penned around 1995-1996, invites writers attuned with Red Ladder's work and interested in being involved creatively with the Company. The second paragraph of this document reads:

> ... How do we create work which combines observable 'learning areas' with narrative that does not reduce to simple 'instructional theatre'? Red Ladder is committed to offering its audiences full, resonating dramas: ones which seek to make connections as opposed to coming to conclusions. This dual responsibility to the writer's craft and to the learning needs of the constituent audience is a fine balance. It has led the Company to look at developing ways in which it can offer strong dramaturgical support to the writer without being prescriptive or limiting...

The keen interest taken by Red Ladder in the kind of scripts that the company could work on is more than enough recognition of the fact that the Company could no longer rely on actual happenings of history to provide themes for plays but rather on enterprisingly crafted dramas to suit their different target audiences. This fact is amply illustrated by Red Ladder's fifth national tour, for young women and girls groups, of <u>Mixed Blessings</u> by Mary Cooper in 1994. What is the colour of love? How is the meaning of a relationship changed by the colour of the skin for those who are involved and those who look on? What does a black man imagine a sexual relationship with a white woman is like? And what do their friends and family say about mixed race relationships when the lovers' backs are turned? These questions and more are explored by the play. Aimed at young women aged 14-25, the play uses comedy and music to explore the nature of mixed race friendships and sexual relationships between young Afro-Caribbean and white people.

Lisette (White, Irish) and Sian (Black, Afro-American) are best friends. They catch the same bus to school, are in the same set for maths, buy the same kind of clothes and both like basketball. But when boyfriends Mark and Jem appear on the scene, their friendship is put to the test. Sparks fly, arguments brew and secrets unfold as Lisette and Sian struggle to stay friends and hang on to their boyfriends.

<u>Mixed Blessings</u> is about friendships, loyalty and relationships with boyfriends. The play forces its audience to recognise and challenge the existence of racial and sexual stereotypes. All these issues are seen through the eyes of Lisette or Sian, from a black woman's point of view and a white woman's point of view. How they perceive boys, how they think boys view them and what they think about their lives. There is a realisation amongst the characters that they are not alone in the way they feel and that problems can be overcome through talking and sharing in each other's experiences.

The play raises issues that affect young women's lives—their dress and identity, relationships with parents and with friends, sex, and different cultures and music. In a report from a performance in a Nottingham youth centre, the reporter said that it was clear from the audience's laughter and nods of recognition, that these issues were realistic to them and they could relate to what was going on.[6] The performance contains a lot of movement, with music and dance playing a large part in each scene, giving the performers a lot of different things to do, but making for a visually interesting piece of theatre.

Before examining the other paraphernalia that Red Ladder used in this production (as it ritually did in other production) it would be worthwhile to analyse briefly how the primary text, i.e., the play itself, sought to reach out to its target audience. Within the play racial stereotypes are constantly challenged and differences of cultures celebrated. Sian is white and Irish while Lisette is Afro-Caribbean, and these different culture are studied. In one scene, Lisette and Sian talk about different music they listen to, and perform the different sorts of dancing they do. They acknowledge that they eat different foods and that their cultural backgrounds are very different in some respects, but similar in others. They both have problems with their boyfriends and parents and, as it turns out, they both have similar expectations of their friendship with each other. The real problems are created when they both get boyfriends and the conflict of seeing each other or seeing their boyfriends develop. Sian's boyfriend Jem is black and Lisette's boyfriend Mark is white.

Lisette tells Sian that she shouldn't go out with Jem because he'll treat her badly, he won't ring her, when they go out he'll ignore her all night and talk to his friends and that anyway, he's only interested in having sex with her. The problems of being in a mixed-race relationship are explored from both the young women's cultural perspectives and sometimes turn out to be the same, although it also becomes clear that there are differences in the acceptability of a white woman seeing a black man and of a black woman seeing a white man. Both young women are afraid that people will stare at them, that their boyfriends will boast to their friends, and that they'll get into trouble with parents for bringing shame on the family. It becomes clear that young women in a mixed-race relationship have a whole range of considerations to think about, due to the existence of racial and sexual stereotypes and some of the lines in the play bring these to the forefront:

> "Being friends is all right but you shouldn't mix blood.' (Friends of Lisette and Sian)
> 'I know you black girls want it.' (Sian's brother, Michael to Lisette)
> 'I've been thinking it might be easier to go out with black eyes.' (Lisette)

'I don't think of you as black. You're just Lisette, my mate, and you just happen to be black." (Sian)

The play uses a lot of stereotypes of black and white people, which raises questions about where they all come from and whether there is any truth in them. Getting back to Mandy Jarvis, again, she says that these questions, along with the whole subject of mixed-race relationships and whether they could work, dominated discussions in the follow-up workshops.

As with all of Red Ladder's productions, the performance of Mixed Blessings was followed by workshops where workers and young women were split up and given the opportunity to share their impressions of the play. The young women were in workshops, facilitated by the actresses and the youth workers, worked alongside Vashti Maclachlan, one of the Company's musicians. The majority of young women and workers who were at the performance and participated in the workshops were black. After the Nottingham performance, the areas (as per Mandy Jarvis' report) discussed by the young women included mixed-race relationships and how parents reacted to them; issues surrounding identity—being mixed-race in all white community, being mixed-race in all black community; people talking about you behind your back; sex and safe sex; sexual harassment—should you tell anybody or keep it to yourself; what other people might say if they found out. Lisa, who played Sian in the play said:

> We've found that in the workshops young women talk to us as if we're the characters that we've played in the performance, although we don't consciously stay in role. It's clear that they feel safe talking to us and they were coming out with a lot of really good stuff. They wanted to tell us about what they got up to and what their relationships and friendships were like. We talked about boys and about how people perceive them as young women, what their parents say to them and how they feel about that.
> I think it's really important that all of these issues are brought into youth clubs. In the workshops there are no youth workers present and the young women do open up. It gives them the space to talk about what they've seen and how they feel about it personally with someone who they see as experiencing the same things that they do.

Amanda who played Lisette, explained that:

> What we talk depends on the make-up of the group. Whether it's a black group, white group or mixed group. Different young women talk about different things.

151

I've found that when I've facilitated a workshop of white young women they want to ask me a lot of questions about what it's like being a black woman. As a black performer, it's good for me to think of why they're asking me those questions, as well as making it clear that I can't speak on behalf of all black women!

The play does throw up a lot of issues. The whole question of loyalty in friendship—having thought about it all and as a result of the conversations I've had with young women, I've found that there are no real right answers. It's a lot about the discussions that young women have to face which are often really difficult. How to handle a relationship with a boyfriend and keep in with your girlfriends. Young women have told me that it's about respect and that you have to give space to both people, as well as space for yourself, which seems like a good attitude to me.

Sitting in on the workshop for youth workers with Vashti Maclachlan, Mandy Jarvis who reported on this play observed that the general feeling was that the play raised some very important issues really well. The workers said that the whole issue of having mixed-race relationships was something that did come up a lot with the young women they worked with and that they do a lot of work around the whole issue of identity—how they see themselves, how they related to their culture. They explained how black young women were constantly bombarded with negative images of their colour. One worker explained, "the lighter your skin is, the less flat the nose is, etc, the more attractive you are seen as being. Black is not perceived as being attractive."

One of the workers talked about how she worked with young people who are of mixed race descent, "It's very difficult for young people who are of mixed race themselves, as they find it even more difficult to formulate an identity of themselves." It seemed that the workers found the production useful, as it related to the ongoing work they do with young women. Expressing it through theatre was another way of encouraging young women to feel more positive about themselves.

However, the whole issue of getting into mixed-race relationships remained a dilemma for some of the workers. "Young women (and men) will go into a relationship because they like the person, but when those involved are of different races there are so many other problems that go with it, like the reactions of family and friends. We try to make the young women we work with more aware of the problems they may encounter if they do go out with a white guy. That's not to say they shouldn't do it, just that they should be aware that it won't be easy."

In the production, both characters have stereotypical image of the other culture, of what a black man is like and what a white man is like, and some of the workers said that although the play uses a lot of these stereotypical images, they worked effectively because they showed them up for what they were—stereotypes based on prejudice and ignorance.

The opportunities for developing the issues raised in the play did not stop with the workshop. As with the other productions, workers took away information and resource listings to do follow-up work with the young women they worked with. Quotes and scenes from the play were extracted in the fanzine to stimulate follow-up discussion and create role-plays while an agree/disagree exercise was provided for further work which included statements like: "It's okay to go out with someone of a different race", "It's okay to put your boyfriend before your girlfriend", "If girls wear short skirts they are asking for it", and "Friends always talk about you behind your back".

The play for which one found extremely elaborate, detailed, resource material (apparently meant for youth workers to use for follow up) was Lin Coughlan's Waking, which toured between April and July 1995. Perhaps the multidimensional themes of the play, its setting, the research that obviously went into its making demanded such well documented, exhaustive resource material to ensure that the play hit home.

Waking is an Irish story which looks at family relationships and the often difficult journey back to one's cultural roots. It explores the emotions, expectations and aspirations that span three generations. Sean is the grandfather who has lived all his life in Ireland. Michael has lost his job and with no place else to go, he returns to Ireland after an absence of twenty years taking his son, Brian with him. Brian is an English boy having lived all his life in England, yet at thirteen years old, makes an instant bond with Sean, his Irish grandfather whom he has never known. The arrival of Sarah (Sean's close friend) on the scene and her strength and determination to bring the family together makes the three men gradually 'wake' to their emotions.

The contents of the 'Resource Material' for Waking are divided into Seven Sections: (i) Useful notes for facilitation/role play, (ii) General themes/issues in 'Waking' to use as stimulus in Youth Work, (iii) How do we fit into the world we live in?—'Identity', (iv) Family Relationships and the 'work' ethic, (v) Loss, (vi) Irish Cultural Traditions in the play, and (vii) About the Red Ladder Touring Team.

Within this broad rubric, however, are carefully worked out details of how to conduct post-production follow up workshops. In the 'notes for discussion' section emphasis is placed on the body language and listening skills of the youth worker/workshop coordinator, as also the kind of questions to be asked to facilitate discussion. Questions that invite yes and no answers are discouraged as they inhibit talk and other open questions are suggested such as "How do you feel about that? Why is it important to you? Could you give some examples? How anyone else felt this way? Who could they talk about this? Are there any other possibilities?" That the kind of venue chosen was an important factor in creating the right atmosphere for interaction is perceived by the fact that the nature of the venue is spelt out, both on this page as also reiterated in the next section to read: "Space to hold the discussion should be 'safe' (not a thoroughfare)," "... should be 'safe' in order to set up a supportive environment for working (there is nothing worse than having an uninvited audience)."

Apart from bringing certain issues to the front, the fact that for Red Ladder, theatre is only a means to a greater end, that of learning about or recognizing individual/societal/other weaknesses and attempting to amend these is reflected in the resource material as well. The resource material reinforces to its user:

> e) After the role-play has taken place, review what has happened with the participants—discuss particular areas of interest: Why did they work? If they didn't, why not? How could this be developed?
> f) The analysis is as important as the role play itself—this is where the real learning takes place.

Empowering the spectators, by making them not just participants in the post-production interactive sessions but in turn becoming actors, is also underlined in this resource material by the suggestion that following the role play, scenes could be taped and then scripted if the group agreed on it. The work could then be developed into theatre, using

154

music, scenery, costume, etc. The ongoing and processual nature of the theatrical project as undertaken by Red Ladder is underlined by such a suggestion. Again, the fact that Red Ladder uses Theatre to help generate greater welfare for people is brought home by the manual's directive that knowledge of other support agencies and availability of their leaflets providing relevant information was essential during the workshops.

The remarkable feature about Waking's resource material is the minuteness and exactitude with which every dimension is worked out so that the section on general themes/issues is a compilation of every possible aspect of the play through key terms; the numerous quotes cited to be used as referral points are aptly chosen from all parts of the play and maintain the connectivity of the workshop with the play. A case in point is the section on 'Loss'. The resource kit actually chalks out the various stages that a person experiencing loss may go through from, both, the psychological as also the physiological angles—the sentiments/emotional confusion of the person as manifest in his/her thoughts and physical symptoms.

The two sections "How do we fit into the world we live in?" and "Irish Cultural Traditions" focus on the whole idea of difference—between individual identities in terms of the impact of their environment, family, social group, cultural group, childhood, adulthood and heritage. The profiles of the actors at the end and in the fanzine accentuates not just these differences but also signals that such differences rather than creating divides in communities, should engender mutual harmony. Only taking interest in and learning about each other can achieve this harmony. Such an educative process can help one see the plus side of another's traditions—a learning that can even affect ones own life positively if one were to adopt beneficial aspects of traditions. Thus the title of the play, Waking, is actually a reference to the ritual where Irish people 'wake' their dead, encouraging the living to celebrate the dead person's life. Metaphorically, 'Waking' implies that knowledge alone can prevent the formation of adverse judgement as well as foster mutual respect among different communities.

This detailed resource kit is documentary evidence of the fact that though the nature of the ritual devices used by the Company and the artistic level of the plays produced may have reformed, the primary mission of Red Ladder, inciting social change, remains very much in place.

Following Red Ladder's successful collaboration with Kuffdem Theatre Company in the production of <u>No Mean Street</u>, 1996 saw yet another such successful venture by Red Ladder. Recognising that in spite of the world becoming smaller due to interconnectivity, there was also increasing separatism and fragmentation and that the need to cut across divides more imperative; Red Ladder felt that artist's have a special function in creating processes of work that prove that one can create, dream and work collaboratively. In doing so one can begin to imagine and produce a healthier future; creative work for and with young people would thus have to naturally be high on the agenda. The collaboration between Red Ladder and Theatre Direct Canada in the production of Noel Greig's <u>End of Season</u> was one such attempt to engage artist's and young people across divides of geography, race and culture; the project involved artists whose histories span three continents, Asia, Europe and North America.

In 1994 a young white woman, Kelly Turner, revealed to the police that her ex-boyfriend was the perpetrator of a vicious, racist attack on a young Bengali boy. The reaction she received from her peer group and her community was both horrifying and yet not surprising. Around the same time, Red Ladder was talking to playwright Noel Greig with a view to him writing a new play for the Company. Red Ladder was concerned by the rise of tribalism particularly amongst young people, and were interested in the stories of individuals who, in different ways, broke ranks with the cultures they were framed in. Kelly Turner's story inspired the Company and, two years on, <u>End of Season</u> was the product fuelled by the stories of individuals like Kelly.

As part of the development of <u>End of Season</u>, a twelve member team of theatre artist's from both sides of the Atlantic came together in Toronto in November 1995. A wide range of voices brought their histories to the project: English, British Asian, Canadian Asian, Czech, Scottish, Ukranian, Indo-Caribbean and Irish. This process reflected the artistic and philosophical concerns of both, Red Ladder and Theatre Direct, Canada: to create a new piece of work for young people on both sides of the Atlantic which was not simply 'about' the world we live in but which, in the manner it had been conceived and executed, challenged the fragmentation we see all around us. It was only by finding ways for artist's to connect, that Red Ladder felt one could produce the art that is now needed.

As anxious and insecure communities begin to close in on themselves, to withdraw from the notion of shared citizenry in a pluralistic culture, Red Ladder through its theatre sought (and continues to seek) to invite young people to see beyond their own constituent group and to make connections—not by abandoning their own cultures, ways and traditions, but by engaging in a dialogue, which enables them to question and challenge the view that 'difference' means 'the other' means 'the enemy'.

The intentions of the Artistic Director (Kully Thiarai), Playwright (Noel Greig) and Canadian Director (John Van Burek) are succinctly spelt out in the programme. While Noel Greig wanted "to tell the story of individuals who are confronted by the choice of self-interest or standing up and speaking out against what they know is wrong"; Kully Thiarai "was interested in making links that were real connections: connections that broke boundaries and safe heavens, crossed divisions of geography, race and culture...", and John Van Burek asks, "... as the world grows smaller, do we, as humans, have to follow suit? The injustices of the world are huge; are their solutions any bigger than our individual responses to them on a daily basis? None of us pretend to have the answers but our play is an invitation to you to join in the search."

What then is <u>End of the Season</u> all about? The play follows the story of five characters: Frances Murphy (mother), Linda Murphy (daughter), Trevor Hipkin (boyfriend/husband to be), Harjit Singh Gill (father: Asian/English) and Rajinder Singh Gill (nicknamed Royce—son: Asian/Canadian). It is set in a seaside town in England.[8] "A world of arcades, ice cream vans, funfairs, chip shops, discos, bed and breakfast. A world away from the world on the TV screen: the faraway world where whole communities, nations, are torn apart."[7]

Here, at the end of the summer, people are preoccupied with more personal matters. Frances worries about the takings of her small guest house. Her daughter Linda, obsessed with the 'soaps', is planning to marry Trevor and longs to leave the house, opened annually to strangers. It was supposed to be a beautiful summer for Trevor and Linda. A summer rich with dreams and desires. A summer full of fun.

Then two strangers arrive: Harjit and his son Royce from their home in Canada. Having visited far flung relatives in India and England, Harjit has now to visit the English seaside town that holds memories dear to him. During their stay, cultures collide with tragic consequences. As events unfold, the sectarian, tribal fractures that appear as distant events on the TV screen cast their shadows over the lives of the people in the town. In a place where the only things that seem to happen are the opening and closing of the season and the ebb and flow of the tides the harsh realities of an increasingly divided world do not seem as remote and incomprehensible as they do each night on the news.

The tensions and pressures people face in that bastion of English tolerance, the seaside town, are exposed—identity and cultural heritage are brought to the fore. When loyalties of blood, family, habit and friendship are tested, where will people stand at the season's end? A symbolic and taunting piece of contemporary theatre End of Season exposes our failure to see what's happening at our own door steps.

Immediately after the messages by the Artistic Director, etc, of the production, is the touring team's profile created through questions answered by the team members. Some of the questions included are: "Where do you come from?", "Where do you live now?" and "What is your ambition?" Seemingly innocuous questions, it is the answers given that drive home the differences in origin, culture and desire between the individuals who hail from Bangladesh, Canada, Ireland and England; who live in different parts of England or Canada; and whose desires (though the seriousness with which these last revelations are made is dubious) range from "making plays with people I like and live in a commune" to "learn the English language". In turn, these differences lead to the idea that there can still be a commonality of interests; the very fact that such dissimilar people can get together and 'act' can be read metaphorically in the sense that agit prop theatre means to.

Directly connecting different aspects of the play to the issues these raise, the next section of the resource programme contains quotes from the play and suitable questions to generate discussion. The themes that crop up through the questions are vast: racism and intolerance, youth violence, gang culture and tribalism, family identity, cultural identity, teenage relationships/teenage pregnancy, peer group pressure and the power and influence of television. The last section focuses on culture and moves from discussion to action, i.e., the idea of cultural difference is explored through project work such as "make a list describing as many aspects of your culture within your group", "Research the culture of a different community", and "Create a 'Cultural Wall' using images from magazines."

To reiterate a point made earlier, this process of moving from discussion to action post-production continues the agit prop traditions maintained by Red Ladder of the 'play' serving only as 'starter'.

The growing ingenuity then, of the fanzines was a natural outcome. For if this was not the time for protest marches or demonstrations and instead was time for persuasive emotional education, what better way for Red Ladder to communicate than through the resource material/fanzines.

Produced in 1996 Autumn, Roy Williams' Josie's Boys looked at single parenting and the choices young people have to make in terms of their friends, family and career. The fanzine accompanying Josie's Boys is significant in the way it persuades young people to look at things from their parents' perspectives—it reveals the flip side of parenting. The significance of this fanzine lies in the humorous tone adopted in conveying its message; obviously a deliberate strategy employed to connect with young people resisting any discourse that appears pontificating. Even the tour profile of the stage manager Fran Maskell is funny as for example the last line that says, "She's a pleasant enough girl as long as she has plenty of chocolate to eat and doesn't have to wear a dress." The suggestion under the tongue-in-cheek heading "How to bring up your parents" continues on this light yet effective plane: "1… Don't be afraid to speak their language. Try to use strange sounding phrases like 'I'll help you with the dishes' and 'Yes'. 2…Try to understand their music Play Gary Glitters' 'D' yer wanna be in my gang on the stereo until you're accustomed to the sound. 3… Encourage your parents to talk about their problems. Try to keep in mind that, to them, things like earning a living and paying the rent/mortgage seems important. 4… Be tolerant of their appearance.

When your mum or dad get a new haircut, don't feel personally humiliated. Remember, it's important for them to look like their peers. 5… Most important of all, if they do something you consider wrong, let them know that it's their behaviour you dislike, not them."

Apart from the difference in tonality (suiting the target group of the play) that one observes in this fanzine, the other feature to be noted is that this is a 'thinking' fanzine rather than a physically proactive one. In other words, the fanzine appeals to the reasoning powers of the audience; it attempts to arouse self awareness as such awareness alone provides scope for change. The questions asked in the fanzine followed by the grouping of the spectators according to their scores is a device used specifically for this purpose. Such categorization though apparently playful is not intended thus. It is meant to lead to introspection. Thus follow up 'action' in Red Ladder's dictionary in the nineties changed in definition, it now read more along the lines of self education and change.

That such self education can only occur alongside discovering/exploring one's identity (ies) is therefore a given fact. Red Ladder's Spring 1997 production, <u>Kaahini</u>, a play by award winning playwright Maya Chowdhry, meant for young people (14+) and adults, explores questions of gender, duty and kismet. Set in 1990s Britain, this intriguing tale of denial, deception and family pride uses rich, poetic language to reveal the dreams, aspirations and frustrations of being young and Asian.

"You want a son for your own life to be fulfilled, you believe you must have a son in order to live. Be careful—where needs and desires cross the path of destiny only chaos will follow."

Neelendra believes his prayers for a son have been answered as he celebrates the birth of his child Esha; but will he ever fully understand the real meaning behind the words of the Mystic? For the Mystic says cryptically as Esha reaches adolescence, the secrets held so long with the family erupt with devastating consequences: Esha is not a boy after all.

Esha is training hard for the school football final and dreams of winning the cup; 'his' parents Neelendra and Anishaa want the best for him but worry. Meanwhile 'his' best friend Farooq is dreaming of girls and wants to hang out as 'Juicy's'. Then there's

Kaahini; is she Esha's 'real self', 'alter ego', 'other'? Farooq is attracted to Kaahini. As if being a teenager was not enough, being an Asian teenager is even more difficult—especially when the past merges with the present, cultures collide and you're a girl.

In researching this play Maya Chowdhry uncovered shamanic rituals in which men and women exchange genders, Hindu philosophy recounts how the 'self' splits into male and female at the beginning of the world. Reflecting on the genderless nature of 'the soul' Maya reread the tale of Sikhandin in The Mahabharata, where King Drupada brings up his daughter as a son after a dream in which Lord Shiva tells him his Queen is bearing a son. Thinking about the implications of the legacy of the Ramayana: boys are told to be like Rama and girls to be like Sita, and the taboos this puts in place, Maya wanted to use this as a background to a play about young Asian people based upon ideas and information gained while working with them.

The Programme/Resource of Kaahini takes the definition of Gender from the Oxfam handbook emphasizing that "whilst sexual identity is biologically determined, gender identity is not. It is constructed by society and therefore can change and be changed. Gender roles and relations are constantly changing, at variable rates and in diverse ways in different cultures." The follow-up work involving the spectators after this definition includes making a list describing different aspects of one's gender; researching how different genders are portrayed in material culture (books, newspapers, television, etc) and questioning whether this shapes our view about how men and women should behave; and creating a gender wall using gender images from different Asian cultures.

One of the interesting facets of this particular fanzine are the questions asked of the touring team in the profile creations. These are searching questions that attempt to project the inner thoughts/beliefs/attitudes of the team members. They read:

1. What did you want to be when you were young?
2. Do you believe in love?
3. If you could be someone else who would you be?
4. What is your image of freedom?
5. What is your favourite food?
6. What is your life's desire?
7. What's great about being a man/women?
8. What does friendship mean to you?
9. Who are you?

10. What did you inherit from your parents?

Undoubtedly, some of the answers given are flippant but the nature of the questions asserts the theme of this play and the larger aims of Red Ladder in choosing it for performance. As observed earlier, such a method of personalising the actors establishes their 'one of us' quality and signals that anyone (among the audience) could well become a 'performer'.

But perhaps the most significant aspect of Kaahini is the language of the play. Classically, agit prop drama would refrain from poetic language, assuming it to undercut the message of the play. However if one keeps in mind that, equally conventionally, agit prop theatre recognises that the play is only secondary—what is of more importance is the follow-up action, then one realises that by staging plays like Kaahini, Red Ladder was in fact following both conventions. For not only were the audience being treated to an artistically sound play but were also being motivated to think along the lines of the ideas propagated by the play. Rather than being a diluted genre, agit prop theatres strength had actually been enhanced.

Completing thirty years in 1998, Red Ladder's horizons had considerably expanded and it had even began to make international connections towards the millennium. In January 1998 the company visited Delhi for two weeks. Kully Thiarai, Noel Greig and Ann Cross worked with arts practitioners, students and young people sharing the company's work and history through a series of workshops in Playwrighting and Performance. The Asian Theatre School, which was collaboration between Theatre in the Mill, Bradford and Red Ladder had held two summer schools in 1997 and 1998 offering young Asian performers an inspiring introduction to the performing arts led by actors, writers, directors and musicians from across the UK. The outcome, Masala Nights, a play performed in Autumn 1998, in which reality and fantasy created a spicy mix when Bradford and Bollywood collided, was the first opportunity for the participants to put their skills to the test in the creation of an original and unique piece of theatre.

Spring 1998 saw the production of Wise Guys by Philip Osment, a hard hitting, stark and engaging play about the lives of four young men, Mike, Skid, Stephen and Darren. Osment says:

There is a widely held belief that there is more and more violence in our society and that more and more people—young men in particular are turning to drugs and crime. There are those who blame this on the breakdown of the family and the collapse of traditional moral values; others say that we have become greedy and selfish because we live in a world where only money matters.

What is certainly true is that there are many young people in present day Britain who do not feel valued and who are not being given the opportunity to realize their full potential. The role of men in our society is changing—they are no longer necessarily the breadwinners and many young men do not feel that they have a role to play.

I decided that I wanted to write a play about a group of young men whose lives reflect this state of affairs and then look at whether they are able to turn their lives around and change direction, find a sense of purpose.

… I wanted to show that whatever choice [he] made it wasn't going to be easy. I think young people know this and so any play that suggested otherwise they would find untruthful.[8]

Obviously Osment was successful in his efforts and as one review reported "Red Ladder and Theatre Centre pour vital new theatrical blood into the old bottle of socially-conscious drama."[9]

The artistic merit of this play and its performance is matched by the gravity with which the follow up work has been undertaken. For there is not just a booklet with notes for youth workers to use as resource material put together with information from Red Ladder's Touring Team and the Oxfam Gender Training manual, but also a booklet of information for young people in the audience.

The information booklet for the young audience contains a large section on and by the actors who answer a number of questions (a) about their selves regarding their origins and what influenced them to join theatre; (b) the main male influence in their lives and (c) a difficult moment with their dad/adult male figure. It is necessary to reemphasise the reason why Red Ladder makes an in depth study of the actors responses to such questions: the boundaries between actor and audience are done away with; the 'sacredness' of the performance space (as maintained by proscenium arch theatre) is erased and the involvement of the performers with the issues propagated by the play is underlined. In other words, the insight provided into the actors' thoughts/lives serves as an entry point to members of the audience to join in the 'play'. This is characteristic of good agit prop theatre.

The actor responses are preceded by the author's words and thoughts from the Director; the latter felt "Directing 'Wise Guys' was an opportunity for me to learn more about why we are violent to each other. In helping to tell the story I wanted to allow others the opportunity to think more about our own/their own use of violence." Yet another instance of the collective approach retained by Red Ladder; each production person was involved with the play as much on ideological as on artistic grounds.

Following the actor responses, are two sections on 'Bullying' and 'Abuse', each defining the parameters within which the two terms operate; as well as suggesting carelines that one can tap if one is a victim of either. The penultimate section is an agreement/disagreement poll allowing scope for interpersonal discussion. The last page contains a little questionnaire for the audience regarding their thoughts about all aspects of the production—the play, the discussions and the booklet; and inviting further comments and discussion—Red Ladder's efforts to facilitate evaluation of the Company's work.

This young people booklet, as said earlier, complements the Youth Workers Resource Pack. Drawing heavily from examples in the play, the pack first highlights the key themes/issues in the play with questions specific to the play as well as general ones. Yet again, as in other resource packs, this one also encourages the movement from discussions to creative activities such as role play, drama scenes, making a video, writing song lyrics and creating a visual art display: i.e., the impetus is towards action than towards speech. The pack then moves on to gender issues, the two major aims being to introduce the term 'gender' to a group and to help male youth to see the pressures on them to adopt certain attitudes. This is done by making the participants respond to statements and then a discussion on the answers by the whole group. Finally, the last pages contain brief biographies of the actors, the latest update on Red Ladder and information on how to become involved in theatre.

One aspect of these resource kits that must be mentioned is their increasing sophistication, their material enhancement. Reflecting the consumerist culture of the times, one notices that the packaging of these resource kits (as regards the quality of paper, illustrations and the obvious labour put into their making) is greatly improved.

While no direct inference can be drawn from this development, it can certainly be perceived as a sign that (a) Red Ladder is materially doing better in its functioning as a Theatre Company, and (b) that there is a recognition on Red Ladder's part that just as the plays needed artistic skill to survive, so did the resource kits need touching up to sustain the attention and commitment of an impatient generation.

For example, the resource kit accompanying the production of Rosy Fordham's Crush, retoured in Autumn 1998, is positively a riot of colours in that single pages of different sizes, each containing notes/information/questions, etc are of different hues. Such an eyecatcher makes for immediate visual impact, and is indicative of a growing awareness on Red Ladder's part of the tactical devices one needs to employ to survive in a world increasingly susceptible to the seduction of good advertising.

Concluding a book such as this is both simple as well as tough. It is simple for one could easily sum up Red Ladder's status by stating that the Company, having weathered all kinds of difficult circumstances is here to stay. But it is tough for one cannot predict how much the Company will change with time; how much it will modify its aims/target groups/methodologies and how much further it will distance itself from pure agit prop theatre.

However it is also visible that the very definition of the term 'agit prop' has undergone change—from inciting the masses to protest and demonstrate against political and social ills of the time; to generating awareness about the same and motivating people to work with social welfare organizations towards a better environment. Earlier agit prop encouraged militant resistance while contemporary agit prop veers towards a more pacifist, mediating stance. This has been traced through both, an analysis of the plays as well as of the follow-up activities.

Thus this study can be said to be as complete as it can possibly be. For with the view that agit prop theatre will continue to survive, one presumes that Red Ladder too will not cease to exist. In what form and structure however, is for this millennium and the courses that history takes, to decide.

Notes

[1] Information from copy of article in 'Youth Clubs with the Edge', September 1990, p.22 given by Red Ladder, entitled 'Red Ladder—The Bus Shelter Tour'

[2] Information from copy of article in 'Young People Now' October 1990, p.39 entitled 'Bus fare' by Tim Burke given by Red Ladder

[3] ibid

[4] The fanzine informs that 'mules are women used by drug smugglers to swallow condoms filled with cocaine, and then to travel to other parts of the world where the drug (which passes through the bowels in the toilet) is then sold for profit on the streets. These women sometimes die of drug overdoses when the condom bursts inside of them. They are called mules and are only ever paid a small amount of the money'.

[5] Set in a mythical Eastern Europe country, Sleeping Dogs using rich classical text and heightened poetic language tells the story of Assan and Marina, two young lovers from different cultures with different religions and different customs. For forty years the leader had ruled with an iron fist, stray dogs slept peacefully in the park and their families lived as neighbours. When the old government was swept away and peace was threatened, Assan and Marina found themselves caught in the crossfire of a community at war. Would their love survive?

[6] Article entitled 'Love see no colour' by Mandy Jarvis in 'Youth Clubs', September 1994, pp 29-31 (given by Red Ladder)

[7] From the programme accompanying the play

[8] Quoted in the information booklet

[9] Donald Hutera, 'The Scotsman', August 1998, quoted by Red Ladder in information flyer accompanying Crush

RED LADDER AT 40

When the Agit Prop Street Players changed their name to Red Ladder Theatre Company, it was a tacit acknowledgement of the shift from an overt declaration of the nature of the Company to a more symbolic one. The politics of the Company, its ideology and methodology as an Agit Prop Theatre Company, underwent little change. It continued to function as a Collective for a long time; address issues, that were of interest to the labour class or look at neglected subjects like gender, in other words, promoted the more peripheral voices of society. However, events detailed in these Chapters proved that if Red Ladder had to continue, it would have to reform in many ways. 1985 was perhaps the most important year in ushering these changes.

With the appointment of an Artistic Director, the very structure of Red Ladder changed from a Collective to a Hierarchy. This led to more efficient management and planning of the Company's schedule of events. The mode of scripting too altered as the Collective scripting of plays gave way to the commissioning of playwrights to write on a particular topic. From catering to the needs of the labour class and propagating measures to lessen their angst, the Company gradually converted to one that saw tremendous potential in the youth of the country. So, it took on youth oriented productions: plays that engaged with problems of the youth be it race or sex or gender or the domestic versus the public, tradition versus modernity, employment or career and so on. Its effectiveness in handling such issues is marked by the fact that today Red Ladder is perceived as one of the foremost youth and community development theatre companies of the country.

Success allowed Red Ladder to take risks with form so that artistic experimentation sneaked into the plays and spilled over to the resource kits, i.e. the fanzines and ragazines. Keeping in mind the consumerist culture of the twentieth century which the target audience, i.e. the youth, was a party to, the language of the plays as well as the resource kits underwent a change with an increase in the personal and social register as against the political. Not just language, the tone of the plays too reflected lesser emphasis on anger at a situation and more stress on furnishing constructive solutions. The 'protest' element seemed to have given way to the idea of 'Help/Care

Lines', the message being that self help was possibly a speedier way out of a crisis than governmental laws.

Red Ladder's heightened artistic endeavours saw training programmes for Directors; Theatre Workshops; Theatre Schools for Asians (a summer training programme); more interaction with theatre companies from outside Britain such as Theatre Direct, Canada (and during their visit to India in 1998 with Theatre Companies in Delhi). In other words, the shift from the aggression underlying 'Agit Prop' to the artistry behind 'Theatre' was now complete.

Or was it?

Red Ladder has not changed its name today when in historical terms, the downfall of the communist ideal has been clearly heralded by the collapse of the Soviet Union and so a symbol such as 'Red Ladder' (red, the communist colour and ladder, the much loved prop of the labour force) has come to stand on dubious ground. The Company obviously apprehends the need to keep alive this symbol as an ideal and as a signifier of all those communities that have remained on the fringes and must be brought to the centre. To reiterate a point made earlier, the plays continue to voice the anxieties of marginalised/oppressed groups. Mainstream, urban theatre; plays meant for sheer entertainment; typically proscenium arch theatre, are still out of bounds for Red Ladder.

Name aside, in aim too the Company may have a façade of a hierarchical structure, but its spirit is still that of a Collective. All decisions are taken collectively; plays written by commissioned playwrights are preceded by intensive sessions with members and actors of Red Ladder thrashing out the selected theme. It still aims to take theatre closer to non-theatre venues and make it accessible to those who otherwise don't get to watch any theatre—thus it persists in using venues such as community centers, the streets and even, as one has seen, a bus. It also continues to use minimalist props, costumes, scenery, etc so that it remains a more affordable alternative to expensive commercial theatre without of course compromising on the artistic merit of the plays or of the performances. Red Ladder's reaching out to Theatre Companies of the same ilk outside Britain reveals an effort to make the foundations for such theatre firmer by giving it a global standing—to build a platform or forum the world over for propagating a certain kind of theatre.

Not all theatre companies last. And especially not all agit prop theatre companies—agit prop theatre being meted the kind of treatment that one typically associates with a foster or Illegitimate child. Ultimately the difference really is between those theatre companies that produce good plays and those that produce bad ones This is true of agit prop plays as well. What is required is more transparency and accessibility on the part of theatre companies that are agit prop whether completely or partially in their ideology and methodology.

Only such openness can assert that the essence of agit prop theatre in however modified a form since its inception, remains even today. The pejorative labels attached to such theatre, the stereotyping and the prejudices that this theatre encounters can be banished only once more and more theatre companies declare their agit prop leanings and make accessible their plays, unabashedly. In an age which believes in cost effectiveness and in value for money, good agit prop theatre can expect (and does receive) a warm welcome. So what will lend strength to this thesis would be more such critical appraisals of agit prop plays so that the range of form and content and of dramaturgy of the theatre companies or activists or playwrights, practicing or writing such plays, becomes manifest.

The book began on the premise that agit prop theatre is here to stay. It ends with the same positive conclusion; the rider being that in its ideological preoccupation and modes of operation when it initially became popular, it has shifted from an extremist position to a more tempered one. That historical conjunctions in the future may rechange the nature of agit prop theatre and make it yet again a forceful cultural mode of protest is a possibility that cannot be ruled out. Its ability to condition psychology is after all intact even today as can be seen in the successful way that Red Ladder uses it to negotiate with the challenges faced by youth in Britain. Thus to announce or assume agit prop theatres' death would not be premature or shortsighted but indeed, a grave blunder.

Postscript

RED LADDER TODAY

Based on a report by Stefanie Gascoigne of Red Ladder in August 2008, the pace of Red Ladder from 2000 onwards can be gauged from their activities as outlined here.

In the Spring of 2000, Red Ladder toured the UK with Mike Kenny's **After the End of the World**. This was Red Ladder's Millennium play, a comedy that explores respect and morality with Stick, a teenage boy living with Chintz, his single parent mum and Wrinkle, his disabled grandma. In Autumn, Noel Greig's **Picture Me** was toured. This is an international story set in England and Mumbai exploring the emotional impact of HIV/Aids on a British Indian teenager.

In 2001, the two plays toured in Spring and Autumn were **Hold Ya** by Chris O Connell and **Lowdown Highnotes** by Andrea Earl. The former play is the story of a single parent Dad and his teenage son, a gritty story about love and change mixing clubland culture and domestic life. The Autumn production is the story of a teenage wannabe who goes off to find her real father, using music, video imagery and live vocals. The following year saw **After You** by Brendan Murray and **Wise Guys** by Philip Osment. **After You** narrates the story of a youth who searches for the truth. A chance meeting with a stranger at his father's graveside sets Chris off on a trail of intrigue and discovery. But Chris uncovers more than he bargained for, forcing him to re-evaluate his relationship with his parents. Cutting edge digital media, design and evocative text are crafted in this gripping piece of theatre. **Wise Guys** has already been written about in Chapter Five.

Apart from the professional touring productions, 2002 also saw the appointment of Madani Younis as Director of the Asian Theatre School. Under his direction, the school created in the Spring of 2002, **Streets of Rage**, a creative response from the young people of Bradford. This play threw light upon the events of the Bradford riots of Summer 2001. Mixing cutting edge digital media, the play gave a new voice to a group of young men and women from Bradford, heard on stage for the first time. In response to the views of the local people from Bradford, the play, devised by the Asian Theatre School participants, gives an opportunity to the local people to retell the events of the riots from their perspective. This is a well researched and innovative piece of theatre which resulted from news footage analysis and interviews with members of the public who lived through the riots, and who are still dealing with the issues that were brought to life.

In 2003, the play **Silent Cry** made a regional Yorkshire tour. This again was performed by the Asian Theatre School. It deals with the voices of an ordinary family who once had an ordinary life but the death of her son in police custody makes the mother embark on a journey for justice in a system that has no answers. The story is based on true documented evidence and interviews. Touring UK that year was the co production with Contact Theatre, Manchester, **The Dreaming of 'Bones'** by Damian Gorman. This is the hard hitting story of a heart scalded young man. Xavier 'Bones' Macmillan, like many young people, dreams of a special and beautiful life for himself. In preparation for a stay at the local 'Thin Bin' he rehearses the story of his past and present life: his over anxious mum, his estranged dad, his cool mate Lenny and his dream girl, Nicola Price all play their part. Weaving dramatic monologue, poetry, movement and original music **'The Dreaming of Bones'** looks at how the strong, true yearning of one young person can overcome the often warped , harsh realities of life pressing in around him.

The Mission Statement for 2003 reads thus:
To inspire and challenge the lives of young people.
Red Ladder Theatre Company is:
- A high quality theatre experience for young audiences
- National tours
- New work
- After show work
- The Asian Theatre School

2003 Artistic Policy:
- To create theatre of the highest quality
- To tour the work nationally targeting young people who have little or no access to theatre
- To continue the Artistic growth of the Asian Theatre School
- To take artistic risks and explore new ways of working
- To create excellent resource material and provide after show work
- To work collaboratively with artists to create new work

- To run development weeks and creative labs for artists to experiment
- To be informed by the young people and audiences we aim to reach
- To embrace new technologies, high quality production standards and highly skilled creative teams to offer a unique artistic experience in non theatre spaces as well as in theatres
- To offer an alternative view of the world through theatre

Recognised as the UK's leading new writing Company for youth audiences producing accessible theatre of the highest quality.
Red Ladder also provide
- After show Chatbacks
- Resource material for young people

Soulskin by Esther Wilson toured the UK between April and July 2004. This story, suitable for 13+ audiences is about fractured families, loyalty, destructive pride and taking responsibility. Chrissie, the child of a teenage pregnancy, has been brought up by her Gran, Mary. She hasn't seen her mum, Bernie, in years until Mary dies. It's the night of the funeral and the eve of Chrissie's sixteenth birthday. She's alone in the house, waiting for Bernie to pick her up. As she packs, Chrissie tries to make sense of the painful memories and secrets that have kept the family apart. But as the sun sets, Chrissie's memory plays tricks, conjuring up strange meetings, with real and imagined situations haunting her until…Mary herself appears and Chrissie has to face up to her part in the fragile relationship between mothers and daughters.

Tagged by Louise Wallwein was developed in collaboration with Half Moon Young People's Theatre, London and toured the UK between September and December 2004. Time is ticking for Chris. He's electronically tagged and on a 70'clock curfew. If he breaks it, he's going down. Two friends, a bike, a pylon, a tractor and a police helicopter conspire to keep Chris from his freedom.

2005 saw two plays by Madani Younis being performed. The first, toured in the UK between April and July, was called **Free Falling**. This was developed with young people in Yorkshire and a team of artists from Red Ladder-inspired by the urban sport of Free running (or le Parkour) with strong visual imagery and story telling and also some strong language. It is a play about success and failure, about a search for beauty, about a generation of youth looking for a future. Multi media, hip beats, cool moves and inspirational words are the highlights of this play reflecting the diversity of British society. The other play, **Caravan**, a local Yorkshire production is inspired from Caravaggio's **The Seven Works Of Mercy.** At the end of a run down street with back to back houses that frown at one another and whose gardens have seen better days, the Caravan sits patiently and quietly. This play looks at the lives of ordinary people and how communities endeavour to continue a normal existence in the face of terror, media hype and a global society at odds with itself.

In January 2006, Madani Younis, the Director of The Asian Theatre School, won the Arts Council England decibel Award at ITV's tenth annual South Bank Show Awards. Presented by Melvyn Bragg, the South Bank Show Awards honour the best in British Arts, with the Arts Council decibel Award recognizing work that contributes to the development and promotion of a more culturally diverse arts sector.

2006 saw the appointment of Rod Dixon as Artistic Director of Red Ladder.

Worlds Apart by Mick Martin made its UK tour between May and July, 2006. This takes us into the life of Sam Harris, a 14 year old girl dealing with life, love, communication and difference in the world around her. At home there's Mum, her step dad Pete and her eight year old half brother, Adam. Adam is autistic. At school there's her best mate Kelly to whom she tells everything. Using multi-media, illustration, original sound and light design, Red Ladder creates visionary theatre that reaches out to teenage and adult audiences. During the making of the play the company was inspired by PECS-The Picture Exchange Communication System-a non verbal communication system that has been successful with adolescents and adults who have a wide array of communicative, cognitive and physical difficulties. September 2006 saw a retouring of Maya Chowdhry's **Kaahini.**

Travelling to 2007, one finds another Mission Statement:
To make theatre which celebrates, inspires and challenges young people, developing in them the desire and ability to express ideas and strengthen social and cultural cohesion.

Artistic policy
- include young people in the creative processes of making theatre
- embellish current text-driven practice by experimentation with new theatre practice-including work with other art forms
- inspire a new generation of theatre makers through the quality and originality of our creative practice

- tour this work nationally targeting young people who have little or no access to theatre
- seek international collaboration actively and to engage with theatre making in troubled parts of the world- helping ordinary people investigate global issues.
- create a reputation for a unique Red Ladder artistic process and a 21st century style- to compliment the reputation that precedes us.
- continue to raise our local and regional profile particularly through enabling and inspiring emerging local artists
- celebrate and build upon Red Ladder's 40 year history of making theatre

The year 2007 brought changes to Red Ladder and demonstrated that the Company is committed to placing young people at the heart of the creative process. In January 2007 was the new development of the Red Grit Project, Red Ladder's New Young Actors Company, a mixed group of young people, selected from city wide workshops in Leeds, all of whom have ambitions to become actors. In June 2007, Red ladder continued with its International connections beyond Europe and Asia to Palestine. This developed out of Red Ladder's relationship as the professional theatre partner of A.R.R.O.W (Art: A Resource for Reconciliation over the World).

Written by Madani Younis, **Doors: This Life was Given to Me** was devised by by the Red Grit Project for production in July 2007. A modern piece of Absurd Theatre made by and for a new generation in which three strangers are caught in a web spun from the mistaken choices of their past. As each one struggles, the web tightens. Giles teases and manipulates like a cruel puppet-master; Jo hides behind his angry mask; Leah comforts herself in fantasy. Frederick arrives. Painful old wounds split open-lies and deceit smother the truth. Can anyone escape this 21st century hell?

In August 2007, the Asian Theatre School became independent and with its new name, Freedom Studios, moved to Bradford. Red Ladder had succeeded in providing an artistic and creative medium to Asian men and women, the paucity of which had been recognised by them in 1997.

2008 and the celebration of forty years of cutting edge theatre by Red ladder began with the play **Where's Vietnam?** This play transports audiences to the year of Red ladder's birth, 1968, a time when the intervention of youth in politics resulted in a world wide revolution. Two brother's, Banks and Arthur are intent on avenging the death of their sister , Cath. They follow their sister's killer, Moz, down to Grosvenor Square and they find themselves face to face with new revolutionary values on the one hand and old fashioned police brutality on the other hand. Using pop culture and filled with soul and funk music, **Where's Vietnam?** deals with family tensions and the pressure to follow in the elder brother's footsteps even when the sibling is a violent gangster in a wheelchair.

The Autumn production for 2008, **Forgotten Things** uses surreal puppetry suitable for teenage and adult audiences to narrate the the story of sixteen year old Toby who believes that he's a failure and wants to end it all. The play deals with issues such as teenage suicide and Alzheimer's.

This book may well end here but as for Red Ladder? Four decades in 2008 and Red Ladder is still going strong. There is no looking back...only a looking forward.

BIBLIOGRAPHY

Red Ladder Scripts

The Cake Play. Unpublished, 1975 version

Nerves of Steel by Steve Trafford and Chris Rawlence. Unpublished, 1979

Power Mad. Unpublished, 1979-80

Taking Our Time. London: Pluto Press, 1979

Strike While the Iron is Hot Three Plays on Sexual Politics. Ed. and intro by Michelene Wandor. London and West Nyack: The Journeyman Press, 1980

Bring Out Your Dead by Peter Cox. Unpublished, 1983

State Agent by Rachel Feldburg and Ruth Mackenzie. Unpublished, 1985

Back to the Walls by Jane Thornton. Unpublished, 1986

On the Line. Unpublished, 1986

Winners by Rona Munro. Unpublished, 1987

Empire Made by Paul Swift. Unpublished, 1987

One of Us by Jacqui Shapiro and Meera Syal. Unpublished, 1988

Off the Road by Rona Munro. Unpublished, 1988

The Best by Mike Kenny. Unpublished, 1988

Bhangra Girls by Nandita Ghose. Unpublished, 1989

Who's Breaking by Philip Osment. Unpublished, 1989

The Bus Shelter Show by Lin Coghlan. Unpublished, 1990

Breaking the Silence by Kate O'Reilly. Unpublished, 1990

The Scrappie by Judith Johnson. Unpublished, 1991

Consequences by Mary Cooper. Unpublished, 1991

Caught by Julie Wilkinson. Unpublished, 1992

No Mean Street by Paul Boakye. Unpublished, 1993

Sleeping Dogs by Philip Osment. Unpublished, 1993

Mixed Blessings by Mary Cooper. Unpublished, 1994

The Wound by Gilly Fraser. Unpublished, 1994

Waking by Lin Coghlan. Unpublished, 1995

End of Season by Noel Greig. Unpublished, 1996

Josie's Boys by Roy Williams. Unpublished, 1996

Kaahini by Maya Chowdhry. Unpublished, 1997

Crush by Rosy Fordham. Unpublished, 1997

Wise Guys by Philip Osment. Unpublished, 1998

After the End of the World by Mike Kenny. Unpublished, 2000

Picture Me by Noel Greig. Unpublished, 2000

CRITICISM

Books

Ashcroft, Bill, Gareth Griffiths and Helen Tiffin, ed., 1995, The Post Colonial Studies Reader. London: Routledge.

Ansorage, Peter, 1975, Disrupting the Spectacle Five Years of Experimental and fringe Theatre in Britain. Pitman Publishing.

Aston, Elaine, 1999, Feminist Theatre Practice A Handbook. London and New York: Routledge.

Aston, Elaine and George Savona, 1991, Theatre as Sign System A Semiotics of Text and Performance. London: Routledge.

Auslander, Philip, ed., 2003, Performance Critical Concepts in Literary and Cultural Studies. Vol III. Roultedge: London and New York

Beckerman, Bernard (ed. Gloria Brim Beckerman and William Coco), 1980, Theatrical Presentation Performer, Audience and Act. New York and London: Routledge.

Bennett, Susan, 1990, Theatre Audiences: A Theory of Production and Reception. London and New York: Routledge.

Bentley, Eric, 1968, The Theatre of Commitment. London: Methuen and Co. Ltd.

Bentley, Eric. ed., 1992, The Theory of the Modern Stage: An Introduction to Modern Theatre and Drama. England: Penguin Books.

Bharucha, Rustom, 1993, Theatre and the World: Performance and the Politics of Culture. London: Routledge.

Bigsby, C.W.E. ed., 1981, Contemporary English Drama. London: Edwin Arnold.

Birch, David, 1991, The Languages of Drama. MacMillan.

Boal, Augusto, 1992, Games for Actors and Non-Actors. London: Routledge.

Boon, Richard, 1991, Brenton: The Playwright. London: Methuen Drama.

Bradby, David, Louis James and Bernard Sharratt, 1980, Performance and Politics in Popular Drama. Cambridge: Cambridge University Press.

Brecht, Bertolt. Brecht on Theatre, 1965, Transl. by John Willett. New York: Hill and Wang.

Brook, Peter, 1968, The Empty Space. New York: Atheneum.

Brown, John Russell, 1982, A Short Guide to Modern British Drama. London: Heinemann.

Brown, John Russell, ed., 1984, Modern British Dramatists: New Perspectives. Twentieth Century Views, Englewood Cliffs, N.J.: Prentice Hall.

Bull, John, 1990, New British Political Dramatists. London and Basingtoke: MacMillan Publishers Ltd.

Butler, Judith, 1990, Gender Trouble Feminism and the Subversion of Identity. New York: Routledge.

Craig, Sandy, 1980, Dreams and Deconstructions: Alternative Theatre in Britain. Derbyshire: Amber Lane.

Davies, Andrew, 1987, Other Theatres: The Development of Alternative and Experimental Theatre in Britain. England: MacMillan Education Ltd.

Edgar, David, 1988, The Second Time as Farce Reflections on the Drama of Mean Times. London: Lawrence and Wishart Ltd.

Elam, Kier, 1980, The Semiotics of Theatre and Drama. London and New York: Methuen, New Accents Series.

Ellis-Fermor, Una, 1964, The Frontiers of Drama. Great Britain: Methuen and Co. Ltd.

Elsom, John, 1979, Post-War British Theatre. London: Routledge and Kegan Paul.

Esslin, Martin, 1987, The Field of Drama: How the Signs of Drama Create Meaning on Stage and Screen. London and New York: Routledge and Kegan Paul.

Foulkes, A.P, 1983, Literature and Propaganda. London and New York: Methuen, New Accents Series.

Freedman, Morris ed., 1964, Essays in the Modern Drama. Boston: D.C. Heath and Co.

Gascoigne, Bamber, 1962, Twentieth Century Drama. London: Hutchison University Library.

Gassner, George. ed., 1964, Ideas in the Drama Selected papers from the English Institute. Columbia University Press.

Gilbert, Helen and Joanne Tompkins, 1996, Post-Colonial Drama: Theory, Practice, Politics. London and New York: Routledge.

Glenn, Lane, 1994 Playwright as Provocateur: David Hare and the British Political Plays of the Theatre Era. Michigan State Theatre: Georg Schutter.

Glover, David and Cora Kaplan, 2000, Genders. London: Routledge.

Glodberg, David Theo, ed., 1994, Multiculturalism A Critical Reader. USA and UK: Blacwell Publishers Ltd.

Goodman, Lizbeth with Jane de Gay, ed., 2000, The Routledge Reader in Politics and Performance. London and New York: Routledge.

Hashmi, Safdar, 1989, The Right to Perform Selected Writings of Safdar Hashmi. New Delhi: SAHMAT.

Hayman, Ronald, 1979, British Theatre since 1955: A Reassessment. Oxford: Oxford University Press.

Hayman, Ronald,1979, Theatre and Anti Theatre New Movements Since Beckett. London: Secker and Warburg.

Herman, Vimala, 1995, Dramatic Discourse Dialogue as interaction in plays. London and New York: Routledge.

Heuvel, Michael Vanden, 1991, Performing Drama/Dramatising Performance Alternative Theatre and the Dramatic Text. USA: The University of Michigan Press.

Holderness, Graham, ed., 1992, The Politics of Theatre and Drama. New York: St. Martins'.

Hornby, Richard, 1979, Script into Performance A Structuralist View of Play Production. Austin, University of Texas Press.

Hubner, Zygmunt (ed. and transl by Zadwiga Kosicka), 1992, Theatre and Poltics. Evanston, Illinois: North Western University.

Hunt, Albert, 1974, Arden: A Study of his Plays. London: Methuen.

Huxley, Michael and Noel Witts, ed., 1996, The Twentieth Century Performance Reader. London and New York: Routledge.

Innes, Christopher, 1992, Modern British Drama 1890-1990. Cambridge: Cambridge University Press.

Itzin, Catherine, 1980, Stages in the Revolution: Political Theatre in Britain Since 1968. London: Eyre Methuen.

Kennedy, Andrew, 1975, Six Dramatists in Search of a Language: Shaw, Eliot, Beckett, Pinter, Osborne, Arden. Cambridge: Cambridge University Press.

Kerensky, Oleg, 1977, The New British Drama: Fourteen Playwrights Since Osborne and Pinter, Hamilton: Taplinger Publishing.

Kertzer, David I, 1988, Ritual, Politics and Power. New Haven and London: Yale University Press.

Kershaw, Baz, 1992, The Politics of Performance: Radical Theatre as Cultural Intervention. London: Routledge.

Kitchin, Laurence, 1966, Drama in the Sixties. London: Faber and Faber.

Kruger, Loren, 1992, The National Stage: Theatre and Cultural Legitimation in England, France and America. Chicago and London: University of Chicago Press.

La Fontaine, J.S., ed., 1972, The Interpretation of Ritual: Essays in Honour of A.I. Richards. London: Tavistock Publications.

Lewis, Gilbert, 1980, Day of Shining Red: An Essay on Understanding Ritual. Cambridge: Cambridge University Press.

Leys, Colin, 1983, Politics in Britain An Introduction. London: Vers.

MacAloon, John J., ed., 1984, Rite, Drama, Festival, Spectacle Rehearsals Toward a Theory of Cultural Performance. USA: Library of Congress catalogina in Publication Data.

Marowitz, Milne and Hale, ed., 1965, The Encore Reader: A Chronicle of the New Drama. London: Methuen.

Mason, Bim, 1992, Street Theatre and Other Outdoor Performance. London: Routledge.

Mills, Sara, 1997, Discourse. London and New York: Routledge.

Morris, Desmond and Peter Marsh, 1988, Tribes. London: Pyramid Books.

Morris, J.A., 1977, Writers and Politics in Modern Britain (1880-1950). Holder and Stoughton.

Nagendra, S.P., 1971, The Concept of Ritual in Modern Sociological Theory. New Delhi: The Academic Journals of India.

Nicholson, Linda L., ed., 1990, Feminism/Postmodernism. London and New York: Routledge.

O'Toole, John, 1992, The Process of Drama: Negotiating Art and Meaning. London and New York: Routledge.

Page, Adrian, ed., 1992, The Death of the Playwright? Modern British Drama and Literary Theory. London: MacMillan.

Parker, Andrew and Eve Kosofsky Sedgwick, ed., 1995, Performativity and Performance. London and New York: Routledge.

Pfister, Manfred, 1988, The Theory and Analysis of Drama (transl. by John Halliday). Cambridge: Cambridge University Press.

Phelan, Peggy, 1993, Unmarked: The Politics of Performance. London and New York: Routledge.

Poulton, Richard, 1981, A History of the Modern World. Oxford: Oxford University Press.

Rabey, David Ian, 1986, British and Irish Political Drama in the Twentieth Century. London: MacMillan.

Read, Alan, 1993, <u>Theatre and Everyday Life An Ethics Of Performance</u>. London and New York: Routledge.

Redmond, James, ed., 1987, <u>The Theatrical Space</u>. Cambridge: Cambridge University Press.

Rees, Roland, 1992, <u>Fringe First Pioneers of Fringe Theatre on Record</u>. London: Oberon Books Ltd.

Roose-Evans, James, 1984, <u>Experimental Theatre: From Stanislavsky to Peter Brooks</u>. London: Routledge and Kegan Paul.

Rozik, Eli, 2002, <u>The Roots of Theatre Rethinking Ritual and Other Theories of Origin</u>. Iowa City: University of Iowa Press.

Salgado, Gamini, 1980, <u>English Drama: A Critical Introduction</u>. London: Edwin Arnold.

Schechner, Richard, 1983, <u>Performative Circumstances From The Avant Grade To Ramlila</u>. Calcutta: Seagull Books.

Scolnicov, Hanna and Peter Holland, ed., 1989, <u>Transfering Plays from Culture to Culture</u>. Cambridge: Cambridge University Press.

Shank, Theodore, ed., 1994, <u>Contemporary British Theatre</u>. Great Britain and USA: MacMillan Press Ltd. and St. Martin's Press Inc.

Southern, Richard, 1964, <u>The Seven Ages of the Theatre</u>. London: Faber and Faber.

Spencer, Jenny S., 1992, <u>Dramatic Strategies in the Plays of Edward Bond</u>. Cambridge: Cambridge University Press.

Srampickal, Jacob, 1984, <u>Voice to the Voiceless The Power of People's Theatre in India</u>. London and New York: Hurst and Co., St Martin's Press.

Striff, Erin, ed., 2003, <u>Performance Studies</u>. New York: MacMillan, Houndmills, Basingtoke, Hampshire RG216X5 and 175 Fifth Avenue.

Studlar, Donley T., 1996, <u>Great Britain Decline or Renewal?</u> USA: Westview Press Inc.

Styan, J.L., 1981, <u>Modern Drama in Theory and Practice, 1 Realism and Naturalism.</u> <u>Cambridge: Cambridge University Press.</u>

............, 1981, <u>Modern Drama in Theory and Practice, 3</u>. Cambridge: Cambridge University Press.

Szondi, Peter (ed. and transl. by Michael Hays), 1987, <u>Theory of the Modern Drama</u>. Cambridge: Polity Press.

Szanto, George, 1978, <u>Theatre and Propaganda</u>. University of Texas Press.

Taylor, John Russell, 1969, <u>Anger and After: A Guide to New British Drama</u>. London: Methuen.

Taylor, John Russell, 1971, <u>The Second Wave</u>. London: Methuen.

Turner, Victor, 1986, <u>The Anthropology of Performances</u>. New York: PAJ Publications.

Wandor, Michelene, 1986, <u>Carry on Understudies   Theatre and Sexual Politics</u>. London and New York: Routledge and Kegan Paul.

Wandor, Michelene, 1987, <u>Look Back in Gender, Sexuality and the Family in Post War   British Drama</u>. London: Methuen.

Wellwarth, George E., 1970, <u>The Theatre of Protest and Paradox: Developments in the Avante-Garde Drama</u>. New York.

Wilson, Edwin, 1980, <u>The Theatre Experience</u>. North Carolina: McGraw Hill Book Co.

Worth, Katherine J., 1972, <u>Revolutions in Modern English Drama</u>. London: G. Bell.

Wu, Duncan, 2000, <u>Making Plays Interviews with Contemporary British Dramatists and their Directors</u>. MacMillan Press Ltd.

Zeifman, Hersh and Cynthia Zimmerman, ed., 1993, <u>Contemporary British Drama, 1970-1990, Essays from Modern Drama</u>. London: MacMillan.

Articles and Essays

"Alternative cabaret: Comedy of Social Comment", Platform New Perspectives on Theatre Today, Summer 1980.

"Red Ladder –The Bus Shelter Show". Youth Clubs with the Edge, Sep, 1990.

Afzal Khan, Fawzia. "Street Theatre in Pakistan: Punjab, The Case of Ajoka, Lok Rehas and the Woman Question". The Drama Review, Vol. 41, No. 3, (T155), Fall 1997.

Anderson, Douglas. "Bums on Seats: parties, Art, and Politics in London's East End". The Drama review, Vol. 35, No.1, (T129), Spring 1991.

Barba, Eugenio. "Four Spectators". The Drama Review, Vol. 34, No. 1, (T125), Spring 1990.

Braun, Kazimierz. "My Long Journey into the American Theatre". The Drama Review, Vol.34, No.1 (T125), Spring 1990.

Brown, J.F. "Aleister Crowley's Rites of Eleusis". The Drama review: Occult and Bizare Issue, Vol. 22, No. 8, June 1978.

Burke, Tim. "Bus Fare". Young People Now, May 1990.

Burke, Tim. "Red Ladder Day". Young People Now, May 1989.

Conquergood, Dwight. "Health Theatre in a Hmong Refugee Camp: Performance, Communication and Culture". The Drama review, Vol. 32, No. 3 (T118), Fall 1988.

Cowan, Suzanne. "Theatre, Politics, and Social Change in Italy since the Second World War". Theatre Quarterly, Vol. 7, 1977: 25-39.

Craig, Sandy. "Reflexes of the Future: The Beginning of the Fringe". Craig, 1980.

Diamond, Catherine. "Quest for the Elusive Self: The Role of Contemporary Phillippines Theatre in the Formation of Cultural Identity". The Drama Review, Vol. 40, No. 1, (T149), Spring 1996.

Drain, Richard. "Spanner at Work2: Some Notes on Style". Platform, Winter 1979.

Drama Review, Nos. 125-128, 1990, section on "On Stage with the Velvet Revolution".

Drama Review, Vol. 30, Nos. 2-4, 1986, section on "Black Protest Theatre".
Elam, Harry J. (Jr.). "Ritual Theory and Political Theatre: Quinta Temporada and Slaveship". Theatre Journal, Vol. 38, December 1986: 463-472.

Erven, Eugene Van. "Resistance Theatre in South Korea: Above and Underground". The Drama review, Vol. 32, No. 3, (T119), Fall 1998.

Etchells, Tim. "Diverse Assembly: Some Trends in Recent Performance". Shank, 1994.

Garner, Stanton B. Jr. "Post Brechtian Anatomies: Weiss, Bond and the Politics of Embodiment". Theatre Journal, Vol. 42, No. 2, May 1990.

Grant, Steve "Voicing the Protest: The New Writers". Craig, 1980.

Graver, David and Loren Kruger. "Dispossessing the Spectator: Performance, Environment and Subjectivity in Theatre of the Homeless". The Drama Review, Vol. 35, No. 2, (T130), Summer 1991.

Hall, Stuart. "New Ethnicities". Ashcroft, Griffits and Tiffin, 1995.

Hashmi, Molayashree. "Drama has to be created and crafted even on the streets". Seagull Theatre Quarterly, Issue 16, December 1997.

Hay, Malcom. "Foco Nocvo". Plays and Players, No. 384, September 1985.

Holdsworth, Nadine. "Good Nights Out: Activating the Audience with 7:84 (England)". New Theatre Quarterly, Vol. XIII, No. 49, February 1997.

Howards, Roger. "Propaganda in the Early Soviet and Contemporary Chinese Theatre". Theatre Quarterly, Vol. 17, 1977: 53-60.

Jarvis, Mandy. "Love see no colour". Youth Club, September 1994.

Jenkins, Ron. "Bali: The Dance Drama Chalonarong". The Drama Review, Vol. 22, No. 2, June 1978.

Kapur, Anuradha. "Notions of the Authentic". The Journal of Arts and Ideas, Nos. 20-21, March 1991

Kershaw, Baz. "Performance, Community, Culture". Goodman and Gay, 2000.

Khan, Naseem. "The Public-going Theatre Community and Ethnic Theatre". Craig, 1980.

Lambert, J.W. "Politics and the Theatre", Drama, No. 124, Spring 1977.

Larlham, Peter. "Theatre in Transition: The Cultural Struggle in South Africa." The Drama Review, Vol. 35, No. 1, (T129), Spring 1991.

Longman, Stanley Vincent. "The Spatial Dimension of Theatre". Theatre Journal. Vol. 33, 1981: 46-59.

Lustig, Veera. "Look Back in Anger?" Plays and Players, No.448, April 1991.

Patraka, Vivian M. "Contemporary Drama, Fascism and the Holocaust". Theatre Journal, Vol. 39 (1), 3-4, 1987: 65-77

Quigley, Austin M. "Creativity and Comittment in Trevor Griffith's Comedians". Ziefman and Zimmerman, 1993.

Riccio, Thomas. "Politics, Slapstick and Zulus on Tour". The Drama Review, Vol. 40, No. 4, (T152), Winter 1996.

Rodriquez, Rafael Gonzalez. "Teatro Escambray: Toward the Cuban's Inner Being". The Drama Review, Vol. 40, No. 1, (T149), Spring 1996.

Rudakoff, Judith. "R/Evolutionary Theatre in Contemporary Cuba: Grupo Teatro Escambray". The Drama Review, Vol. 40, No. 4, (T149), Spring 1996.

Seeds, Dale E. in interview with Thomas Riccio. "trickster by Trade: Thomas Riccio on Indigenous Theatre". The Drama Review, Vol. 40, No. 4, (T152), Winter 1996.

Shank, Theodore. "Multiplicity of British Theatre". Shank, 1994.

Smith, Jonathan Z. "Bare Facts of Ritual". History of Religions, Vol. 20, 1980-81.

Sobieski, Lynn. "breaking the Boundaries: The People Show, Lumiere and Son and Hesitate and Demonstrate". Shank, 1994.

Suleri, Sara. "Woman Skin Deep Feminism and the Post Colonial Condition". Ashcroft, Griffiths and Tiffin, 1995.

Sukin, Darko. "Approach to Topoanalysis and to Paradigmatics of Dramaturgic Space". The Journal of Arts and Ideas, No. 8, July-Sept, 1984.

Symposium entitled "Theatre in Thatcher's Britain: Organising the Opposition". New Theatre Quarterly, vol. V, No. 2, May 1989.

Taylor, Diana. "Theater and Terrorism: Griselda Gambaro's Information for Foreigners". Theatre Journal, Vol. 42, No. 2, May 1990.

Theatre Quarterly, Vol. 7, 1977, section on "Theatre in Australia".

Thiongo, Ngugi Wa. "Enactments of Power: The Politics of Performance Space". The Drama Review, Vol. 41, No. 3, (T155), Fall 1997.

Encyclopedias and Dictionaries

International Encyclopedia of the Social Sciences, David L. Sill, ed., Vol. 13, MacMillan and Free Press, 1968.

Reader's Digest Universal Dictionary. London: Reader's Digest Association, 1987.

The Dictionary of Dates and Events. Dr A.N. Kapoor and V.P. Gupta, ed., Delhi: Ambe Books, 1995.

The Encyclopedia of Religion. Mircea Eliade, ed., Vol. 12, MacMillan, 1987.

The New Encyclopedia Britannica: Macropedia, Vol. 1, Vol. 4, Vol. 15 and Vol. 28.

VDM

Verlag
Dr. Müller

Wissenschaftlicher Buchverlag bietet

kostenfreie

Publikation

von

wissenschaftlichen Arbeiten

Diplomarbeiten, Magisterarbeiten, Master und Bachelor Theses
sowie Dissertationen, Habilitationen und wissenschaftliche Monographien

Sie verfügen über eine wissenschaftliche ¨bschlußarbeit zu aktuellen oder zeitlosen
Fragestellungen, die hohen inhaltlichen und formalen ¨nsprüchen genügt,
und haben **Interesse an einer honorarvergüteten Publikation**?

Dann senden Sie bitte erste Informationen über Ihre ¨rbeit per Email
an info@vdm-verlag.de. Unser ¨ußenlektorat meldet sich umgehend bei Ihnen.

VDM Verlag Dr. Müller ¨ktiengesellschaft & Co. KG
Dudweiler Landstraße 125a
D - 6612¨ Saarbrücken

www.vdm-verlag.de

Printed in the United Kingdom by
Lightning Source UK Ltd., Milton Keynes
136822UK00001B/224/P